THE MYTH OF THE BLOOD

JULIUS EVOLA

THE MYTH OF THE BLOOD

THE GENESIS OF RACIALISM

ARKTOS
LONDON 2018

ORIGINAL TITLE	*Il mito del sangue*
ISBN	978-1-912079-42-1 (Softcover)
	978-1-912079-41-4 (Hardback)
	978-1-912079-40-7 (Ebook)
TRANSLATION	John Bruce Leonard
EDITING	Martin Locker and John Bruce Leonard
LAYOUT	Tor Westman
COVER DESIGN	Andreas Nilsson

⊕ Arktos.com   ▪ fb.com/Arktos   🐦 @arktosmedia   📷 arktosmedia

Contents

Translator's Preface

$\mathcal{T}$*he Myth of the Blood* was published twice by Julius Evola, the first time in 1937, and the second time, in a slightly expanded and redacted form, five years later in 1942. In the arc of that half decade much had happened, both in the world at large and in Evola's literary career, to warrant this double publication, and it is hardly superfluous of us to identify the principal of these events. This for the simple reason that *The Myth of the Blood* is in some ways a very peculiar book in the Evolian *oeuvre*, and one that demands a special explanation. One might be tempted to say on a superficial reading that it is a book in which *Evola* does not appear at all. He himself gives his purpose in it as follows: "In the present volume we have set ourselves the task ... of presenting with the greatest objectivity the various motifs which, up to the advent of Germanic National Socialism, have nourished the racist current." That is a curiously scholarly aim for one of the great thinkers of the past century. One can countenance such a man striving for objectivity in his analysis of the works of another worthy thinker — say, a Guénon or a Jünger — but to see him stoop to grant his neutral gaze to men, many of whom are patently his inferior, one must certainly ask, wherefore? Was he not wasting his time? And perhaps — ours?

This objection appears all the stronger, since Evola, in the time between the publication of the two editions of *The Myth of the Blood*, published yet another work on race — this time a *most* Evolian study which seeks in a piercing and metaphysical fashion to get to the bottom of the racial question in its deepest and most essential elements, and which submits simultaneously a powerful critique of the false directions and blind alleys into which racism in Evola's day (and, we might well add, in our own) tended to stray. This second work, *Synthesis of the Doctrine of Race*, can be taken as Evola's final judgement on the question of race. Yet Evola considered his *Synthesis*, as he himself states in the Introduction of that work, the *second half* of the *Myth of the Blood* — one therefore predicated on, following on, fundamentally *dependent* on, the present book. *The Myth of the Blood* was indeed so important to this progression, that Evola saw fit to republish it shortly after the first issuance of his *Synthesis*, and this time specifically with an eye toward his *Synthesis*. The present work, we might say, was the *preparation* for Evola's final statement on race. But in what way? Or, put otherwise, why did Evola feel the need to dedicate himself to such a scholarly task of merely presenting ideas that were not his own, before he could dedicate himself to what was surely his loftier and more characteristic task, of winnowing these ideas out and giving the best of them depth and meaning?

By his own proclamation on this score:

> The task that we propose to ourselves in this work is ... to trace a kind of genesis of racism, or, better say, of the various motifs which figure in it, after having clearly defined their meaning; we wish to give a sense to the wellsprings that have nourished this 'myth,' of the influences which have gradually favored its formation and affirmation in the most recent history. [Introduction of 1942]

Several points emerge from this. In the first place, *The Myth of the Blood*, despite its appearance as a somewhat technical recapitulation of the thought of other men, in truth is anything but. It is, in point of fact, a *genealogy* in the original sense of the word, a work dedicated to exposing the antecedents of an idea which Evola considered so important that it might be capable of "affirming, against [the materialistic, democratic, rationalistic] conception, the value of blood, of tradition, of race," perhaps even to such an extent that "racism might have the meaning of restoration and of recovery of higher values" (*Myth of the Blood*, Conclusion). One can pass no judgement on these matters, save as one has due clarity on them; objective investigation into the origins necessarily precedes any objective determination of the value of the ideas that stem from these origins. This genealogical work was therefore considered by Evola to be of special importance on account of two related factors: first, the unique, inimitable promise possessed by the idea of race; and second, the ease with which that same idea might be spoiled or miscarried.

This returns us to the historical question, the question of what had been happening in Evola's time, such that he supposed the necessity of publishing not one, but two books on race in a very brief period of time. The most striking historical developments, without doubt, were surely the emergence of the German-Italian Axis in the year preceding the first publication of this book on the one hand, and both the Italian Manifesto of Race (a "slipshod piece of work," as Evola calls it in *The Path of Cinnabar*) and the decree on the Racial Laws in the year following it on the other. The Racial Laws were modeled explicitly on National Socialist legislation, to such an extent that some have supposed they should never have seen the light of day, had it not been for Italy's alliance with Germany — a thesis, incidentally, with which Evola disagreed.[1] Evola held that these laws were necessary in Italy principally due to the Italian Empire which was emerging in Africa; they were needed to establish a *pathos of distance* on the part of the Italians in their dealings with the Africans.

Be that as it may, the introduction of these laws marks a most sensitive moment in the history of Fascism — one of those decisive moments in which an idea of great price first makes its appearance in a people's spirit, and everything suddenly hinges on how that idea *will be interpreted*. Evola threw himself to the task of making this concept of race show its higher qualities, by molding it, rectifying it, directing it in the *right* way, imprinting it with all his marvelous talents of clarification, so as to make it the carrier of "a recovery of a spiritual heritage which we have forgotten" (see his Conclusion) — a heritage capable, perchance, of carrying modern man

---

1 On this and on many related matters of interest see "The Issue of Race" in *The Path of Cinnabar*.

toward that Traditionalist Order which Evola never ceased to seek with all the power at his disposal.

It seems indeed that his call was not without answer; after the publication of his *Synthesis* no lesser a figure than Mussolini himself contacted Evola, praising Evola's work and expressing his fervent hope that Evola's ideas might give rise to a specifically Italian doctrine of race, which could inform the Fascist regime and, as Evola put it, "elevate the Italian people." This was complicated by the outraged response of certain Italian Catholics and vulgar racists upon learning that Mussolini had been in contact with the Baron; they set about obstructing a rapport between the two men in every way possible.

Enough; that is a drama, as we well know, which was not permitted to play out to the end. The plot was interrupted violently and conclusively by a *diabolus ex machina*, and the Evolian project was brought with it to a ruinous and premature halt; nor can we say how it might have unfolded had it been permitted its due life. But in the same breath, let us respire hope as much as sadness; for in truth, in our day, that attempt *is being reborn*—

The reawakening of the racial idea after a long slumber is certainly one of the salient characteristics of our time. The Right in our day — the Alt-Right or the New Right as one prefers, but at any rate, the *True* Right — is characterized by many features, but one of the most visible is without question the *racial* frame of reference it takes when contemplating human societies and peoples. It declines to close its eyes to differences that have been indelibly incised in the human clay itself; it resolutely refuses to turn away, to avert its gaze in either modesty or shame. On the contrary, in a spirit of intellectual courage which is fundamentally *Western*, it insists on looking full on the reality of the matter, perhaps despite the consequences, and certainly despite all mores and morals which would prudishly deflect its glance. This contemporary *racial awareness* is on the verge of becoming, as we might say in Evolian language, an awareness of the "race of spirit" — a transformation which we must do all in our power to facilitate and to favor. For this is an integral and indispensable condition for the *awakening of the Occident*, through which we might once more strive toward *our* heights, and without which we are surely doomed to fade away from the history of the world, to be canceled out from the Book of Life.

There is patent urgency contained in this; but urgency, as always, is by itself a poor counselor. It would incite us, first and foremost, to neglect the *foundational work* of what we are building, and to proceed straight to the steeple. But if we be not merely architects of sky-castles and air-temples, it behooves us to heed the warning contained, not so much in the words as in the deeds of greater men: we should follow Evola's example and dedicate ourselves, first and foremost, to a comprehension of the origins, a contemplation of the *points of departure* of the modern idea of race. Only then might we position ourselves to embrace the idea of race with clarity and caliber, neglecting its pitfalls, avoiding its hazards, bravely countering its points of degeneration and boldly embracing those elements of it which can bring our renewal — that cultural and spiritual part of the idea of race which, if it be but rightly cultivated, might force a new renaissance of the West.

To our great fortune, Evola himself has broken trail in this preparatory work, with a lapidary succinctness of which he alone is capable. *The Myth of the Blood* is a guide through this parlous terrain.

A Comparison of the 1937 and 1942 Texts

So much for an apologia of the present work of translation — supposing such were necessary. We proceed now to a question which might appear on the surface, like this book itself, to be of a merely technical or scholarly nature, but which in point of fact is a doorway permitting us entry into a number of vital questions, both about Evola and about the wider question of race as such. The question is simply: what changes did Evola see fit to make to *The Myth of the Blood* in its second publication?

Apart from various smaller or purely stylistic additions or alterations, and a few intriguing subtractions (which I have noted in the footnotes), the most substantial differences between the two editions of *The Myth of the Blood* occur in four chapters: the Introduction; Chapter I: The Origins;

Chapter IX: Racism and Antisemitism; and the Conclusion. Let us articulate these differences.

In the present English edition, I have opted to provide translations of both the 1937 and the 1942 Introductions, despite the fact that some of their material thereby becomes redundant. Both introductions are of intellectual and literary excellence, and it is my hope that the reader may find his profit in comparing the two, keeping in mind the historical context which we have sketched above. It is always interesting to follow the transformation of a great man over the course of his life, and it seems to me that certain key points in Evola's development show forth, if only ever so subtly, in contrast between the two introductions he wrote. We shall presently have moment to speak of a few of these points.

Surely some of the most interesting material which Evola added in this interim period is to be found in the first chapter. The original edition of *The Myth of the Blood* began its investigation into the idea of race peremptorily with the modern period, seeking the roots of contemporary racism directly and explicitly in the Enlightenment. The second edition, on the other hand, opens with several dense and extremely suggestive pages on certain pre-modern seeds or analogues to contemporary racism, touching on everything from the Zodiac to Galen, from Emperor Julian to the Biblical tradition. The Renaissance origins of racism are also duly expanded, and several very interesting figures make their novel appearance in Evola's analysis.

Considering Evola's general worldview, this change, despite comprising only a handful of paragraphs, is deeply significant. A man like Evola, who tends to view almost everything modern with an almost invincible suspicion, surely would have balked before adopting any idea originating in that same period, the idea of race included. The expansion of the first chapter, we may say, indicates a parallel expansion of Evola's perspective. With the benefit of several *more* years' reflection, insight, and study, Evola had sharpened his appreciation of the racialist philosophy of his time, and had concluded that its roots sank deeper into the past than he had originally suspected. Indeed, I would argue that the course of these years represents

Evola's discovery of a *pre-modern and Traditional doctrine of race*, and the consequent birth of Evola's own and strikingly original racialist doctrine. The publication of the *Synthesis*, together with the republication of *The Myth of the Blood*, therefore represents the transformation from Evola's interpretation of race as a preeminently modern phenomenon in need of resistance and rectification, to his view of it as a concept of potentially crucial importance in the battle to save the West.

This Evolian transformation of viewpoint can be neatly summarized in a phrase which occurs, not on the 1937 edition of *The Myth of the Blood*, but exclusively in the 1942 edition, in the Introduction of 1942: "[I]t rarely happens that one encounters, in the ancient world, the word 'race': one did not feel the need to speak of race in the modern sense, because one *had* race" — a sentiment he echoes, incidentally, in the work's closing pages. The idea of race, so far from being a modern invention, is a modern *necessity*; it was *presupposed* by past ages, because they possessed the quality in question. We, by implication *no longer possess it — we must strive to get it back.*

Race as a spiritual task — that is the fundamental idea behind Evola's entire doctrine of race, and the fundamental key to many of the riddles that plague the contemporary day. The racial task, in turn, requires due preparation, which must, for reasons we have made clear, dally more on the modern period than on any more Traditional period. Race is a challenge for *our* time, made necessary by our special exigencies and contingencies. The present work represents a kind of intellectual and spiritual training in preparation for that challenge.

As for the expansion of Chapter IX, let us call the historical context once more to our service. The Italian Racial Laws unsurprisingly targeted the Jews in particular, sparking off heated debate and in many cases fierce opposition. The social situation in Italy was not what it had been in Germany at the time of the Nuremberg Laws. In the first place, the Jewish-Italian population was not always so easily identifiable as it was in Germany, having been historically much less numerous, and much longer in the country. As but an example of the difference, Evola in Chapter XI of the present work indicates a law in Germany which prohibits people from changing their names, since it was by their names that Jews could most readily be identified in that country. This was not so clearly the case in Italy, just as it is not so today; though of course there are exceptions, some of which are very visible indeed, in many specific cases the Italian Jew has been fully and invisibly assimilated into the Italian national fabric. (As Nietzsche put it, Italy had a "stronger digestive system" than Germany in this respect.) Mussolini himself received the support of several Jews, and he tended to waver on the racial question — an ambivalence which is in some ways but the reflection of the ambiguity of the Italian context itself.

It is therefore most significant that of all the chapters in the present book, that on the Jewish question strays most from Evola's clear intention to be expositor and not adjudicator of the ideas he presents. In part, we can explain this variance with reference to the fact that several of the ideas which Evola identifies in this chapter can be traced back to works that he himself had written. In the years preceding the second publication of this book, Evola had penned several essential articles on the Jewish question, making him, together with Giovanni Preziosi, one of the foremost Italian intellectuals to address this prickly problem; Evola had moreover written the introduction to the Italian publication of *The Protocols of the Elders of Zion*. This put him, in the chapter in question, into the somewhat awkward position of having to provide an objective third-party critique of ideas that in many cases he himself had originated. It is only to be expected that he should have tended in certain cases to break from his neutrality.

This peculiar aspect of the situation, however, does not fully explain the chapter in question. Evola could as easily have referred the reader to his relevant works, and dedicated himself merely to considering the published statements of the antisemites. There was no shortage of such material in his day, no limit to the list from which he might have fished a few pertinent names. Evola's reworking of this chapter thus indicates his recognition of the centrality of the Jewish question in his day. Its centrality, however, is not due to the centrality of the Jewish influence in history; it is due rather to the overwhelming importance which was ascribed to antisemitism in Germany. The chapter in question, its more evaluative tone, was made necessary by Evola's will to limn the Jewish question as clearly and briefly as possible, in order to give the Italian perspective on this question a condign form.

In what did such consist? We might suggest two points. In the first place, it can be said with surety that Evola had nothing to do with what he called the "vulgar antisemitic" position, which likes to blame everything on the Jew, from globalism to indigestion, from the decline of the West to head lice. As Evola points out, to reduce the crisis of the West exclusively to Jewish meddling, is to admit the shameful inferiority of the European, his abject genuflection before a manifestly greater Jewish power. But this, as Evola reminds us, is to mistake cause for effect; Jews did *not* bring about the decline of the West, but rather were permitted to exert a certain influence *because of* that decline.

In the second place, we might venture an interpretation of Evola's critique, as follows. Evola summarized the Jewish problem in this way:

> For the non-Jew who departs from his tradition as a religious law, there are yet a series of supports: there is the soil, there is blood, there is the fatherland. But in Judaism the Law takes the place of all these. At the point therefore that the Jew disbands, he becomes automatically a disintegrating force. Thus it is that he who is raceless becomes anti-race; he who is without nation becomes the anti-nation.

The fundamental aspect of the Jewish problem, as Evola is certainly not the first to note, is the Diaspora; the Jew belongs to no people, to no nation, to no soil. He is eternally a Jew who has been born, by a mere accident, in such and such a place, and who might as easily have been born in any other. Naturally, the intensity of the problem varies from individual to individual, as should go without saying. In our fundamentally unhealthy day, however, many things that *should* go without saying must be said.

Evola directs us, however, to an aspect of this problem that is less well recognized: that is, the spiritual tendencies of that Jew who *detaches himself from his tradition*. Such a one, having no natural point of reference, innately seeks out that kind of society which best accommodates his kind — the cosmopolitan, placeless, amoral, traditionless, rootless, borderless, unqualified and uncharacterized society which corresponds in large part, both to the situation of the "nonobservant Jew," and to the globalist order emerging in our day. On account of the rampant, indeed virulent secularization of society, this difficulty is aggravated tenfold, as it promotes a drifting within the Jewish community away from the Jewish tradition — a problem which is observed with due concern, incidentally, by many Jews. It thus seems to emerge from Evola's analysis that the Jewish problem has but a single viable solution, one which should be desired as much by Jews as by non-Jews: *Zionism.* The nationless people must be given its nation.

We mention finally the changes that Evola made to the closing chapter of this work. The original Conclusion was but a single page in length, and stated almost nothing on the value of the idea of race. The much-expanded Conclusion of the 1942 edition, on the contrary, comes nearest to expressing Evola's own idea of race, contrasting that idea, most significantly, with the claim that race is the product of Enlightenment Humanism — that is to say, the same claim that Evola himself had adopted only five years before, in the first publication of *The Myth of the Blood.* This new Conclusion opens with four brief but brilliant paragraphs in which Evola establishes two broad meanings of racism — the humanistic, rationalistic, scientistic meaning, and the traditional, spiritual, higher meaning which he himself embraced, and in large part created. This distinction prepares the way decisively for the *Synthesis,* for Evola's presentation of the views on race which he himself had developed over the course of a lengthy and penetrating study of the origins of modern racism.

The present work is the fruit, not of the *conclusions* of that study, but of the *study itself.* It is a masterly summation, an essential condensation, of the years of research that Evola dedicated to the perusal of racialist works. It is thus a synoptic invitation to all of us to prepare ourselves for a *higher doctrine of race* — to prepare ourselves for the Myth of the Blood.

The Myth of the Blood in our Contemporary Moment

What then ought we, in our very peculiar historical juncture, to bear in mind as we proceed along this path, whose contours have been indicated to us by the Baron?

In a broad survey of the idea of race in our day, it is clear that it has been brought to reawakening principally through the scientific approach to the study of man. It is likely, if not certain, that the question of race should never have arisen in our day and in our intellectual atmosphere if not for the *logic of biology* which sustains it and so often justifies it in our ranks. Any man, of course, even the rudest and most ignorant of scientific method and research, is capable of observing the manifest divergences between human groups, and of deriving therefrom certain appropriate conclusions. But such a one, standing as it were naked before the shame-slinging armies of egalitarianism, is not likely to resist their onslaught, save as he be particularly independent, cantankerous, or stubborn. Not for nothing has racism in our day been associated so closely with *shameless ignorance* — though one should not draw from this the facile conclusion that is too often drawn, namely, that racialist thought itself is the *product* of shameless ignorance. Rather, it is manifestly true that in a day like our own which is governed by unnatural lies and distortions, it will be the steadfastly ignorant man who will often be most capable of resisting the errors of his time, even as a gnarled and dense briar root might be but hardened by the same forest fire which withers leaves and swallows the straight-grained trunk.

But at the same time, it has not been ignorant men who were primarily responsible for the rebirth in our time of racialist thinking, for the simple reason that they lacked the intellectual quality to prepare it. It has rather been men of great independence and great intelligence to bring about this marvelous shift, and in order to do so, they have urgently required armor and arms to resist the ideologies of the day, which immediately set about attacking them with fervor and rage. These pioneers found their most ready defense, and *off*ense, in science — Darwinism, evolution, genetics, research into IQ, anthropology, etc. Racialism in our day almost invariably bears the watermark of science — if not of scientism.

The usefulness of science in this respect cannot be underestimated. Science itself is indeed, from a certain point of view, nothing but *usefulness* incarnate — for both good and ill. The issue is therefore not the desirability of scientific thought in the defense of racialist propositions, but rather its limitations in that domain. Science, in our materialistic and spiritually hollow day, is peculiarly equipped to bring certain men to the brink of an initiation into non-modern or nobler thought; but it cannot guide them over the threshold, for the simple reason that science itself is part and parcel of the modern world. Science, like a mole in a cage, can but paw at the borders of modernity; it cannot see past them.

Let us try to express this insight in Evolian terms. The title of the work the reader holds in his hands is not *The* Genetics *of the Blood*, not *The* Biology *of the Blood*, not *The* Evolution *of the Blood*, but — *The* Myth *of the Blood*. That is a most evocative phrase, taken from one of the central racialists of the National Socialism regime, Alfred Rosenberg, a man that Evola knew personally. Now, it is evident — it is indeed almost definitional — that science, no matter how long it strives, no matter with what sophistication and intricacy it manages to reveal the secrets of that double-helix which it so reductively considers the source of all living order, will never come near to giving birth to anything like a *myth* of the blood. It would not even know the meaning of such a thing, and would gaze with utter stupidity upon a phrase like "race of spirit" — supposing it did not dismiss these words out of hand. Nor could it ever, on account of certain of its rigorous self-restrictions, suggest for any human society a good or bad, a yea or a nay, based on race, or on any other standard for that matter. More to the point, for all its ability to isolate measurable or pseudo-measurable differences between human groups, it, alone and unsupplemented, can never furnish real *grounding* for ideas such as the preservation of the race, the continuation of the race — not to speak of the thriving, the exaltation, the consummation of the race. It is more helpless than a babe before questions of spirit and value: and thus so are we, insofar as we rely on it in these matters. It can at best recognize the existence of differences; as for *evaluating* these differences, or encouraging them, or seeking to realize them, we must turn elsewhere. We are in need, that is to say, of other and richer founts from which to draw these living waters. We must go back.

One might of course ask — and why not *ahead*? Why not attempt to *create* that which we lack, to bring from the bowels of nothing a new value, a new ideal of race? Evola, naturally, would regard any such Nietzscheanism with deep skepticism, for he believed that the unaided powers of man alone were necessarily destined to failure and fundamental inadequacy. Nonetheless, by his own admission, the texts of the Tradition are largely silent on the problem of race, for their writers and protagonists were able to take their *own* race simply for granted. This leads to a most peculiar quandary; the idea which has the greatest potential in our day of reawakening our higher beings and the reestablishing the greater qualities and mission of our people, is simultaneously the least accessible to us in the Tradition to which Evola eternally and imperiously directs us.

Our "going back" is then not like the going back of *Revolt Against Modernity*; it is a going back to the *modern* origins of race, rather than their *Traditional* origins; it is an action of rectification and investigation of those origins, which will permit us to prepare ourselves and our kin for the adoption of a *new doctrine of race* — one that transcends the scientistic boundaries of our modern intellectual schema — one that opens up the possibility of conscious and creative action in our day toward the spiritual and cultural resurrection of our people, our way, our *West*—

As for the rest — as for Evola's particular solution to this grave problem — we must here leave off as Evola himself does, by referring the reader to *Synthesis of the Doctrine of Race*, whose English publication, the translation of the present work has *finally* made possible.

JOHN BRUCE LEONARD
Cagliari, March 2018

Introduction of 1937

T**HE THEORY OF RACE, OR RACISM,** as it has taken form in Europe in the latest quarter of the century, and which ended up being affirmed in a way known by everyone in National-Socialistic Germany, should be conceived as more than a properly scientific, philosophic, or historical concept, such as might be evaluated objectively, in and for itself; it should be conceived of as a "myth."

When we say "myth," we do not mean a simple fiction, the arbitrary offspring of the fantasy, but rather an idea which principally draws its persuasive force from non-rational elements, an idea which has worth for the suggestive force which it condenses, and thus for its capacity to translate itself, finally, into action.

After all, it is more or less in these terms that Alfred Rosenberg, who is one of the most official exponents of the new doctrine, today presents the new theory of race: as a "new myth of life" called upon to create a "new type of life," and so, of state and of civilization. For, in every age, a people's irrational will to believe has need of a mainstay, almost we would say a center of crystallization, to gather itself and to manifest itself practically. The "myth" which he offers them is just such a mainstay, or center. The myth of the blood, of race — and thus more specifically of the Nordic blood and of the Aryan race[1]—is for Germany the "myth of the twentieth

---

1   The Italian here is *ario*. Evola uses this unconventional transliteration of the original Sanskrit term *ārya* here and almost exclusively throughout the present work, though

century," the symbol obscurely chosen by the new will to believe, the new will of this nation to rise. And in the same manner is surely to be found in the judgement of Mussolini, according to which "race," in part, is a fact of sentiment, not a reality.

The sum of its single elements and of its single motifs does not alone suffice to explain the mysterious force of a passion. In the same way, "myth" transcends the various elements which compose it, be these scientific, philosophical, or historical — the elements from which it is drawn and with which it claims to justify itself. And for this, the analysis worked by a coldly rationalist critic on a myth leads to little or nothing. It never reaches the deepest nucleus, the intimate necessity, the fact of sentiment, which grants support and force to the myth itself. This applies directly to the theory of race, and yet it instructs us regarding the fittest way to bring it to the consciousness of our public. We must consider racism as essentially a "symptom" and a "symbol of the times." Racism, certainly, lays claims to its own historical, philological, anthropological, philosophical, even juridical and religious, foundation. All these elements ought to be taken into consideration, but without letting ourselves be deluded by them, and so also without lingering too much on their objective value. It would be much more worthwhile to examine and to expose, in its various phases, the genesis of racism, its development up to its present extremist-political form, according to which it is founded absolutely with the "conception of life" (*Weltanschauung*) that National Socialism has placed at the center of its action.

In this development, three epochs can be distinguished. The first refers to the antecedents of racism, those preceding the man who is considered as its father, Gobineau. In the second epoch, in connection with the theses of Chamberlain, racism associates itself with politics, and develops itself in

---

ariano is much more common in Italian, even as "Aryan" in English. *Ario* is, however, clearly much nearer to the original, which might be Evola's reason for preferring it. At any rate, I have preserved Evola's choice through the use of a similar term in English; wherever the commoner "Aryan" appears, Evola himself has elected to use the commoner *ariano* in Italian.

connection with the Pan-Germanist ideologies of the immediate post-war period.[2] The third epoch comprehends the most recent post-war forms of racism, at times of its scientific and at times of its historico-speculative aspect, in which the politico-social moment determines itself ever more, up to the official ideology formulated by Hitler himself.

Thus, it will naturally become clear that it is impossible to separate one from the other these diverse aspects of the question, so as to isolate that which is relative to the problem of racism in a restricted sense — that is, the ethnic and anthropological sense. As we will see, racism has as its basic idea the strict correlation between blood and spirit, between race and culture. Thus it is that, from the very start, the problem of race was ever fused together with that of the origin, of the development and of the destiny of civilizations, and that therefore the urge to return to that point at which one might speak of "pure" race has ever determined new conceptions regarding the remotest prehistory, for which one has put one's hand on traditions, symbols, cults, myths, and testimonials of every kind. We therefore consider the theory of race in its entirety, in all that which, according to various domains, is most characteristic of it, and best able to bring us to understand its content of "myth," that is of an idea emerging with a momentary force of evidence in this special moment of the history of Western man.

Only the future will be able to tell us what meaning and what consequences this "myth" might bring in the development of our tormented European civilization.

J. Evola

---

2   As this book was first published in 1937, Evola means here, of course, the period following the *First* World War.

Introduction of 1942

*T*HERE ARE THREE POSSIBLE WAYS of understanding the concept of race: as a reference to reality; as a reference to a certain order of scientific knowledge; or, finally, as a "myth."

According to the first acceptation, the awareness of the value of race is betrayed already in a whole series of norms which can be found in ancient civilizations, especially wherever the system of castes and the laws of endogamy ruled, norms which in part continued up until relatively recent times in the traditions proper to the aristocracies. This racism was not theorized, but lived. Thus, it rarely happens that one encounters, in the ancient world, the word "race": one did not feel the need to speak of race in the modern sense, because one *had* race. One was more strongly interested in the mystic forces which could be felt behind the forces of the blood and of the *gens*: as in the patrician Roman, and in general Arya, the cults relative to the Lares, the Penates, and the *archegetes* heroes.[1] There was a very clear idea of the necessity of preserving the blood, of maintaining and transmitting a precious and irreplaceable patrimony connected to the blood in its integrity. Therefore, in various cases, the contamination of the blood appeared to be a true sacrilege. In the Orient, especially in Japan, very precise forms of racism of this kind live and rule even today.

---

1 The Lares were guardian deities in Rome, and were associated with the ancestors or with particular places, such as homes, buildings, fields, etc. The Penates, also deities of the Roman tradition, were deities of the household and hearth. *Archegetes* comes from the Ancient Greek Ἀρχηγέτης, meaning "leader" or "founder," and referred therefore to the heroes who were the founders of new cities or settlements.

The word "Anthropology" originally signified the science of man in general, taken in his physical and spiritual completeness. The term was used in the ancient world with such a significance especially by ARISTOTLE, and it was conserved also in certain Western philosophical schools, up to the time of KANT. But in the development of Western culture a gradual change of point of view came about. One was accustomed ever more to consider man, not as a privileged being in creation to be understood above all on the basis of his origins and of his supernatural essence, but as one of so many natural and, in the end, even animal species. Thus, Anthropology ended up taking on a new meaning: it was no longer the science of man as such, but of man as a being of nature, to whom it was possible to apply classificatory methods similar to those used in Zoology and Botany: Anthropology became a natural science of man.

By such a route, ever greater attention was brought to the corporeal and physical differences of human beings, and one arrived gradually at a consideration of the various races of humanity. Thus the idea of race became familiar in modern Anthropology, and defined itself increasingly through various elements furnished by biology and by genetics. Race, therefore, became a scientific concept, not to say a scientistic one: it founded itself on knowledge of "positive" character obtained by the classificatory and experimental method.

In the third place, we have race as a "myth" — and it is above all in these terms that the idea of race has taken form in Europe in the last quarter century, and has thus come to play a role in renovative political movements, first in the early days of National Socialism and then in Fascism itself. When we say "myth," we do not mean a simple fiction, the arbitrary offspring of the fantasy, but rather an idea which principally draws its persuasive force from non-rational elements, an idea which has worth for the suggestive force which it condenses, and thus for its capacity to translate itself, finally, into action.

Alfred ROSENBERG, who is one of the most official exponents of the new doctrine, presents the new theory of race in these terms: as a "new myth of life" called upon to create a "new type of life," and so, of State and of civilization.

The sum of its single elements and of its single motifs does not alone suffice to explain the mysterious force of a passion. In the same way, "myth" transcends the various elements which compose it, be these scientific, philosophical, or historical — the elements from which it is drawn and with which it claims to justify itself. And for this, the analysis worked by a coldly rationalist critic on a myth leads to little or nothing. It never reaches the deepest nucleus, the intimate necessity, the fact of sentiment, which grants support and force to the myth itself. This applies also to modern political forms of the theory of race: these forms, certainly, lay claim to historical, philological, anthropological, philosophical, biological, even juridical and religious, bases. But there is something more, beyond all of this, something with respect to which all of this has nothing but a "func-tional" meaning. This "something more," this "differential," in the highest forms of modern racism, should be understood as something which has arrived to us and which has conserved itself in the profound meaning that blood and race held for ancient, traditional man: as the reemergence — in new forms of expression, making use of the most various materials — of an internal heredity, which seemed to be dissipated in the development of various civilizations of modern type.

What formulations the doctrine of race ought to have if it is to be well cognizant of this, its deepest root, the wellspring of its power as myth and "idea-force"; from what deviations it must guard itself; what use ought to be made in it of contributions of anthropological, and, in generally, strictly scientific character; by what route it might reflect the traditional spirit, while at the same time expanding the potential of Fascism as a restorative revolution — we have spoken of all this in our book *Synthesis of the Doctrine of Race* (ed. Hoepli, 1941). The task that we propose to ourselves in this work is another: we wish to trace a kind of genesis of racism, or, better say, of the various motifs which figure in it, after having clearly defined their meaning; we wish to give a sense to the wellsprings

xxvi   THE MYTH OF THE BLOOD

that have nourished this "myth," of the influences which have gradually favored its formation and affirmation in the most recent history.

This task of ours will be carried out in the following way: we will first of all mention certain premodern antecedents of racism; we will then examine the principal formulations of that man who can, from a certain point of view, be considered the father of modern racism, GOBINEAU. We will study then the epoch in which, in connection to the theses of CHAMBERLAIN, racism "politicized" and developed itself above all in solidarity with the Pan-Germanic ideologies of the immediate post-war period. We will finally pass to the most recent post-war forms of racism, now of a "scientific" intonation, now of a historico-speculative intonation — forms in which the politico-social moment defines itself ever more clearly, and to which the ideology belongs which was formulated in this connection by HITLER.

In this exposition, we will keep ourselves faithful to the principle of the greatest objectivity, because, so far as critique and orientation go, the reader will find everything he might desire in our other work, which we have here mentioned. The impossibility of separating the various aspects of this question will thus appear by itself — the impossibility of isolating that aspect relative to the racist problem in the restricted sense, that is, the merely ethnic, anthropological, and biological sense. Precisely from the multifarious variety of the influences which the racist myth has gathered and has crystallized within a central nucleus, this myth has drawn its most recent meaning as a *Weltanschauung*, that is, of a general vision of life.

CHAPTER I

Origins

The fundamental axioms of racism. The idea of race in ancient traditions. Theory of the stars and of temperaments. The Biblical theory. Polygenism. Mystic races. The soul of the nations. Fichte and the "originating people." The philological Aryan thesis.

IN ITS ESSENCE, racism rests on two fundamental principles:

1) Humanity, humankind, is an abstract fiction. Human nature is fundamentally differentiated and its differentiations correspond to blood, to races. There stands amongst the various races a fundamental inequality — not an inequality determined by external causes, but an inequality of nature. Inequality, not equality, is the original datum and the normal condition.

2) To each one of these racial differentiations of human type corresponds a determinate "spirit," which constitutes its internal aspect — and, according to some, also its formative cause: in which case this "spirit" is the counterpart of that which manifests itself in the physical characteristics of a race and which stands at the basis of

the form proper to its civilization, to the creations and to the deeds of those individuals which compose it.

To these two fundamental principles, one might add a third, somewhat in the quality of a corollary:

3)   A race can keep itself more or less faithful to its spirit and to its type, it can correspond more or less to its original characteristics. A race can therefore be more or less "pure." The purity of race is subjected to special laws, maxims such as that of heredity and of the non-mixing of blood. The importance attributed to the purity of race in a people might be indicated by these words, excised from certain official directives for racial education in Germany: "Peoples and civilizations can truly acquit the mission entrusted to them when they realize in their history the tasks defined by their race — that is when they tend to their proper ends, commencing from their proper nature. Every mixing with races which are physically or psychically foreign signifies, for every people, a betrayal of its proper task, and, in the end, a decline."

According to the likeliest conjectures, the word "race" comes from *radix*, thus proving itself etymologically equivalent to the word "stock": both words refer to the continuity of the originating lineage, which produces individuals always like to each other. Whence the current definition: "race is a living unity of individuals of common origin with equal bodily and spiritual characteristics" (WOLTMANN): "Race represents a human group which, for a commonality of physical characteristics and of psychic qualities which are proper to it, distinguishes itself from every other human group and generates elements which are always similar to one another" (GÜNTHER), or, yet more concisely: "race is a hereditary type" (TOPINARD).

Taking this as our premise, let us say something regarding the most distant antecedents of racism. We might observe in the first place that certain of the starting points of the racists, certain of which are of no little moment, can already be found in the theory of planetary and zodiacal influences, a doctrine which dates back to the eldest antiquity. It was a traditional teaching that not only individuals, but also various peoples are differentiated by way of supersensible influences, connected to the stars and to the spiritual forces of which the stars are, according to this teaching, the symbolic manifestations: and as the appearance of men and of the races on earth were connected to such influences, one might through their study come to an already almost racist classification which comprehends the temperament, the character, the tendencies, the physical constitution, and sometimes even the color, of the peoples. In this connection, the points of reference were either the seven planets or the twelve signs of the Zodiac. We owe to PTOLEMY a Zodiac-based classification which, as Guéydan de ROUSSEL has justly noted, "is the fount of all the dualistic and multiplistic classifications encountered afterward. Thus, for example, the great dualistic classifications based on the nineteenth-century principle of conquering races and races destined to be subjected, into diurnal peoples and nocturnal peoples, into masculine races and feminine races, are already found implicitly in the divisions of the Zodiac into signs that command signs that obey, in diurnal signs and nocturnal signs, into masculine signs and feminine signs."

We therefore find already in antiquity the idea of differences between human beings which are innate, congenital, and, to a certain degree, even "fatal," because they draw their origin from a state anterior to the human state. Thus, for example, we find a tradition, also a Roman tradition, that whoever were connected to the influences of the sun would be *dominus natus*, the man destined naturally and fatally to dominion.

The ancient Biblical tradition too has certain racist elements in the theory of descendance of the principal peoples of the earth from the three sons of Noah: Ham, Japheth, and Shem. We are dealing therefore with three lineages differentiated not only in matters of blood and body, as distinct "seeds," but also in matters of spirit, given that one of these bears a "curse," and another a "predilection." From Ham, a name which also means heat, multitude, the "torrid" race of the Hamites, of the ancient peoples inhabiting Egypt and the eastern Mediterranean, of the

Phoenicians and the Ethiopians, etc.; from Shem, Noah's firstborn, were derived the Semites — the Jews, the Assyrians, the Caldeans, etc.; and finally, from Japheth, were supposedly derived the principal lines of the white race, the Celts, the Scythians, the Medeans, up to the Greeks and the Romans. Proper to the Biblical tradition is also another racial classification, referring back to the twelve Jewish tribes which were supposedly dispersed throughout the world, thus giving rise to distinct stocks. Quite singularly, certain English circles, and traditionalist to boot, have had no difficulty in making these Jewish views their own in the present day; the result is a racism *sui generis*, which maintains the idea that the most ancient Brittonic stocks are derived from one of those tribes.

It is little known that EMPEROR JULIAN — or, as he is also and abusively known, Julian the Apostate — was a decided subscriber to the racist idea, to such an extent that Cyril felt constrained to write a work in refutation of its theses. Emperor Julian upheld the thesis of *polygenism*; considering Teutons, Phoenicians, Scythians, Ethiopians, and other peoples, he refused to believe that the physical and spiritual differences which these present might be derived from external factors, from environment, climate, etc.: he held rather that it was necessary to refer to essential differences, differences of nature, of genesis; thus he came to oppose the Judaic-Christian idea of monogenism, which is to say the supposition that the entire human race was derived from a single couple, issuing therefore in the last analysis from a single blood. The immortal gods rather created, in his opinion, together with the world and *ab initio*, different human stocks.

Moreover, the term *genos* in its turn, which means generation, ancestry, or race, appears rather often in the ancient Christian literature, and particularly in the Pauline and Gnostic writings: here it essentially designates, however, a "race of the spirit," *theoû génos*, a *genus mysticum*. Gnosticism moreover articulates this notion by distinguishing between three races: those of the *pneumatic* men, the of the *psychic* men, and that of the *hylic* men — races characterized by the predominance which one or the other of the three fundamental elements has in the human being in each of them, these elements being the spiritual (*pneuma*), the psychic (*psyche*), or the material (*'ulé*). These differences have an "ontological" character: they regard substance, they manifest themselves in the very subtlest makeup of the body. In the Medieval Age and in the Renaissance, racist elements persist in the doctrines on the human being which take their bearings from the ancient teachings on the astral presence and on the correspondences between man and world, between "microcosm" and "macrocosm." The *doctrine of the four humors* in particular was developed, with reference to the theories of HIPPOCRATES and GALEN. This doctrine almost even stood in for the definition of four great human races: the humors manifest themselves in individuals both through clearly identifiable psychic and physiological marks, and also through various forms of character and of predispositions in the soul. One might observe that this doctrine of the humors, for which one might cite, along with the others, Paracelsus, after having fallen into disrepute and after being considered "outdated," today has been made the object of renewed attention in various circles, which recognize in it many valid positive aspects. Jean BODIN in 1593 and Pierre LE CHARRON in 1601 employed it, moreover, in their properly ethnic classifications; these classifications were meant to specify the general qualities of the various peoples, which were divided, not only by their location, but also by their intimate constitution, into southern peoples, central peoples, and northern peoples.

Nor should one neglect the curious racist anticipations, now in an almost modern sense, which are found in Tomaso CAMPANELLA (1589–1639). In the "city of the sun" of his utopia, the idea of race receives specific recognition. The "Solarians," who rule in his hypothetic State, mock the Europeans of the time, who "dedicate themselves with great care to the improvement of the race of dogs and horses, and do not deign to occupy themselves with the race of men." The Solarians have rather created in their State a ministry which, aided by competent men, by doctors and astrologers, controls all unions between men and women. The authorization of this ministry is necessary in the "city of the sun" not only for marriages, but also for engendering and baptizing children. The purpose is the formation "of the most beautiful race possible"; the "Solarians religiously entrust the care of this race, which is the prime element of the Republic, to the magistrates." This brings de ROUSSEL to say, in recording these passages of the work of the Italian philosopher, that "such a clear vision of the future certainly justifies our calling Campanella, who was considered in the past century as a prophet of the socialist State, the prophet of the racist State."

And now let us turn to more recent times. Here we find developments of the idea of race in connection to the gradual formation of the Romantic conception of nation.

However much his conception remains decidedly indeterminate, MONTESQUIEU as early as 1748 had spoken of a "spirit of nations" which arises surely from various factors — climate, creeds, customs, history, etc. — but which is different for every people and which constitutes the principal from which any normal legislation should take its inspiration. This concept was however developed only later, in the epoch of German Romanticism, first of all with HERDER, then with FICHTE.

In contrast to LESSING, for whom the causes of the differences between nations in affects, talents, and bodily abilities are solely physical, which is to say is accidental, exterior, reducible to environment, to climate, etc., Herder took up a nearly theological position, speaking of the "spirit of the nations" (*Völkergeist*) as of so many divine manifestations which characterize the substance of various human groups from within, making of them almost as many persons; such a spirit, flowing through the generations of a people, connects the individuals into a single unity and a single destiny. "Through the nations God proceeds on earth," wrote Herder. Nevertheless, the conception of the individuality of peoples in Herder does not yet arrive at the specific domain of race. Faith, language, and literature, more than blood and ethnic characteristics, are for him the decisive witness to the spirit of peoples.

In this connection, one can also observe that those determinations and those oppositions to various kinds of civilization originally developed

on a similar plane that, finally giving life to the famous concept of "Arya."
First Franz BOPP, and then his successor August Friedrich POTT, who was
already author of a work on the *Inequalities of the Human Races*, and finally Jakob GRIMM, all drew their hypotheses about the common origins of
Indo-Germanic civilizations from essentially philological studies, as well
as their hypotheses about the opposition of these civilizations to Semitic
civilizations. From the research of this group of thinkers, who would be
joined subsequently by the Englishman Max MÜLLER and his school, the
existence of a common originating "Indo-Germanic" or "Arya" language
and of a corresponding common ideology was revealed. Thence also the
hypothesis of an originating Indo-Germanic or Arya race surfaced, a race
which was the bearer of the language and the common mythology in those
various European and Asiatic civilizations which conserve the remnants
of such a race. The formulation of this hypothesis, together with the coin-
ing of the term "Arya," dates back to the aforementioned Franz Bopp, author of a *Comparative Grammar of Sanskrit, Zend (Avestan), Greek, Latin,
Lithuanian, Old Slavonic, Gothic and German* issued in Berlin already in
1833. According to Müller, this originating Aryan race existed "in a specific epoch in a region of central Asia" and from there was diffused into
the Persian, Indian, and European regions in various nomadic waves: the
corresponding languages and civilizations had, therefore, a common root,
and their diversity could be related to various circumstances and various
forms of adaptation. Only later did the properly racist interpretation arise,
and really in an abusive way, because it ended up uniting to the concept
of a given language of a determinate anthropological and ethnic type,
speaking of "Arya" peoples in places where one should have spoken only
of peoples of "Arya" culture and language. Such are however the origins
of the modern Arya myth (which in this phase does not yet mean Nordic,
because an originating Caucasian fatherland was attributed even to the
Teutonic Arya, as has been said): origins, therefore, marked by a visible
ambiguity, because if we could infer race from language, we should, for
example, suppose a single race for all those who, having been absorbed by
the Anglo-Saxon culture and education, today speak English: but in fact

we find Americans and Negros, Hindus and Australians, who all speak that tongue. However, regarding this, and regarding that further legacy of research which attempted to complete and further define the concept of the Arya, we will speak presently. Here we shall only observe that the best-known terminology of racism has taken its origin less from racial and ethnic, than from philological and cultural, considerations.

Following in the steps once more of Herder, we come to recall the conception of Fichte, who already stands nearer to an ideology of the racist type. Naturally we cannot here explicate the metaphysical premises of this conception, which are linked to the general principles of so-called idealistic philosophy. We will limit ourselves to saying that, for Fichte, the world is the theater of a gargantuan effort of the Idea to become identical to itself in nature and in history. In every domain, we find therefore a greater or lesser degree of this correspondence, of this transparency or conformity to the natural element, as compared to that idea which manifests it. In the application of this conception to the ethic plane, there arises in Fichte the concept of a "primordial people" (*Urvolk*) as distinguished from derivative peoples, and of a "normal people" as distinguished from "mixed peoples" — concepts already very near to the successive concept of the "pure race."

Fichte meant by people "the totality of men continuing to live in society with each other and continually creating themselves *naturally and spiritually* out of themselves, a totality that arises together out of the divine under a certain special law of divine development."[1] He says, moreover, that:

> Spiritual nature was able to present the essence of humanity in extremely diverse gradations in individuals and in individuality as a whole, in peoples. Only when each people, left to itself, develops and forms itself in accordance with its own peculiar quality, and only when in every people each individual develops himself in accordance with that common quality, as well as in accordance with his own peculiar quality then, and then only, does the manifestation of divinity appear in its true mirror as it ought to be; and only a man who either entirely lacks the

---

1   All quotations by Fichte, except as otherwise noted, are taken from *Addresses to the German Nation*, trans. R. F. Jones, M.A.

notion of the rule of law and divine order, or else is an obdurate enemy thereto, could take upon himself to want to interfere with that law, which is the highest law in the spiritual world. Only in the invisible qualities of nations, which are hidden from their own eyes qualities as the means whereby these nations remain in touch with the source of original life only therein is to be found the guarantee of their present and future worth, virtue, and merit. If these qualities are dulled by admixture and worn away by friction, the flatness that results will bring about a separation from spiritual nature, and this in its turn will cause all men to be fused together to their uniform and conjoint destruction.

Here one can recognize the mainstays of what will become the racist ideology: the differentiation of peoples; the principle of purity; and the condemnation of every intermixing and adulteration; the deduction of the characteristics, virtues, and dignities of single peoples from the qualities innate to the originating stock.

Fichte's "normal people" is precisely a people to which corrupting intermixing is alien, a people faithful to its originating type so far as to appear as "a pure image of the idea." While mixed peoples have nothing but a "historical I," meaning a spirit forged solely by earthly contingencies, the "normal people" has a "metaphysical I." The concept of "normal people" in Fichte proceeds then to associate itself with the concept of a "primordial people," which in prehistoric times was dispersed through various lands, "carrying civilization even to the savages." Anticipating GOBINEAU and CHAMBERLAIN, Fichte recognizes two distinct ethnic elements even in Rome: "it is very clear that in Rome, originally, there were two principal classes, the patricians descended from an aristocratic colonizing stock and the people descended from the original inhabitants of Italy."

Fichte distinguishes himself from many of his contemporaneous Romantics, who were full of nostalgia for the distant lost spiritual light of the origins, by not reducing the "primordial people" to a mere reality of the past. He believed that there exist to this day peoples which conserve a certain purity, rendering them capable of maintaining uninterrupted contact with their "idea," and a kind of perennial freshness and originality. In his *Speech to the German Nation*, Fichte attributes precisely to his people the dignity of being a "primordial people," therefore anticipating

another fundamental concept of the Pan-Germanic racism which followed him: the Teuton, supposedly the direct heir to the primordial Arya
race. Fichte affirms that "only the German, the original man, who has
not become dead in an arbitrary organization, really has a people and is
entitled to count on one, and that he alone is capable of real and rational
love for his nation."

For Fichte, the differentiation of the pure Teutons from the impure
Teutons (the Franks) at the dawn of the Medieval, was a great turning
point in European history. To the stock of the pure Teutons remained
the patrimony not only of the "originating language" (*Ursprache*), itself
free from any intermixing, but also as it were of a certain metaphysical
sensitivity. This brings Fichte to some rather curious affirmations, such as
when he asserts the presumed identity between every "originating" philosophy (that is, every philosophy arising from the one, pure, divine life)
and German philosophy—or when he states that only to the Germans
was it given to comprehend Christianity in its pure state. If together with
such views one recalls Fichte's conviction that "the metaphysically predestined people has the moral right to realize its destiny with all the means
of cunning and strength,"[2] one realizes that those who have seen in Fichte
the father of post-war Pan-Germanism are not altogether mistaken.
Regarding that which really interests us here, if Fichte, in his conceiving
the difference between peoples as conforming to a spiritual law and in his
connecting the privilege of special gifts to conditions of race and origin,
really is a precursor of racism, then one must allow that these racist drives
are turned on their heads in Fichte, that they transform into precisely
contrary ideas (which some extremist racists today[3] would not hesitate
to call Jewish or even ... Catholic) when Fichte assigns to the German
people, conceived as primordial and as the carrier of the Idea, the task of

2   In both this and the following Fichte quotation, I am uncertain as to the origin of this
     phrase, and have provided the translation of Evola's Italian. The nearest equivalent I
     was able to find for the present quotation reads as follows in the original Fichte: "To
     you has fallen the greater destiny, to found the empire of the spirit and of reason, and
     completely to annihilate the rule of brute physical force in the world."

3   In the 1937 edition Evola here indicated Rosenberg by name.

"realizing the postulate of a single empire, of a state which is intimately and organically homogeneous" according to the principle of "a liberty founded on the equality of every being that has a human appearance." This is a contradiction which derives from two aspects of Fichte, who was on the one hand an "idealist" philosopher, and on the other the herald of liberal and Jacobinizing democratic principles, toward the emancipation of his people.

The idea likewise peeks out of HEGEL that each people has its determinate spirit and that "this spirit of a people is determined in itself ... and determined also by the historical degree of its development," beyond being a particular manifestation of the World Spirit. However the racist significance of this view disappears in the entirety of Hegelian philosophy, both because the "Spirit of the Nation" for Hegel finds expression more in the State, and even in its Head, its Monarch, than in race or in the blood; and also because intrinsic to this Spirit is an impulse toward the universal, therefore, toward a point of reference which necessarily relativizes and transcends whatever might be proper to a single anthropological type or ethnic group, or to its particularistic traditions. Let this suffice as a sketch of the antecedents of the racist idea. In the end, we find it yet entangled with nationalistic ideology. Only with Gobineau does it overcome this entanglement, taking a precise and decided form, becoming conscious of itself. In the meantime, it would be well to mention also the scientific and anthropological precedents for the theory in question.

CHAPTER II

The Doctrine of the Count Gobineau

The beginning of anthropological racism. The problem of the
decadence of civilizations. The first racist typology: the Aryans,
the Blacks, and the Yellows. The Arya heroic cycle. A new
historical method. "Semitic" Rome.

OWARD THAT END, it is necessary to turn to the German Johann
Friedrich BLUMENBACH (1752–1840), who with his specification
and description of the various forms of human crania, and with
his attempts to reach, on that basis, a scientific subdivision of the various
human races, can be called the forerunner of contemporary anthropological science.

The well-known but by now superseded classification of the five fundamental races dates back to Blumenbach: the white or Caucasian, the
yellow or Mongolic, the black or African, the olive or Malaysian, the red
or American. We owe to him the introduction of methods whose application and extension were encouraged ever more in the general climate of

the new epoch. This was indeed also the epoch of DARWIN's evolutionist materialism, and LAMARCK's transformist materialism. It became ever more customary to consider man in his naturalistic, biological part, the part of him conditioned by heredity and by natural selections. Thus one arrived also at a natural science of man, which employed more or less the same criteria and the same methods that had been adopted by the other forms of natural science. Genetics, Phrenology, Skeletology, and above all Biology transformed themselves into the helpmeets of the new discipline. Prehistoric investigations began to enter into the question particularly in the field of Phrenology, wherein use was made of research into prehistoric man and fossilized man. TROTSKY defined racism as "zoological materialism." There is something in this Jewish definition which fits, if one considers certain one-sided forms of the theory of race which feel the effects precisely of this anthropological materialism, this mutilated and materialized way of conceiving of the human being.

Already the Dutchman Peter CAMPER (1722–1789) had introduced the criterion of "facial angle" for the specification of racial characteristics. The Swede Anders RETZIUS (1796–1860) in his turn introduced the famous subdivision of dolichocephalic crania and brachycephalic crania, meaning lengthened types and shortened types of crania; and it was he who on the basis of this criterion made a new attempt at the classification of human races, which was to serve as racism's *pièce de résistance.* On this basis, Anthropology developed rapidly in the last century somewhat in all countries, conserving ever its distinctly positivistic hues. Here one might recall the Frenchman Paul BROCA (1824–1889),[1] founder of the Anthropological School of Paris. The current that takes its inspiration from him so early as 1841 enunciated its principle thus: "In a nation there are always diverse races; it is necessary therefore to seek to distinguish the pure types from those produced by intermixing." With this principle, the movement from a Romantic conception of "nation" to that of "race" was virtually already effected, and a new order of research began, which sought to get to the bottom of racism properly understood, to rediscover and to define what

---

[1]   There is a small error in the original: BROCA died in 1880.

could be considered equivalent in the field of ethnology and anthropology to the pure and originating "normal people" theorized by Fichte in the philosophical field.

Moreover, a work of VIREY entitled *Natural History of Human Kind* dates back to 1801, to the epoch of the Revolution (the work even declared itself to have been written in the "year IX"); this work contained a "genealogical table of the intermixings of the various human races": it thus heralded the special importance granted by modern biological racism to the laws of heredity, which by then had been carried onto the experimental plane. Virey also employs Camper's science of facial angles, since it is also on the basis of facial indices that he distinguishes in human kind "the beautiful white races" and the "ugly brown and black ones." Simultaneously, it is here that various attempts at integration arise; sketches of a racism connected to a classification which is also spiritual. Thus in 1824, with evident polemic reference to the work now cited by Virey, a book written by Fabre D'OLIVET was issued, a work of no little interest entitled *Philosophical History of Human Kind*. This book also contained a scheme of general racial classification, beyond the attempt to identify the influence that each race has exercised by turns on history, starting in primordial times. The denominations are: the red or Austral race, the yellow race, the black or Sudic race, the white or Boreal race. The most important aspect of this categorization is that Fabre d'Olivet was the first in this epoch to maintain the *remote Nordic-Arctic origin* of the white race, its Boreal or Hyperboreal origin. In him, this thesis however no longer has the character of a scientific hypothesis, but rather that of an exposition of a traditional teaching, which was yet conserved in the very closed circles with which he was in contact.

Here we will cite once more KLEMM's division into "active races" and "passive races," and also the division into "feminine races" and "masculine races" of Gustave D'EICHTAL. The principal motifs of this subdivision were taken up in 1849 by Victor COURTET DE L'ISLE, not without specific polemical intentions: there was yet humming in France the polemic for and against the abolition of slavery, and, in this connection, the abolitionists took their bearings naturally by the humanitarian theses and by the democratic conception of the absolute equality of all the human races. Against this, Courtet de l'Isle proclaimed himself a subscriber to the existence of "naturally preponderant races" and "naturally weak races" in the terms of a true and proper antithesis, drawing all the logical consequences to come of this in terms of racial and colonial politics. He thus developed a theory which remains interesting even today, one based on the difference between the "conquering races" and those "born to serve," between "noble races" and "races of slaves," between "adult races" and "infantile races," bringing to bear also the distinction between "masculine races" and "feminine races" in the German d'Eichtal, and affirming on this basis the necessity for very different relations in dignity and supremacy between the various parts of humankind.

At the beginning of the second half of the last century, three principal components favored the formation of the racist myth, one *philosophical*, one *anthropological*, and the third *philological*. The philosophical component is represented by the Romantic conception of the soul or spirit of peoples; the anthropological component is represented by the distinction between dolichocephalic man and brachycephalic man, which is associated more or less with other ethnic traits, as well as with the first starts of the theory of heredity; and finally the philological component is represented by the discovery of the common origin of groups of Indo-European languages, and by the hypothesis of a primordial "Arya" language anterior to their differentiation.

These elements awaited only a synthesis, which then would necessarily enter into the domains of history and of the philosophy of civilization, introducing into these a criterion hitherto unknown, namely the racial criterion:

The so-called spiritualistic (or idealistic) consideration of history had recognized in spiritual forces and in ethical ideas the potency that molds the historical life; the so-called materialistic consideration of history had attributed to environment and to economico-social circumstances and in general to material conditions the historically forming function. In opposition to this, the racist narrative of history posits man himself as the historically formative force, but man as a

member of his particular race, of the special spirit from which proceed the oc-
currences of an epoch and of a nation, which race itself conditions.[2] (GÜNTHER)

Arthur de GOBINEAU was the author of just such an investigation.
Gobineau was pressed to conceive and to formulate his theory of race by
the problem of the decadence of human civilization, "the most striking,
and at the same time the most obscure, of all the phenomena in history."[3]
It would seem that he was originally brought to this problem in the Orient,
in Persia, where, after having passed a long period in a diplomatic role,
he came to feel the living bitter contrast between the Persia of that time,
fragmentary and decadent, and the splendid grandeur yet conserved by
the mute monumental traces of the antique Middle-Iranian civilization.
Naturally, Assyria, India, Greece, and Rome itself presented the same
enigma, from which Gobineau came to ask himself why such marvelous
civilizations had declined — civilizations which seemed almost to reflect
on the earth the greatness and the power of superterrestrial things.

Gobineau commenced by affirming that various causes usually ad-
duced to explain why civilizations die are only apparent; that, beyond the
superficial side, apart from cases of violent death, the existence of a general, uniform, and precise cause for the life and death of all civilizations
can be observed. He distinguished also between the ruin of States and
that of civilizations, observing that "the same kind of culture sometimes
persisting in a country under foreign rule and weathering every storm of
calamity, at other times being destroyed or changed by the slightest breath
of a contrary wind."[4]

---

2   Evola had read Günther extensively, and cited fully nine of his books in *The Myth of
    the Blood*. Unfortunately, only some of these have been translated. In all quotations
    taken from Günther, I have therefore translated from Evola's translation, save where
    otherwise noted.

3   All references to Gobineau, unless otherwise noted, are taken from *The Inequality of
    the Human Races*, translated by Adrian Collins (1915, London: William Heinemann).
    The present sentence is the opening line of the first chapter of that book.

4   Chapter I, p. 2.

After positing this, Gobineau dedicated himself to demonstrating, little by little, the insufficiency of the various causes usually admitted to explain the phenomenon of decadence.

1) This phenomenon is not owing to the absence of religious sentiment nor to bad customs. As for the first point, he recalls that for example the Persian Empire, the Tyrian Empire, the Carthaginian, the Hebrew, the ancient Mexican, fully maintained their national faith when they were stricken with death. Regarding customs, he observes that these exceedingly frequently show oscillations which little enough influence the general course of a civilization. Far from discovering a superior morality in young societies and in societies in which the force of civilization is yet intact, there is good reason to think that nations which grow old and crystallize, and consequently which are nearing their fall, present to the eyes of the censor a much more satisfying state; for their usances are sweetened, their men are of better accord with one another, each one having discovered how to live more easily, and reciprocal rights having had the time to better define themselves. This gives a more positive and precise content to the concepts of just and unjust, of good and bad.

2) Nor does the greater or lesser perfection of the system of government, that is, the political moment, have influence over the longevity of civilizations. Gobineau recognizes that a good government and good laws certainly influence the general well-being, but he contests that these are the only cause of social aggregation, or that the state and the laws alone give to a social group its unity and its true strength. Moreover, he believes it imprecise to say that peoples and civilizations can live only under the condition of a state of well-being and of political order. "[W]e know that, like individuals, they can often go on for a long time, carrying within them the seeds of some fell disease, which may suddenly break out in a virulent form." If civilization and nations were to perish for the imperfection of their political system, "not one would survive the first years of its growth; for it is

precisely in those years that they show the worst administration, the worst laws, and the greatest disorder."[5] A government for Gobineau is bad above all when the principle from which it has drawn its life lets itself be corrupted, ceases to be healthy and vigorous as it was before; when it rests on conquest pure and simple; or when it stirs up antagonism between the various classes or between the supreme power and the nation. But Gobineau dedicated himself to demonstrating that never have such conditions in and of themselves meant the death of a civilization, nor the decadence of a civilization and of a people.

3) Nor can influence over the destiny of a people and of its civilization be found in the degree to which the well-being of the people is accommodated by the country in which that people is established. "[A] nation does not derive its value from its position; it never has and never will. On the contrary, it is the people which has always given — and always will give — to the land its moral, economic, and political value."[6] A race which conserves its strength and finds itself in its ascendant phase will always liberate itself from unfavorable geographical considerations, transporting itself elsewhere, and the destiny of its civilization will not suffer from this.

4) Finally, Gobineau excludes the possibility that simple domination or subjection of one people by another might decide the problem of the life and the death of their respective civilizations, so long as we are not dealing with the case of complete destruction. In the face of foreign domination, the civilization of the conquered, if it is yet vital, grows often stronger, even to the point of conquering its own conquerors. The civilization of the conquerors develops itself and bolsters itself from its conquest only when the people that brings this conquest has in itself superior vital possibilities, which will give place to superior creations, by way of which the conquest, the strength,

---

5   Both quotations here are from Chapter III, p. 19.

6   Chapter VI, p. 61.

and the life of the victor will be transmitted, and it will find itself called to participate in a new and better destiny.

If, however, all of this does not suffice to explain the mystery of the life and the death of civilizations, on what principle must one lay one's hands? Gobineau responds: the principle of *race*.

It is race which gives origin, strength, value, and life to a nation and to its civilization. Every living civilization is the expression of a young race, an integrated and originating race. So long as the intimate vital possibilities of such a race remain intact, so long as its blood remains pure, the corresponding civilization maintains itself, defends itself, reaffirms itself in the face of every contingency and every obstacle. When the race declines, when the originating blood alters or disperses, its civilization fatally dies, or else it conserves itself in mere cadavers possessed of an illusory semblance of life, which collapse to the ground at the slightest blow. Likewise, every effective variation or modification of civilization has a biological background, which is parallel to a corresponding variation or modification or hybridization of the race.

The secret of the decline of civilization for Gobineau is therefore ethnic degeneration. A people is degenerate "because it has no longer the same blood in its veins, continual adulterations having gradually affected the quality of that blood. In other words, though the nation bears the name given by its founders, the name no longer connotes the same race."[7] It is therefore the *intermingling of blood* which appears to Gobineau as the cause of degeneration. But such an idea leads one directly to an originating diversity and inequality of human races and, in particular, to the opposition between superior dominating races on the one hand, and inferior races on the other, which, as subjects, offer the former the object of their affirmation.

Here Gobineau seems to tend toward fatalism, insofar as he recognizes almost as an inevitability that the superior races by their very nature expand in order to affirm themselves and to dominate. But with dominion a

---

7   Chapter 4, p. 25.

fusion is necessarily brought about, an interpenetration of the elements of the dominating race with those of the inferior dominated and conquered races, which unite themselves with the former, absorbing and at the same time altering its blood, its civilization. Beginning at this moment, the originating ethical and spiritual qualities of the conquerors are diminished and obfuscated and their civilization enters into its descending arc. Superior peoples, precisely on account of their civilizing genius, gather around themselves those elements by which they must be absorbed and corrupted. On the other hand — according to Gobineau — they become victims of a primary cause, namely their small originating number, then of secondary causes, such as for example that, for the special role that the elements of the superior race play in the whole complex of civilizations and of the states founded by that race, and being by their very nature lovers of battle and of danger, they are particularly exposed to destructive effects of battles, of banishments, of revolts. Thus it happens that a civilization often subsists after the generating cause of its life has ceased to exist, and this posthumous, contingent survival of a civilization misleads the superficial observer and induces him to accept abstract and unreal principles as the causes of the civilizations of peoples, neglecting the true cause of race.

For Gobineau, the fundamental equality of humankind is naught but the truth of the bastard, the crossbreed: "[W]hen the majority of the citizens have mixed blood flowing in their veins, they erect into a universal and absolute truth what is only true for themselves, and feel it to be their duty to assert that all men are equal."[8] "[T]he more heterogeneous the elements of which a people is composed, the more complacently does it assert that the most different powers are, or can be, possessed in the same measure by every fraction of the human race, without exception."[9] And, extending that which is true only for them to the entirety of the generations which exist, have existed, or will exist on earth, it ends precisely

---

8   Chapter V, p. 36.

9   Chapter V, p. 37.

by proclaiming words "which, like the bag of Aiolus, contain so many storms—'All men are brothers.'"

The *normal* truth, which relates to the origins, to humanity in its pure state, so to speak, is rather inequality, which Gobineau defines by distinguishing three great ethnic lines or originating racial types: the *white Arya* type, the *yellow* type, and the *black* type.

The black race is considered worthless by Gobineau. In his narrow and vanishing brow, the man of the black race carries in his cranium the imprint of potent energies. But there is no intellectual dominion corresponding to these energies. Whence the Negro is characterized by desire and by an often fearful will. In the very lust for the sensations which he feels, one finds the most evident sign of his inferiority. Added to this is an instability of humor and of sentiment, an obtuse indifference both to his own life, and to that of the others ("[he] shows, in face of suffering, either a monstrous indifference or a cowardice that seeks a voluntary refuge in death").[10] The supersensible is conceived under demonic form by this race: it is a product of an imagination in delirium; it is a projection of the most elementary and subconscious forces of human nature, like the Al of the Melanesians.[11]

The yellow race presents itself as the antithesis of the black. The cranium of the yellow man, rather than slanting backward, is carried forward. The large, bony, often protruding forehead develops upward, and the countenance does not present those coarse protuberances which characterize the Negro. Poor physical vigor, and a disposition to apathy. Weak desires, a will more obstinate than it is strong. In everything, tendencies toward mediocrity, love for that which is useful, respect for all rules. Yellow man does not dream, has no taste for abstractions. He invents little, but he has the capacity to appreciate and to adopt all that which might guarantee him a secure order in his life. "He represents the type of that petty bourgeois, that every civilizer would desire to have as the base of his society."

---

10 Chapter XVI, p. 206.

11 There does not appear to be any such god in the Melanesian mythology. Evola might have in mind the trickster god Olifat, who was associated with fire.

And now for the white race. The white race is essentially composed of blond dolichocephalics, of tall and slender figure. The superiority of this race for Gobineau is to be found in its total dominion of intelligence as reflexive energy; dominion which is associated to a lesser vehemence and immediacy of sensations. The practical spirit of the whites has a greater significance, is more courageous and more ideal than with the yellows. An extraordinary instinct for order, a pronounced taste for liberty, personality, and dignity, and above all, finally, the cult of *honor*, are associated in the whites with the joy for battle and for conquest. The concept of honor, known by names which are almost identical amongst the various lineages of the white race, is for Gobineau fused with the very essence of the civilizing strength, and is unknown as much to the yellows as to the blacks. "The white race originally possessed a monopoly on beauty, intelligence, and strength, while from its union with other varieties arose mixed races, beautiful without being strong, strong without being intelligent, and also some which were neither intelligent nor strong." To these orders belong for example the *Semitic peoples*, which Gobineau believes derive from an intermixing of white blood and black blood.

In order to designate the primordial elements yet exempt from every intermingling of the white race, and also its parts which destiny has preserved from the contamination of the species by conserving them in the breast of now mixed peoples as sparse fragments of this superior humanity, Gobineau uses the term *Arya*.

We have already noted that this term was at first adopted by Bopp. The term is of Indo-Persian origin. In Sanskrit it designates the "nobles," those who are worthy of honor, and it is applied to the entire group of the superior castes, to contrast them with the caste of the servants, or the *çûdra*. This last caste is also called the "adversary caste" and the "dark caste," while that of the *ârya* is called also the "divine caste." The Sanskrit term for caste — *varna* — likewise means "color." From all of this arises the idea that the Hindu system of castes was nothing other than the result of a stratification of races that were originally of different colors: the whites and the "divine" *ârya* being the conquerors and the dark and servile "adversary" strata being rather the aborigines they subjected.

The *Rig-Veda*, the originating text of the Hindu tradition, calls the *âryas* those who speak the same language in which that text has been transcribed, and *âryâvarta*, that is "terra degli Arya," the regions which they conquered.

The term "Arya" or "Aryan" belongs also the Iranian tradition. The great king Darius, in a description of Behistum (520 A.D.), is defined as "Aryan of the Aryan race" and calls his God "the god of the Aryas." HERODOTUS relates that the Medi were first called "Aryas," and some claim that the name of Persia itself, as Iran, and first Èran, meant the land of the Aryas. The Iranian tradition in any case gives to the legendary originating fatherland of the extreme Northern races which created the Middle-Persian civilization the name of *airyanem vaêjô*, which means "seedbed of the Aryas"; and this was considered the first creation of the God of Light, Ahura Mazda. The Aryans are conceived as the friends, the faithful, and the allies of the God of Light, who combat for him against the God of Shadows, Ahriman, and against his emissaries. In this battle, which constitutes the central theme of the entire Persian religion, many racists come even to see a fantastic transposition of the memory of the battle between two races, corresponding respectively to those that in the Hindu hierarchy of the castes constituted the "divine *ârya*" and the "dark servants."

The name *ârya* has been sought also in Europe. The ancient name of Ireland, *Erin, Erenn*, has been referred back to it, and a corresponding trace is thought to be found in the Irish term *aire*, which means "lord." Pliny and Tacitus speak of the Aryas, referring to certain Germanic lineages. Names like Ariovisto, Arimanno, Ariberto, Aribello, etc., which contain the *ar* root from Arya or *ârya*, were in any case very common amongst the Teutons, probably together with patronymic names, the names of the *clans*.[12]

---

12 Evola uses the English word "clan" here.

As for Gobineau, he believes he finds the root *ar* of *ârya* in the German word *Ehre*, which means "honor," and in the Irish *air*, meaning "to honor," which he takes to confirm the inherency of the concept of "honor" in the pure white race; in the Greek word *aristos*, which implicates the idea of superiority and returns us to the same root; finally in the Latin *herus* and in the German *Herr*, words which signify "lord" — whence again the idea of the Arya race as the race of born dominators.

Gobineau finds the concept of light, of splendor, at the center of the spirituality of the Arya race. The Aryan gods are essentially divinities of light, of solar splendor, of the luminous sky, of the day. The most significant national gods of the subspecies of the race derive their names from the root *du*, which means to illuminate: the *deva* and the *dyaus* of the Hindus, the *Deus* of the Latins, *Zeus* of the Hellenes, the Gallic *Dus*, the Nordic *Tyr*, the *Tiuz* of the ancient Germans, the Slavic *Devana*. This idea of light stands moreover in the strictest relation with intellectual principle, it is the very light of the creator and dominator intellect in opposition to the conception of the *Al* of the negroid aborigines, which is the personification of frenetic forces and of the wild imagination.

The Aryas before their gods felt neither fear nor servility. They believed the gods to be not only of their same race, but believed it was the same as that of the Heroes, to whom was reserved the privilege of the highest forms of immortality, not rarely one attributed the possibility of a battle against the inhabitants of the skies, the seizure of their scepter.

Having defined the concept of the white Arya race, of the Arya civilization and spirituality, Gobineau does not hesitate to affirm that "all civilizations derive from the white race, that none can exist without its help, and that a society is great and brilliant only so far as it preserves the blood of the noble group that created it, provided that this group itself belongs to the most illustrious branch of our species,"[13] the Arya branch. To demonstrate this formulation in some way and also to demonstrate that so soon as a principle of death manifests itself in a given cycle, this manifestation derives from the inferior races admitted by the civilizers,

_____

13   Chapter XVI, p. 210.

Gobineau dedicated himself to analyzing the development of the principal civilizations that have ruled in the world.

He believed that there were ten of these civilizations. Arya groups created the Hindu civilization, and the Persian and Greek civilizations, which then were modified by Semitic elements. Of two groups of Arya colonizers deriving from India, one created the Egyptian civilization, around which the Ethiopians and Nubians gathered above all, and the other brought a certain light of superior civilization into China, whose development was arrested with the exhaustion of the blood of those dominators and of the analogous elements that had come to China from the North. Also, the Assyrian civilization is of Aryan origin: after being adulterated successively by the Jews, Phoenicians, Lydians, etc., who joined with it, it owed its rebirth anew to the Aryas of the Persian period. The ancient civilization of the Italic peninsula from which the Roman culture arose was the expression of a cross between Semites, Celtic Aryans, and Iberians. Even the antique civilizations of Peru and of Mexico according to Gobineau were derived from mysterious Arya colonies. Finally, the last civilization of the history of the world is essentially Arya — that arisen from the Nordic-Germanic Medieval Period.

There is no need for us here to follow that reconstruction of the birth, of the development, and of the twilight of all these civilizations, which Gobineau undertook: first because the value of this reconstruction is in large part conditioned by the times and the poorly selected material which Gobineau had at hand; also because in expounding the ideas of other racists we will have occasion to return to insights of the kind, brought up to date with richer, more select and modern, historical material. What is important here is to bring into relief the appearance of a *new historiographical method*. Gobineau is the spokesperson of the *dynamic* racial method, that is of a method which divides and separates heterogeneous qualities in what seemed unitary in a given civilization, and which, in function of the dynamism of these heterogeneous elements traced back to ethnic factors, causes the events in the life and death of various civilizations to open before our eyes.

Here we will add only a few detailed considerations. If the essential gifts of the Arya race are obfuscated in its intermixing with a different blood, even Gobineau maintains that from such a mixture other, and not contemptible, gifts might at times draw their origin. For example, aesthetic sentiment and artistic creation are, according to him, several derivatives of the combination of Arya blood with black-Melanesian blood. In epic poetry, the Arya component predominates; in artistic creation wherein lyricism, vehement imagery, and sensuality stand out, meanwhile, the predominance of characteristic qualities of black blood is betrayed.

In this connection, it should also be remembered that Gobineau takes up from D'EICHTAL one of the most important ideas of the philosophy of racially intoned civilization: the opposition between the masculine and the feminine races. "The Melanesian (negroid) species appears to have a feminine personality, while the masculine sex is almost always represented by the white element." The product of their crossing, "less vehement in the absolute individuality of the feminine principle, less integral in intellectual potency than the masculine principle, enjoys a combination of the two forces which permits aesthetic creation, forbidden both to the one and to the other of the two disassociated races."[14]

Another product of the intermixing of blood for Gobineau was the feeling for fatherland and for authority, which he believed arose from the union of the Aryas with the Semites, from a Semitic mitigation of the Aryan taste for isolation, independence, and personality. We will see this theme often repeated in certain extremist racist writers, in relating every form of sovereignty and statolatry containing ethnic-national elements to "Semitic" origin.

Moreover, the expression "Semitic Rome" is to be traced back to Gobineau, by which he designated the imperial period of this civilization, "not in the sense that it indicates a human variety identical to that which

---

14 These two quotations were evidently taken from an untranslated and rare work by d'Eichtal entitled *Lettres sur la race noire et la race blanche* (Letters on the Black Race and the White Race). I have translated directly from Evola's Italian. Gobineau's reflections on the gendered quality of the races, and of the civilizations they produce, can be found in Chapter IX of *The Inequality of Human Races*.

resulted from the ancient Chaldaen and Chamite combinations," but in the sense that "in the multitudes dispersed by the fortune of Rome on all the peoples subjugated by the Caesars, the greater part was marked with black blood and represented therefore a combination not equivalent, but analogous to the Semitic fusion."[15]

Predominant "black" qualities, well contained within certain limits and compensated for through certain white qualities, were for Gobineau essential factors in the development of Imperial Rome. Gobineau's stance with regard to Christianity seems negative at more than one point: too much does this faith betray "a religion of slaves, disheartened because pacifistic and egalitarian and, in a word, unworthy of the races that yet conserve some spark of the Arya flame." In any case, for Gobineau Christianity was slowly purified as, from being Semitic and Greek, it was made Roman (Catholicism), and from Roman, German.

For Gobineau, the Germans and the other Nordic lines of the period of the invasions appear naturally as races of pure Arya blood. But they were attracted by the mirage of the Roman symbol, and they could not withdraw from the destiny of dissolving themselves into the potent detritus of the races amalgamated by Rome, through which the energy of the Romans and their blood were to decline. This assimilation was not so rapid as to drag society to the point of the "Semitic" departure proper to the Early Empire: at first the Teutonic elements surely were absorbed, but not to such an extent as that. So it was that "Teutonic Rome," Medieval civilization, arose. Every normal society, for Gobineau, founds itself on three classes or originating castes, corresponding to distinct ethnic states: "The nobility, in greater or lesser likeness to the glorious race; the bourgeois, composed of cross breeds similar to the great race; and the people, a servile class belonging to an inferior human variety: black in the South, Finnish in the North."[16] The Medieval period yet knew such a subdivision.

---

15   I have been unable to find the sources for the present quotations.

16   I have been unable to find the source for the present quotation. It might be noted in clarification, however, that Gobineau considered the Finnish blood to pertain to the yellow race; see Chapter 12, p. 146.

But it demonstrated itself ever more devoid of its racial basis, and thus of its strength. This hierarchical image was destined slowly therefore to dismantle itself, as the last veins of pure Arya blood were extinguished and dispersed. Everything was plunged toward the "repulsive atmosphere of the democratic manure heap" of modernity.

The conclusion of Gobineau's views, which are expounded in his major work, the famous *Essay on the Inequality of the Human Races*, which came to light between 1853 and 1855, is pessimistic. The dominating impulse of the white race, which brought it to all lands, has shattered the last ethnic barriers, has created a world in which distances no longer exist and wherein vicinity, aggregation, and the confusion of the times are fatal and rapid as never before. "No pure Aryans are any longer to be found." It is an inexorable law that everything which has power of civilization attracts other races, it extends itself, it carries itself ever farther geographically, it dissipates, it degrades. Gobineau at the end of his book states that the history of the world most likely will carry, by its present road, toward that "supreme unity" which he had moreover already declared to be nothing more than the truth of raceless crossbreeds.

CHAPTER III

Developments

The selectionistic doctrine of VACHER DE LAPOUGE.
WOLTMANN and "Political Anthropology." The "Northern"
thesis and the Prussian myth.

ACISM IN GOBINEAU appears essentially as the manifestation of an aristocratic instinct, as an aristocratic reaction against times of democracy, of egalitarianism, of the ascent of the masses. Against the democratic myth of the sovereign people, Gobineau affirms the myth of the dominating noble race. Against the democratico-Jacobin principle of equality, he affirms the principle of human difference. Against the Enlightenment cult of reason, he affirms the superiority of gifts that are not learned and that have root in the blood, in the race. However much it might be invalidated by not a few confusions and arbitrary and fallacious constructions, Gobineau's doctrine presents indisputable characteristics of nobility at the bottom, and even of spirituality. This distinguishes it from the most recent racism, which often takes up these principles only to place them at the service of an entirely opposite instinct, as we will observe in due time.

Gobineau's ideas did not have an immediate repercussion. So long as he was alive, and apart from a little circle of friends and admirers, his work remained almost unknown. The repercussion came afterward, and above all in Germany.

In the development of racism, immediately after Gobineau we should mention another Frenchman, the Count Georges VACHER DE LAPOUGE. With Vacher de Lapouge, the "scientification" of the racist ideology began. Its properly historico-philosophical aspect is not maintained save in a series of other writers — a series which, intermixing with the Pan-Germanists, carries us, with Houston Stewart CHAMBERLAIN, up to the threshold of the World War. We will have something to say about all of this.

Vacher de Lapouge wishes to have little to do with Gobineau, whom he considers a "literatus," and likewise with the Aryan theories of philology and of "political charlatans." He proclaims himself rather a disciple of DARWIN, of GALTON and of HAECKEL and he wishes to bring the problem of race out of the plane of philosophical constructions and philological hypotheses, into that of positive anthropological data. He seeks therefore to define from a strictly biological point of view the various racial components of European humanity, and with him begins the classification of "Alpine men," "Atlantic-Western men," etc., exposition of which classification we will conserve for when we speak of the most recent forms of this research.[1] In all this, the cephalic index plays a key part for Vacher de Lapouge. Arya man is defined by him in anthropological terms as the "blond dolichocephalic," which in its turn is associated in the strictest way to the Nordic type, which has imposed its domination on the other two European races, the brachycephalic and Mediterranean races. He attempts to reconstruct the history of this race. As for Gobineau, so also for Vacher de Lapouge: there is no doubt as to the superiority of Arya man as the creator of civilization. "The supreme quality of the Aryan race," he writes in his work L'Aryen: son Role Social, published in 1899, "that which characterizes it and places it higher than the others, is his cold,

---

1   See Chapter VI below.

precise, tenacious, will, superior to every obstacle. ... That which makes races dominant, is the aptitude to command." "This temperament is often opposed by that of the peaceable, brachycephalic, laborious whipping boy, the dolico-blond, a race inured to servitude, ever in search of masters and little fastidious in its selection of them."[2] "The light that certain other races have diffused should be ascribed to the presence in them of a blond dolichocephalic element, which the obscurity of time has revealed." This is the case for Persia, for Assyria, for Caldea, for India, for China, for the Greco-Roman civilization itself, and lastly, for the present civilization. "In our time the meaning of nations almost depends on the quantity of blond dolichocephalics, who have contributed to the formation of their ruling classes." The antagonism between the civilization of the brachycephalics and that of the dolichocephalics is recurrent throughout history, and Vacher de Lapouge goes so far as to prophesize: "I am convinced that in the next century [that is, in the twentieth century] millions of men will come to the field of battle on account of the difference of one or two degrees of the cephalic index. In this way kin races will recognize one another, and the last sentimental thinkers will witness the mighty upheavals of the nations."

The type of civilization varies profoundly so soon as the brachycephalic element gains the upper hand over the Arya. The history of France, for instance, is according to Vacher de Lapouge the history of the triumph of the brachycephalic, the inferior bastard race to whose influence Vacher de Lapouge attributes the French Revolution itself, with the egalitarian ideology relative to that race, and, generally, the mutation of the ancient French mindset.

---

2   I have translated this directly from *L'Aryen: son Role Social* (1899, Paris: Albert Fontemoing), p. 371–372. The last part of the present quotation, "ever in search of masters and little fastidious in its selection of them," is not to be found in the text from which I have translated; either Evola was working with a different version of this book, or else he extracted this from another section. I have not been able to source the following quotations, which probably occur in other books by Vacher de Lapouge.

However, even in the Nordic countries, in America, in England, in Germany, the representatives of the Arya race are according to him in danger of extinction, destruction through hybridism and through the advent of elements of an inferior type. Here the concept of Gobineau returns regarding a natural and fatal law of decadence. Vacher de Lapouge expounds on it in a work entitled *Social Selection*, demonstrating that natural selection has always acted as inverted selection, that is, as selection which eliminates superior ethnic-social elements and brings inferior ones to the fore. Vacher de Lapouge studied this phenomenon in various societies. Wars, civil wars, phenomena such as the persecution of heretics, the massacre of the Huguenots[3] and the great Medieval monastic orders which attracted valid elements and then condemned them to sterility, etc.; all of this has resulted in the decimation and the twilight of the Arya elites through natural selection. The action of capitalistico-bourgeois society is added to this in our time, and also international Judaism which brings us to the ultimate consequences of inverted selection. But while Gobineau limited himself to constating the process of decadence, Vacher de Lapouge wishes to react, and thinks it is possible to do so by opposing to this blind and destructive natural social selection, a systematic and rational one, based on a plan and on the active intervention of man, meant to safeguard the purest elements.

For Vacher de Lapouge, such an end could be reached by two means: by prohibiting or obstructing the descendants of inferior and undesirable elements, or by multiplying the descendants of pure elements of the Arya race. As we will see, it is precisely this view which Hitlerism has

---

3   The Huguenots were French Calvinist Protestants of the sixteenth century, primarily extracted from the noble classes of France, who came to control a sizeable portion of France in their day despite forming a minority of some ten percent of the population. Resentment against them grew from the more populous Catholic contingent of the country, both on account of their influence and due to years of prior tension between the Catholics and the Protestants. A number of political events finally sparked off the famous St. Bartholomew's Day massacre, in which mobs took to the streets and massacred whatever Huguenots they could find. It is unknown how many were slaughtered; contemporary estimates range from about 10,000 to about 30,000.

espoused, which moreover finds in the selective program of Vacher de Lapouge even the very principle of sterilization of individuals who are noxious to the race.

The historical research of Vacher de Lapouge regarding inverted selection recalls certain views of the "philosophy of the overman," of Friedrich NIETZSCHE. Although one certainly cannot place Nietzsche amongst the racists, nonetheless one must recognize that certain concepts of his philosophy, which was anything but homogeneous, at bottom draw from the general premises of the ideology which we are here analyzing. We could make reference to the "Nietzschean religion of life" which basically excludes from human personality the reality of any transcendent principle, and gives to every ethical valuation, to good and to evil, a simply biological meaning and justification. The sense of the Nietzschean "inversion of all values" is as follows: for centuries, a whole group of ethical, social, and religious conceptions have conspired against "life," exalting as value and as spirit everything which mortifies and emasculates the instinct, which veils or abases the sensation of vital strength. These are the values of "decadence" and of *ressentiment* proclaimed by the slaves, by the weak, by the disowned, by those rejected by nature, the which with these values have slowly eroded the basis upon which, in strong and healthy times, the "overman" stood, and the right of the "overman" as lord of men; and they have triumphed. Nietzsche proclaims the revolt against these "values of decadence" (amongst which Christianity is located), he denounces the poison in them, and as the principle of a new valuation posits the biological criterion: only that which confirms, justifies, and enhances the vital instinct can be called true, moral, spiritual, and beautiful, the greatest expression of which is the "will to power"; all that which distances itself from life, which limits, condemns, and suffocates the will to power, is false, immoral, ugly, and subversive. If one unites to this the lower sense of the Nietzschean "overman," according to which the overman presents simply the blond, indomitable conquering beast, one can admit an interference of Nietzschean philosophy in racist ideology, and it is licit to think that the first has not been without influence on the formation of the second. In reality, we can ascertain also in Nietzsche an aristocratic reaction misled by the naturalistic and evolutionistic ideas which were fashionable in his time.

We now pass to Ludwig WILSER (1850–1923), in whom first appears the attempt to investigate the prehistory of the Arya race in the field of Anthropology. Here an essential shift of point of view is carried out. We have already said that in the current idea the originating fatherland of the white Arya races is thought to have been a region of central Asia, perhaps the Pamir uplands. It is therefore from the Orient that civilization emanated, carried by the Aryas. Apart from the already mentioned FABRE D'OLIVET in 1824, first Theodore POESCHE in 1878, then Karl PENKA in 1883, and finally Wilser himself opposed to this a fundamentally different idea: the originating home of the Aryas was the North, was indeed even the *Arctic region*. The blond dolichocephalic European, states Wilser, has a skin color and a quality of pigmentation which can be developed only in the North and, moreover, they bring us back to a period which is very remote indeed: that which is called the "glacial era" by the geologists.

According to these thinkers, there was a center of the Arya race located in the Arctic region, which has since disappeared. As the sea of ice in that period, both in America and in Asia, precluded the emigratory path of these races, the only direction possible toward the south was that across Europe, and in this way the Arya emigration proceeded. Thus, from Greenland to Ceylon we find a diffusion of dolichocephalic cranial form, which is however more frequent amongst the blond and blue-eyed men of tall stature of Europe and the North.

Wilser recalls an ancient Longbardo-Byzantine tradition, according to which the "Scania" — Scandinavia — was a *vagina gentium*, a crucible of those peoples that pullulated out of it and emigrated from it. All the Aryas were therefore descended from Scandinavia: by way of the West the Celts and certain Italic lineages; the Thracians, the Lithuanians, the Hellenes, the Mediterraneans, the Slavs, the Persians, the Hindus, in a series of great waves aiming toward the Orient; and finally, at the center, across Jutland and the Scandinavian islands, groups of Teutonic Aryas came to establish themselves, the four tribes of the Ingvaeones (Cimbri), the Istvaeones (Marsi and Franks), the Irminones (Suebi), and finally the Vandals and the Goths. As they were the last to detach from the originating trunk, it was these races to best conserve the blood and the traits of the pure Arya. Wilser affirms once more the idea we have already mentioned, namely that if in the historical period following these peoples, other grand cultures were manifested, like the Assyrian, the Egyptian, and the Cretan, this is because such civilizations in their origin bore strains of Nordic blood. The Persian civilization, the Macedonian, the Roman, are naught but triumphs over aboriginal races and cultures. Wilser also says that heredity of qualities acquired in the battle for existence in the terrible Arctic winter is the heredity of warrior virtue, of an internal invincibility, of the spirit of initiative and of invention — gifts proper to the Nordic men more than to any other race; cause of their past glories, pledge of their future dominion. Indeed, Wilser does not believe with Gobineau that the pure Arya type has by now vanished. The Teutons in his opinion are to this day the most legitimate and genuine heirs of the ancient Nordic race, and Wilser, dreaming at this point the dream of global hegemony of the most elect race, winds up at the vanguard the Pan-Germanic idea.

Wilser's principal work, *The Origin and the Prehistory of the Aryas*, dates to 1899. With this work the "Northern" myth appears for the first time in decisive form in German science, a myth which subsequently was to find ample development. Not *ex Oriente Lux*, but: the *light from the North*. Here surfaces already the theme of Thule, the legendary polar island, original fatherland of the dominating white race.

Along these same lines, another contribution to the development of the Arya ideology was furnished by a philosopher, Friedrich LANGE, who, in a work entitled *Pure Germanism*, also anticipates various themes of the subsequent religious racist polemic. Indeed, for Lange, Christianity was naught but a worm-eaten carcass which ought to be substituted by a new religion of Protestant intonation, but essentially with biologico-racist basis. "In general," affirms Lange, "it is of key importance today to consider our blood as a specific good, all the more as it is the most precious of all our goods."⁴ The fact that Christianity might protest in name of that right by which all men can consider themselves sons of one god, cannot make one forget the decisive virtue of the blood, nor the truth that such a virtue has always possessed for whomever has, in the history of the common white race, conquered and conserved his superiority. "Even though every intelligent farmer, every horse or dog breeder has long known or at least experimentally employed the laws according to which the various races of animals are produced, and on which their betterment or their degeneration is based, still such every-day experiences no longer find an echo in social legislation; they do not risk shining even the weakest light on the usances and customs of the European peoples." Amongst the foremost principles of this failure of recognition is on the one hand the rising tide of democracy, which in the name of the "immortal rights" of man willingly authorizes every intermingling of blood and every hybridism; and on the other hand, a poorly understood religious spirit. "In the modern world," Lange continues, "a whole group of circumstances combine to extirpate yet more radically, to cover in yet greater contempt, every traditional respect for powers and privileges founded on recognized descent and on the genealogical tables — that is, on breeding regulated by blood." The aristocracy itself, in this respect, fails in its principles and at the same time loses awareness of the profound reason for the privilege to which it lays claim. Lange already indicted the scandal constituted by the fact that officials and functionaries of the nobility might marry Jewesses for love of Mammon and nonetheless expected to be treated as their peers, "the which can unfortunately be seen in an ever greater number of cases." Against which Lange affirms: "the future depends entirely on the force that the decisive virtue of the blood might acquire in us and in the other peoples of the white race."

For Lange, the sense of honor, basis of the personality, distinguishes good from bad, the sublime from the abject, in the warrior spirit of individuals and of nations, and, in general, civilization from barbarism. "If

---

4   This work by Lange is neither translated nor accessible. I translate from Evola's Italian.

however, already since the remotest times, the Arya people have uninter-ruptedly demonstrated themselves as the bearers of every lasting civiliza-tion, one must consider the fact that these called themselves by the name of Arya — that is, men of honor — not as a secondary circumstance, but as the key itself to the mystery of their noteworthy superiority with respect to other peoples. They knew indeed the sense of honor as their distinctive characteristic as compared with the other peoples who did not implanted this sentiment."

And therefore, *Blood and Honor*. This is the watchword of Arya rac-ism. In 1894, Lange founded the *Deutschbund*, association of evidently Pan-Germanic hue. In this atmosphere, the Romantic concept of the "spirit of peoples" regains its life, as applied to the German nation. This spirit gives the basic premise for the task of selecting a race which is pure and, as such, aware of its own superiority and of the impulse to carry itself forth, to expand, to take the initiative in attack toward the end of imposing its own will on foes of inferior race, cleverness, or courage. In this reintegration, the Prussian military element — which is considered by Lange to be the marrow of German civilization — must constitute the central nucleus and to assume the directive part. "We have the duty to consciously fortify that which by good luck we have salvaged from the Christian influence, and toward which an innate impulse impels each of us: the warrior spirit." Already here the accusation of Judaism is moved against the myth of universal peace: "a parasitic people like the Jewish one, is carried by its ambitious and avaricious instincts to work toward eternal peace, since in such a regime it would no longer encounter any obstacle to that dismantlement which it works on the living body of the nations." Lange recalls the saying of Moltke: "Eternal peace is a dream — and not even a beautiful dream." — And with this, he seals the myth of the aggres-sive imperialism of the superior race.

After which, we can occupy ourselves with Ludwig WOLTMANN (1871–1907), who, in connection with what presently interests us, is one of the most significant figures of the period prior to the war. Racism in him takes above all the name and the form of "political Anthropology." Political

Anthropology takes as its purpose the study and the judgement of social institutions, laws, and political constitutions, in function of the selective action that these exert. Such a science as this, to Woltmann's mind, would be absolutely necessary for the development of a superior civilization, since for Woltmann no superior civilization exists which is not overseen by conditions apt to assure the primacy and the potency of an ethnic elite. If man is, in general, a dominating animal, this quality of his is not equally distributed in all individuals and in all nations. Therefore, political Anthropology — which, as we will see, is attached in the strictest way to the selectionism of Vacher de Lapouge — must before all establish the characteristics of that people which, more than any other, can be called dominator in the eminent sense. For Woltmann, such characteristics derive from race.

Woltmann accentuates in an entirely materialistic way the concept that racial qualities are the unavoidable and visible support of every intellectual and moral gift, whence he is brought to consider the biological substrate as an essential part in the development of every civilization. Woltmann, therefore, first defines a biological type and then inseparably connects to it a given spirit. His biological research does not stop at the most visible characteristics, such as the cranium, complexion, stature, but already calls genetics to its aid, utilizing the principles enunciated by WEISMANN regarding germ cells to confront the problem of the physiological basis of the hereditary transmission of characteristic moral and spiritual gifts amongst the races. We will consider this aspect of racism further on, in our treatment of so-called "Mendelism." So far as the purely morphological and anthropological side of this matter goes, Woltmann brings us back once more to the same point, declaring that "The man of tall stature, well-developed cranium, with frontal dolichocephalia and fair pigment — in short, the Northern-European race — represents the most perfect type of the human race and the highest product of organic evolution." The ascending hierarchy of intellectual capacities and of attitudes toward dominion in the various races corresponds, according to Woltmann, to a correlated diminution of pigmentation, and proceeds in this way: Negroes, Indians,

CVS pharmacy

SUBTOTAL	-19
NY 8.625% TAX	-19
TOTAL	2.38-
CHARGE	-2.13
************	

REFUND	2.38-

SEPTEMBER 10, 2019 11:18 AM

THANK YOU AND 24 HOURS AT CVS.COM

❤CVS pharmacy®

1 GUSSACK PLAZA   GREAT NECK, NY
PHARMACY: 829-3300 STORE: 829-1294

REG#03 TRN#0873 CSHR#1379692 STR#1934

Helped by: SHONAE

REFUND SLIP

SUBTOTAL	2.19-
NY 8.625% TAX	.19-
TOTAL	2.38-
CHARGE	2.38-
************9175 CH	
REFUND	2.38-

SEPTEMBER 10, 2019   11:18 AM

THANK YOU. SHOP 24 HOURS AT CVS.COM

Mongols, Mediterraneans, Northern Europeans. Taking as his own one of the worst materialistic superstitions of evolution, Woltmann, with REIL, defines the brain as "the supreme efflorescence of creation" and the "origin of history," so that the brain is made to correspond to that condition which has the principal part in the predisposition of the races.

Thus, according to Woltmann, the Nordic races possessed a quality of brain which had the maximum degree of creative faculty, and the faculty to assimilate in an original way. For this it was possible for them to embrace the elements of even diverse civilizations into new forms without altering them in their innermost nature. The negro and the other inferior races were absolutely resistant to this, and for this reason, for example, they never adopted the Nordic-Mediterranean civilization to which they nonetheless lived so near. For Woltmann, exterior social and even psychological contact do not suffice to produce a true and durable transfusion of civilization. "The potency of ideas breaks against the organic limits of natural faculties."[5] "The transmission of a superior civilization to inferior races is not possible without an intermingling of blood, in which the elements of the more gifted race blend with those of the less gifted races." For the superior races the piercing of civilizations is the easier and more fecund, the more that civilization originates from similar races. "It is thus that the Germanic races swiftly and spontaneously mastered the Greek and Roman culture, while they did not assimilate the Jewish, save in its Hellenized form; and to this day a Germanic aversion to the Semitic spirit of the Old Testament can be observed." More generally, "a physiological crossbreeding of races is not a factor in lasting progress, save when one treats of two similar races of the same value. The degree of culture that their historical circumstances have brought them to attain is not the decisive element; only their equality from the anthropological point of view is divisive, in this respect. Thus it is that the Germans and the Romans felt themselves to be reciprocally of equal value."

---

5   Woltmann's work has not been translated into English, and the German originals are not easy to come by. I have translated from Evola here and in the quotations that follow.

In order to specify the spirit correlated to the anthropological Nordic type, Woltmann took up and developed the ideas of KLEMM, who, as we have seen, had divided the human race into *active races* and *passive races*:

> Among the first there predominates that aspiration of the will to dominion, to autonomy, to liberty, activism and perseverance, the urge toward the conquest of distant horizons, progress in all its forms, but also the inclination to observe and to critique the spirit of non-submission and of doubt. This manifests itself clearly in the history of those nations which have been formed by active men: the Persians, the Arabs, the Greeks, the Romans, and the Germans. These men emigrate or immigrate; overturning all the most solidly established kingdoms, they found new ones; they are audacious navigators. They form a political constitution imprinted with liberty, taking as its condition continual progress. Theocracy and tyranny do not prosper amongst them, insofar as such nations are open to the sublime, and consign their strength to it. Science, study, faith take the place in them of blind belief. The spirit of such nations is always in movement — movement now ascending and now descending, but always pressing out ahead. They have swept the world in all of its parts up to the poles, tolerating every clime and bringing to their fatherlands the treasures of all lands.

As for the passive races,

> ... that is, all those different from the Caucasian, [they] content themselves with the first results of their observations and of their discoveries. They happily remain in their regions without showing any desire to explore distant countries. Stability is their law of life. In their arts, in their public and private institutions, no free and personal form is developed. The active race is the less numerous, and it is that which appears latest. In principle, it leaves agricultural work properly speaking to the passive races which it finds on its arrival, reserving to itself those occupations proper to the intellectual and to the warrior, to the navigator and to the merchant.

Such a view, in its breadth, is however not easily reconciled with the horizons proper to racist particularism, to the degree that in Woltmann the racist ideology assumes so pronounced a Teutonic hue that he cannot even tolerate the union of Germans with other branches of the Nordic-Teutonic family; that he keeps his distance from the "Pan-Aryan" ideas of the type that we will see defended by Chamberlain; that it is indeed even the Teutonic man which he strives to discover in all the superior

personalities which appeared in the peoples near to Germany; that, finally, it is to the Teutonic race that he attributes the function of "embracing the earth in its domain" and of "making of the passive races simple
subordinate organs for the development of its civilization." "Papacy and
empire," Woltmann adds, "are both Germanic institutions, instruments of
a dominion destined to subjugate the world."

The theses contained in Woltmann's two works, *The Germans in
Italy* and *The Germans in France*, take on a particular character of ex-
travagance. The central idea is the usual one: for all peoples, "the value
of their civilization depends on the quantity of the blond race that they
contain." He recalls the race of the blond Heraclids,[6] come to Sparta from
the North. He recalls the testimony of TACITUS regarding the decadence
of the Romans, which began with the scarcity of blond men. But above all
an analysis is made, aimed toward demonstrating that the Renaissance is
a racial event, much less the result of a rediscovery of classical antiquity
than a transfusion of Teutonic blood into an otherwise infertile substance;
so that all the noble families of all the major Italian and French cities, all
the names of the exponents most representative of the Italian and French
civilizations, are of Teutonic origin, in the same way that that these last
in their somatic characteristics always betray something of the anthropological characteristics of the dolichocephalic blond. For example, the
following names were, according to Woltmann, Teutonic: Dante Alighieri
(Aigler), Boccaccio (Buchatz), Leonardo da Vinci (Winke), Buonarroti
(Bahnrodt), Tasso (Dasse), and so forth, up to Benso di Cavour (Benz)
and Garibaldi (Kerpolt). Dante, Donatello, Leonardo, Christopher
Columbus, etc. are of the blond type. In France: Mirabeau, Napoleon,
La Fayette, etc. are Germanic types, Voltaire, Montaigne, Victor Hugo,
etc. are mixed types, and so forth. Extravagancies of the kind are here
recorded purely for curiosity's sake. They can do nothing other than offer
arms most generously to the enemies of racism.

---

6   That is, the Dorians. They were considered to be a branch of the Heraclids, the di-
    rect descendants of Heracles, and often claimed the right to rule on account of this
    ancestry.

We have mentioned that the "political Anthropology" of Woltmann agrees with the views of Vacher de Lapouge, in observing the phenomenon of inverted selection. "The extinction of the blond race of tall stature is one of the inevitable consequences of his dominating function in society, and of his psychological characteristics." The more that the races are of the active type, and likewise gifted with superior qualities, the more vital competition unleashes a tragic struggle amongst them. And since it is essentially the "Teutonic" races which find themselves in such conditions, so Woltmann sees the most decisive events of history and of global civilization proceed from the antagonism and the struggle between Teutonic races and heroes. A grave internal destiny therefore burdens those to whom the laws of political anthropology should assure conditions of life and of power in any normal civilization. Here Woltmann's ideas oscillate, ending with an acceptance of the "tragic," which he wraps in the cloth of the "heroic." On one hand, as we have seen, he cultivates the dream of universal Teutonic hegemony. On the other hand, he writes, "Certain sentimental political men have dreamed of an alliance of all the Germanic races. However Pan-Germanism is a historically realized fact; it is now asked in amazement against whom this alliance should be directed. Indeed, German man is the greatest enemy of German man, and the most dangerous. To uproot this animosity from the world would mean to suppress the fundamental conditions for the development of civilization: it would be the puerile attempt to oppose certain chimerical dreams to certain natural laws." Such laws would seem therefore to call the members of the various species of the family of the active and dolichocephalic race to battle amongst themselves to the bitter end, toward the aim of producing an additional selection and the most complete development of the superior civilizations. The battle for the conquest of the world would be closed therefore within the circle of the nations of pure Teutonic race. The unity of the elements of the "active race," according to the expression of Alfred WEBER, is an "explosive unit." Woltmann's imperialistic and tragico-heroic conception therefore seems to take on greater weight than those considerations he makes regarding international struggles and the factors of decadence, greater weight also than the views of Gobineau regarding the fatal dissolution of the pure race at the moment of its expansion as dominator and founder of empire. On this last point, political anthropology should be called on to formulate adequate laws of preservation and of "internal ethnic colonization."

We note also that even outside of Germany we can find tendencies analogous to the political Anthropology of Woltmann. We cite for example V. COURTET DE L'ISLE, who with a much better sense of equilibrium sought to draw, in works written toward 1883, the basis for a new political science from the science of the human races.

Before passing to the last great exponent of the postbellum phase of this ideology — namely, Chamberlain — let us yet mention the theories of Heinrich DRIESMANS (1864).[7] In them, the Nietzsche of the "philosophy of life," while on one hand absorbing a good part of the biologico-scientistic armament, on the other hand passes into the meaning of a metaphysics *sui generis*, with which the Fichtean conception of the "normal people" returns almost to renewed existence. Indeed, for Driesmans the essence of every civilization is metaphysical, in the sense that it expresses contact with the originating powers of life — contact, however, which not all the races are capable of making. In these terms, civilization is something primordial; it is a hard and naked style of life that makes one think more of the vulgar concept of "barbarians" than of that decadent and aesthetic concept one usually has for "civilized" people.

With this as his premise, Driesmans passes to racial antitheses of a kind already known. In the first place, that between the Hellenes and the Semites. The barbaric intensity of the first Hellenes could not have carried itself to its known cultural level, if it had not been in contact with elements of the Semitic race, gifted with a much greater sensitivity, plasticity, mercuriality and mobility. The Greece that we know, mistress of the arts, of the sciences, of thought, is a Semitized Greece, however not past the point of a fecund equilibrium of the two ethnic stocks. But brief is this

7   Driesmans was actually born in 1863, and died in 1927.

condition of equilibrium. The tide of Jewish blood rises from out of the bottom of the plebeian element. From this point on, decadence: skeptical Greece, sensualistic Greece, Alexandrine Greece, which dissolves rapidly in the currents of history.

According to Driesmans, the same process repeated itself, or sought to repeat itself, with the contact between the pure Teutonic races and the Celtic or Celtico-Latin element. The Celts, beginning from the moment at which "Irish or Gallic missionaries brought their arts and the narcotic of their religion to Germany," from the moment in which they transmitted "a wisdom for eunuchs in Latin words" and various traditions in which the sensualistic cult of the woman circulated, represented for the pure Nordics a principle of profound change, if not even of decomposition. The Reformation, before being a religious phenomenon, was a racial phenomenon. For Driesmans, it matters not if one condemns Luther from the Catholic point of view or if one recognizes him as the renovator of genuine Christianity. There remains the fact of a revolt of the German nature against foreign civilizing influences, against elements of intoxication, against "the seductress culture of humanism — pleasant, facile, but inconsistent." "Like Cato, Luther incarnated the ancient times in the face of his contemporaries, who had been corrupted by civilization." Beginning from the Reformation, two civilizations come to battle: the one Celtico-Roman, humanizing, sensual, refined, figurative, aestheticizing; the other rude, iconoclastic, penetrated through and through by a rigid moral and military sense, and still the bearer, in its blood, of that *furor*[8] which is nothing if not the overwhelming thrust of the races in direct contact with the originating forces of life.

The problem of an opportune coexistence of this blood is, for Driesmans, the problem of the future culture of Europe. "In France, the Germanic element was almost in a constant state of siege by the Celtic element, and in the end was conquered and rejected. In England, a division of labor, so to speak, established itself, according to which the Germanic element was confined to the domain of politics and business, and the

---

8   The word is Latin, meaning madness, rage, or frenzy.

Celtic to the domain of arts. Finally in Germany the primitive Germanic nature combined with Celtic nature, and this Celtico-Germanic nature even united with a third element."[9] The most fecund mixture, for our Author, would be however the *Slavo-Teutonic* (Slavo-Saxon) one. This corresponds to the *Prussian* element which Driesmans, along with Lange, considers as the bulwark and as the principal renovator of Teutonic civilization. But here the term "civilization" must be taken in the special sense we have already recalled. In the Prussian, the warrior qualities conserve primacy over intellectual ones. Contempt for "civilization" was, according to Driesmans, an ancient Prussian tradition, which brings out the contrast between these Germans and their nearest relatives established in the South-West. "When Frederick William, the spiritual father of modern Prussianism, led the president of his academy about in the garb of madmen, and pleased himself by playing games with this personality at every turn, to the great amusement of his officials, we ought not however be scandalized by such wild conduct: we should rather recognize here the Slavo-Saxon spirit which in wishes to strike out, in the form of the scientist, at a kind hated and despised, the bookish, lymphatic and bourgeois type of the Germans of the Empire." However, Driesmans believes that the Slavo-Saxon element, if not in its present form, at least in a modified form, reuniting and harmonizing opposite racial elements, might attain to physical and intellectual gifts superior to all those seen hitherto, and present itself as the type and the basis for super-European humanity.

---

9   Here, too, the author in question has not been translated into English, and his work is not easily accessible.

CHAPTER IV

The Views of Chamberlain

The superior race as task. The Slavo-Celtico-Teutonic complex.
The historical vision of Chamberlain. "Teutonic" science.
"Ethnic chaos." The "Anti-Rome." Racism and the modern
world. Pan-Germanic racism.

WE SHALL NOW TURN TO Houston Stewart CHAMBERLAIN. Alfred ROSENBERG begins an essay dedicated to this writer with the words, "It is said that the peasant seeds, plows, and harvests, with his gaze fixed on the earth, without looking at the sky which stands above him, the forests, the lakes, the mountains. Only at the coming of a foreigner does he begin to realize also of the beauty of his fatherland."[1] The comparison regards the German people, which in truth seems to have been carried to consciousness and esteem of its characteristics and of the faith in its primacy through foreigners — such as Frenchman GOBINEAU, but also the Englishman Chamberlain (who became a naturalized German) and Vacher DE LAPOUGE himself, almost

---

1 I was unable to find the source of this quotation.

unknown in France, while he was highly esteemed in the circles of Frederick William. The resonance awoken in Germany and in France by Chamberlain's principal work, *The Foundations of the Nineteenth Century*, was much more rapid and much wider than it had been for Gobineau. Undeservedly, for the inferiority of Chamberlain with respect to Gobineau, in terms of originality, of choice of thesis, and of construction, is evident to every unprejudiced observer. One is rather disturbed by Chamberlain's a-systematicality, by his continuous flitting about between one domain and another, movement which bears the pronounced mark of the dilettante, and with his decided entrance into politics and Pan-Germanic exaltations. One can charge him with an aestheticizing overestimation of the simply artistic expressions of a civilization, which in contrast with other racist views, for example in the iconoclastic rudeness of DRIESMANS, in the end elicit more sympathy — and in the end, one can also charge him with a curious racist but rather Enlightenment evaluation of technical and scientific civilization. In the "Arya" concept, Chamberlain offers views which are more placating, but also more compromising. His racism is considerably more modern and traditional and, at bottom, even as myth, lacking in a true spine.

The premise of Chamberlain is already known to the reader: "Certain anthropologists would fain teach us that all races are equally gifted; we point to history and answer: that is a lie! The races of mankind are markedly different in the nature and also in the extent of their gifts."[2] The most favored of them is the group of the Arya races. We will see what the "Arya race" means for Chamberlain. We observe in the meanwhile that, differently from other racists, this author leaves the problem of the common descendancy of the Arya undecided. The concept of the "primordial race" is for him a problematic one. "I do not know if the words Arya and Semite correspond, generally speaking, to concrete facts of descendancy, or if they are rather artificial concepts, convenient for indicating men

---

2   All quotations in this chapter are taken from *The Foundations of the 19th Century* (1912, London: Ballantyne & Co. Limited); the present is found in Division II, Sixth Chapter, p. 542.

belonging to one kind by way of their equal nature."³ And again: "Is this human family united and uniform by bonds of blood? Do these stems really all spring from the same root? I do not know and I do not much care; no affinity binds more closely than elective affinity, and in this sense the Indo-European Aryans certainly form a family. [...] Physically and mentally the Aryans are pre-eminent among all peoples; for that reason they are by right, as the Stagirite expresses it, the lords of the world."⁴

Detaching himself in this from the idea of the greater part of racists, Chamberlain thinks therefore that this superiority, rather than being innate, is *acquired*. The races are nor originally noble or pure, but *become so*. As an enthusiast of vegetal physiology, Chamberlain seems here to recall the virtues that cultivation and grafting exert, and takes up the selectionistic theme of Vacher de Lapouge. The superior race is not a point of departure, but a point of arrival. We could almost say: it is a task. And indeed, Chamberlain goes so far as to write, "Though it were proved that there never was an Aryan race in the past, yet we desire that in the future there may be one. That is the decisive standpoint for men for action."⁵ According to Chamberlain, the formation of the elect race is subordinated to five great natural laws:

1) The preexistence of excellent ethnic materials is indisputably the first and fundamental condition. However, "if I am asked, 'Whence comes this material?' I must answer, 'I know not,' I am as ignorant in this matter as if I were the greatest of all scholars. [...] Only one thing can be asserted without leaving the basis of historical observation: a high state of excellence is only attained gradually and under particular circumstances, it is only forced activity that can bring it about; under other circumstances it may completely degenerate. The struggle which means destruction for the fundamentally weak race steels the strong; the same struggle, moreover, by eliminating the

---

3   I was unable to find the source of this quotation.

4   Again from *Foundations*, Division II, Sixth Chapter, p. 542.

5   *Foundations*, Division II, Fourth Chapter, p. 266.

weaker elements, tends still further to strengthen the strong. Around the childhood of great races, as we observe, even in the case of the metaphysical Indians, the storm of war always rages."[6]

2) But the presence of superior elements as *materia prima* is not sufficient. The second condition is the uninterrupted conservation of the purity of the race.

3) But not even this is enough. It is necessary that in the very breast of the pure race those racial eliminations operate, which the technicians call "selective breeding." This law, says Chamberlain, "We understand this law best when we study the principles of artificial breeding in the animal and vegetable worlds... When one has come to understand what miracles are performed by selection ... one will recognise that the same phenomenon is found in the human race, although of course it can never be seen with the same clearness and definiteness as in the other spheres."[7] For example, the exposure of ill-born infants amongst the Greeks, the Romans, and the Germans was, for Chamberlain, one of the most fruitful laws. Here emerges the theme of "eugenics" and of "racial hygiene."

4) Another law, which likewise finds empirical confirmation in the theme of scientific breeding of animals, is the following: the formation of superior races has always and without exception, as its preliminary condition, an "intermixing of blood." Those pure racists who today pay the tribute of their admiration to Chamberlain prefer, naturally, to pass this conviction of his over in silence, insofar as it is specified and limited through the last law, namely:

5) "Only quite definite, limited mixtures of blood contribute towards the ennoblement of a race, or, it may be, the origin of a new one. Here again the clearest and least ambiguous examples are furnished by animal breeding. The mixture of blood must be strictly limited as regards time, and it must, in addition, be appropriate; not all and any

---

6   *Foundations*, Division II, Fourth Chapter, p. 276.

7   *Foundations*, Division II, Fourth Chapter, p. 277.

crossings, but only definite ones can form the basis of ennoblement. By time-limitation I mean that the influx of new blood must take place as quickly as possible and then cease; continual crossing ruins the strongest race."[8] Thus, for example, the cross between the Attic and the Roman races.

In this connection, Chamberlain recognizes also the role that historico-geographical conditions have played in the formation of the noblest races, insofar as from these conditions proceeds the refinement of the *materia prima* through internal and external selection. The concept of racial purity in Chamberlain is thus relative: it is the quality resulting from a certain intermixing, which has to be preserved — not that of a unique blood, which is only itself. However, in our author all of this soon passes to the background. Whatever might be their origins and their components, Chamberlain has no doubt that races exist with very clear characteristics, and he experiences an authentic horror and panic at "ethnic chaos," the principle of general bastardization and inevitable decadence. There is no doubt that he professes the general principle of racism — namely, the relation of dependency or inter-dependancy between a given blood and given moral gifts: "Men who do not inherit definite ideals with their blood are neither moral nor immoral, they are simply 'without morals.' If I may be allowed to use a current phrase to explain my meaning, I should say they are neither good nor bad, equally they are neither beautiful nor ugly, deep nor shallow. The individual in fact cannot make for himself an ideal of life and a moral law; these very things can only exist as a gradual growth."[9] The characteristics of race betray themselves, according to their irreducible diversity, in physical forms, in bone structure, in coloration, in musculature, in the proportions of the cranium. "[T]here is perhaps not a single anatomical fact upon which race has not impressed its special distinguishing stamp."[10]

---

8   *Foundations*, Division II, Fourth Chapter, p. 282.

9   *Foundations*, Division II, Fourth Chapter, p. 309.

10 *Foundations*, Division II, Sixth Chapter, p. 309.

Chamberlain admits that "the nation is a crucible in which race is formed." Within it work mixtures which are sometimes happy and sometimes unhappy, and the best condition is found when the State decides to protect itself for centuries against every hybridization of pure and noble elements, so as to give them the time to compose a homogeneous and stable ethnic substance.

When the States open themselves to the latest comers, on the other hand, it is the end so far as race is concerned. "[W]hen ... these States are thrown open to every stranger, the race is ruined, in Athens slowly, because owing to the political situation there was not much to get there, and the mixing in consequence only took place gradually and then for the most part with Indo-European peoples, in Rome with frightful rapidity, after Marius and Sulla had, by murdering the flower of the genuine Roman youth, dammed the source of noble blood and at the same time, by the freeing of slaves, brought into the nation perfect floods of African and Asiatic blood, thus transforming Rome into the *cloaca gentium*, the trysting-place of all the mongrels of the world. We observe the same on all sides."[11]

Except that the concept of the "superior race" in Chamberlain is rather poorly defined. In the Arya family, examples of superior races would be the Teutons, the Celts, the Slavs. But he sometimes ends up generalizing the concept of Teutons, so far as to include in them all the great races of the world, making of the Teutons a prehistoric race from which precisely the Celts, the Slavs, and the Teutons properly speaking were formed by selection: sometimes he conceives a species of mixture of the three elements, speaking comprehensively of a race and of a "Slavo-Celtico-Germanic" blood of Northern Europe, and attributing to this the creative force of civilization which has radiated out over the world in modernity.

The characteristics of the race of the Teutons, according to Chamberlain, are the usual ones:

---

11 *Foundations*, Division II, Fourth Chapter, pp. 285–286. *Cloaca gentium* is Latin for "sewer of the nations."

Ideal and at the same time Practice.[12] [...] The Teutons are characterised by a power of expansion possessed by no race before them, and at the same time by an inclination to concentration which is equally new. We see the expansive power at work — in the practical sphere, in the gradual colonisation of the whole surface of the globe; — in the scientific sphere, in the revelation of the infinite Cosmos, in the search for ever remoter causes; — in the ideal sphere, in the conception of the Transcendent, in the boldness of hypotheses, and in sublime artistic flights which lead to more and more comprehensive means of expression. At the same time, however, we are inclined to return within more and more narrowly circumscribed limits, carefully cut off from everything external by ramparts and trenches; we return to the idea of blood-relationships of the Fatherland, of the native district, of the village of our birth, of the inviolable home (my home is my castle, as in Rome), of the closest family circle; finally we return to the innermost central point of the individual, who now, purified and elevated to consciousness of absolute isolation, faces the outer world as an invisible, independent being, a supreme lord of freedom, as was the case with the Indians.[13]

Liberty for Chamberlain is not an abstract good to which every man has a natural right. Only the superior races can arrogate to themselves the right to liberty, and to consider themselves as naturally free — on the basis of special gifts, first amongst which is "the organizing force. Only a race capable of forming States is worthy of liberty." This too would be the Arya prerogative, and, more specifically, the Teutonic prerogative.

Chamberlain invites us to distinguish between *knowledge, civilization,* and *spirituality*. Knowledge for him is equivalent to science, that is to a system of notions capable of giving account of nature. Civilization consists in technical development, industrial, agricultural, statal development; it consists in the organization of a social order. Spirituality includes finally every manifestation of culture and above all the arts, as the expressions of a superior moral and religious life. These elements can be uncoupled, but they remain forever racially conditioned. There are races which by nature and more gifted in the sense of knowledge and civilization, without being so in the sense of spirituality — as, for example, the Jews and the Chinese.

---

12 *Foundations*, Division II, Sixth Chapter, p. 551.

13 *Foundations*, Division III, Ninth Chapter, Part A, pp. 226–227.

In the Hindus on the other hand we find the example of a high spirituality, which is not accompanied by gifts of economic and political civilization.

Only the Teutons, for Chamberlain, are so gifted as to develop simultaneously these three aspects into an integral civilization. We have already seen that the "organizing force" is, according to him, a Teutonic monopoly. Here those gifts which most characterize the Teutonic social organizations enter into consideration, and we find the famous theme of "Teutonic loyalty" — *deutsche Treue*. "[I]f we wish to sum up in a single word the historic greatness of the Teuton — always a perilous undertaking, since everything living is of Protean nature — we must name his loyalty," says Chamberlain. "That is the central point from which we can survey his whole character, or better, his personality."[14] It is true that loyalty generically understood does not appear to be an exclusively Teutonic virtue. As Chamberlain concedes, this virtue appears indeed in all those races which have remained pure, the Negroes not excluded. But Germanic loyalty has as its characteristic liberty, the fact that it determines itself by itself, consciously. "The Negro and the dog serve their masters, whoever they maybe: that is the morality of the weak, or, as Aristotle says, of the man who is born to be a slave; the Teuton chooses his master, and his loyalty is therefore loyalty to himself: that is the morality of the man who is born free."[15]

In the domain of consciousness, Chamberlain, referring to modern science, does not hesitate to derive it from the psychological and moral gifts of the race of the Teutons, gifts which in the other races are either absent or sporadically present. "Experience — that is, exact, minute, indefatigable observation … the capacity of observation, the passionate enthusiasm, self-sacrifice and honesty with which it is pursued, are essential features of our race. […] Obedience on the one hand towards experienced nature; autocracy on the other in reference to the human intellect: these are the hall-mark of Teutonic Science."[16] And again: "The whole secret

---

14   *Foundations*, Division II, Sixth Chapter, p. 548.

15   *Foundations*, Division II, Sixth Chapter, p. 547.

16   *Foundations*, Division III, Ninth Chapter, Part B, Section 2, pp. 302–303.

of discovery lies in this, to let nature speak. For this self-control is essential: the Greeks did not possess it."[17] Above all, by way of its discoveries, modern science is for Chamberlain inseparably connected to the role that Teutonism has played in history.

Finally, as regards the *spiritual* side, after the other two, social and knowledge-related, Teutonism presents two characteristic aspects, which are not antagonistic but intimately complementary: *humanism* and *mysticism*. Humanism is given as the faculty of recognizing and appreciating that which is particular and individuated, connected to personality and to genius, a faculty which is an instinct of race and which gives place to a special culture. As we will see, also in its historical aspect (the Renaissance), Humanism, for Chamberlain, as already for WOLTMANN, is a Teutonic phenomenon. As for mysticism, it is conceived as the impulse to consider religion as an internal and immediate experience, rather than as a chronicle of sacred history and a dogmatic mechanism. "The real High School of freedom from hieratic and historical shackles is mysticism, the *philosophia teutonica*, as it was called. A mystical philosophy, when completely worked out, dissolves one dogmatic theory after another as allegory."[18] And so "religion is then no longer a creed, a hope, a conviction, but an experience of life, an actual process, a direct state of mind." Masters in this respect were the Aryas of India. "[B]ut scarcely a hair's-breadth separates our great Teutonic mystics from their Indian predecessors and contemporaries," Chamberlain affirms; "only one thing really distinguishes them: Indian religion is genuinely Indo-Teutonic, mysticism finds in it a natural, universally recognised place, but there is no place for mysticism in such a conjunction as that of Semitic history with pseudo-Egyptian magic, and so it was and is at best merely tolerated, though mostly persecuted by our various sects."

Contrary to the Teutonism of various of his contemporary successors, Chamberlain's Teutonism does not stop far short of professing itself

---

17 *Foundations*, Division III, Ninth Chapter, Part B, Section 2, p. 272.

18 This quote, and all those in the present paragraph, are from *Foundations*, Division III, Ninth Chapter, Part B, Section 6, p. 411.

even anti-Christian. But in order that the opposition between the Aryas and Jews might remain well fixed, and with it, the inferior, materialistic, idolatristic, and disintegrating character of Judaism, Chamberlain, in order to resolve the incongruence, creates the singular myth of Jesus as a "Blond Arya." Jesus came from Galilee, a region devastated by Assyrian wars, then restored by groups of blond colonists come from the Nord, and thence purified of the last Jewish residues some time before the birth of Jesus. It is the lineage of those colonists which gave birth to Christ. "There is … not the slightest foundation for the supposition that Christ's parents were of Jewish descent," says Chamberlain.[19] Bringing us back to the simple idea that "the kingdom of God is within you," he believes that Christianity originally had Aryan characteristics, and so only by Aryas could it be understood in its purity. "Are we to believe — to dive deeply into the subject — that it is an accident that St. Paul's epistle on redemption by faith, on the gospel of freedom (in contrast to the 'slavish yoke' of the Church law), on the importance of religion as not consisting in works but in regeneration 'to a new creature' — was addressed to the Galatians, those 'Gallic Greeks' of Asia Minor who had remained almost pure Celts — an epistle in which we seem to hear a Martin Luther speaking to Germans credulous indeed but yet incomparably gifted for understanding the deepest mysteries?"[20] Moreover, we see that it is the Celtic race to furnish the greatest figures of ancient Christianity for their metaphysical thrust and their theological profundity, from Scotus Eriugena and Duns Scotus to Peter Abelard.[21] "[T]he present spreaders of the Gospel

19   *Foundations*, Division I, Third Chapter, p. 206.

20   *Foundations*, Division II, Sixth Chapter, pp. 500–501.

21   Scotus Eriugena (c. 815-c. 877) was an Irish theologian. A Christian Neoplatonist, he was steeped in the ancient philosophies and wrote several philosophical works, foremost among which is his classic synthesis of previous philosophy, *The Division of Nature*. Duns Scotus (1266–1308) was a theologian of prime importance during the High Middle Ages, and, together with Thomas Aquinas, was responsible for one of the great attempts to reconcile Christian theology with classical philosophy. Peter Abelard (1079–1142), also an important theologian, presented his ideas in various

throughout Europe are all Teutons," says Chamberlain;[22] and setting off down this road, after glorifying those German mystics who were more or less suspected of heresy, he naturally sets off down the path also of the Reformation.

This is a glorification, to be sure, which logically takes as its counterpart a violent anti-Catholic and "anti-Roman affect." The tragedy of Europe, according to Chamberlain, consisted in the fact that Arya spirituality had to cross the "Syrio-Semitic quagmire" and that a youthful Teutonism could not connect itself directly to spiritual forms congenial to it, but received the heritage of the Hellenes, of Ancient Rome, and of Christianity itself only through the mediation of a people Africanized and mixed with Syrian bastards.

If Chamberlain grants recognition to the first Roman times, he nevertheless proceeds to lay ethnic chaos to the account of Imperial Rome, the mongrel spirit of slavishness and in general, anti-race. "The Roman Empire in the imperial period was the materialisation of the anti-national principle; this principle led to racelessness and simultaneously to intellectual and moral chaos."[23] Rome became the center of a gathering of all the castaways of the ancient world. Pseudo-Persians, Syrians of every kind, Phoenicians, Egyptians, Africans, degenerate Hellenes, and so forth — all came to seek their fortune in Rome, to seek splendor and power. According to Chamberlain, the Church assumed this tradition of promiscuity and made it its own, uniting it with a fanatical intolerance, with a blind spirit of authority, and with a battle undertaken systematically in all directions to immediately nullify every spiritual liberty. Here, within a Syrio-Semitic ritualistic apparatus and a materialistic monotheism, Chamberlain believed that "the real 'sin against the Holy Spirit,' ... [v]iolence to the inner man, the robbery of personality" was celebrated.[24] Whence, "Let us

---

works, one of the foremost of which is his autobiographical *Historia Calamitatum* ("A History of my Calamities," as it is sometimes rendered in English).

22 *Foundations*, Division III, Ninth Chapter, Part B, p. 258.

23 *Foundations*, Division II, Fourth Chapter, p. 295.

24 *Foundations*, Division III, Ninth Chapter, Part B, p. 241.

honestly admit the fact; between Christianity, as forced upon us by the Chaos of Peoples, and the innermost soul-faith of the Teutons there has never been any real agreement, never,"[25] and "The Roman Church, on the other hand, was unavoidably the shield- and armour-bearer of all Anti-Germanic movements."[26]

Consequently, "Nowhere does the organic unity of Slavonic Germanicism manifest itself more convincingly than in this revolt against Rome."[27] In the hands of this Englishman Chamberlain, the tradition of race proper to Germany is thus transformed, most deplorably, into nothing else than the tradition of all rebels and heretics.

By this view, CHARLEMAGNE committed a fatal error when he accepted the Roman consecration, and when from that "mediocre African mongrel" Saint AUGUSTINE, he borrowed the idea of conversion by iron, using it at once to destroy, in the Saxon wars, the best Teutonic blood. The Empire and the Church, these two Roman ideas, these two absolutisms, both destructors in their centralism and in their universalism, were therefore for Chamberlain (as opposed to WOLTMANN who, as we have seen, rather saw in them two Teutonic creations to seize upon for the conquest of the world) foreign to the Teutonic essence, and thanks to a fatal equivocation had for eight centuries suffocated and prostrated this essence. LUTHER, "the turning-point in the history of the world"[28], is the liberator: he throws down the pontifical absolutism and prepares the revolt of the national principle and the restoration of the "old Teutonic law of freedom."[29]

If the decline of the Teutons already appeared to Chamberlain as a force of salvation for an agonized humanity, notwithstanding "'Latinising,' that is, the fusion with the chaos of peoples,"[30] the Renaissance, in its turn,

25 *Foundations*, Division III, Ninth Chapter, Part B, Section 6, p. 492.

26 *Foundations*, Division II, Sixth Chapter, pp. 556–557.

27 *Foundations*, Division II, Sixth Chapter, p. 512.

28 *Foundations*, Division III, Ninth Chapter, Part B, Section 5, p. 375.

29 *Foundations*, Division III, Ninth Chapter, Part A, p. 224.

30 *Foundations*, Division II, Sixth Chapter, p. 495.

presents itself in the guise of a new racially conditioned Teutonic phenomenon, as Woltmann believed. For Chamberlain, the idea according
to which the Renaissance was a return to the ancient civilization is "an
idea worthy of the soul of a crossbreed of degenerate Northern Europe,
for which culture is something that man can externally appropriate." The
creative force of civilization is conferred only by race. "[The] Renaissance
... [was] not the rebirth of antiquity, and least of all the rebirth of inartis-
tic, unphilosophic, unscientific Rome, but simply free man's regeneration
from out of the all-levelling Imperium: freedom of political, national
organisation in contrast to cut-and-dried common pattern; freedom of
rivalry, of individual independence in work and creation and endeavour,
in contrast to the peaceful uniformity of the *civitas Dei*; freedom of the
senses of observation in contrast to dogmatic interpretations of nature;
freedom of investigation and thought in contrast to artificial systems after
the manner of Thomas Aquinas; freedom of artistic invention and shaping in contrast to hieratically fixed formulas; finally, freedom of faith in
contrast to religious intolerance."[31] It is an explosion of life, "a completely
Teutonic fact and so, decidedly anti-Roman."

It is clear that here Chamberlain's racism lays its hands fully on the most
trivial and banal commonplaces of a profane, liberaloid-Enlightenment
and anti-traditional interpretation of history, which unfortunately — it
must be recognized — apart from the gratuitous racial justification, was
and in a certain sense still is the byword of a certain "modern education,"
even in our country: and have not even we, in the very midst of Fascism,
seen [Giovanni] GENTILE take up analogous motifs in regard to the
definition of a presumed "Italian tradition"?[32] Chamberlain's incompre-

---

31 *Foundations*, Division III, Ninth Chapter, Part A, p. 190. *Civitas Dei* is Latin for "City
    of God"; it was also the title of St. Augustine's great political tract (*De civitate Dei
    contra paganos*, On the City of God Against the Pagans). The phrase with which
    Evola concludes this paragraph is taken from page 191 of the same part.

32 Giovanni Gentile (1875–1944) was a neo-Hegelian intellectual of the Fascist Period;
    he was a very important figure during Mussolini's rule, and remained a rigorous pro-
    ponent of the Fascist regime throughout all its vicissitudes, for which loyalty Evola
    elsewhere praises him. Gentile eventually lost his life for his beliefs, for he refused to

hension of the true spirit both of the pontifical idea, and of the imperial one, joins an equally great failure to recognize the aristocratic German traditions themselves. The very man who wishes to see one of the causes of the decadence of Renaissance Italy in the dissipation of the "Teutonic patriciate" present in it, comes then to define those German Princes who saved the life of his Luther and irresponsibly subscribed to Luther's doctrine, as a brood of criminals, and to associate the Teutonic "Renaissance" with the civilizations of those Commons which were more or less in revolt against the authority of the Ghibelline nobility:[33] quite beyond associating it with those naturalistic, laic and scientist "conquests" of the new civilization, which were precisely destined to lead the West to the second "ethnic chaos" denounced by Chamberlain: to the chaos of contemporary internationalistic civilization. But it would be too easy to demonstrate all the contradictions, all the miscomprehensions, all the confusions which pullulate in these dilettante historical views; they truly have both their beginning and their end in purely personal opinions — indeed, not even personal in the superior sense, or, as we were almost about to say, in the "Arya" sense, but rather obscurely suggested by the *pathos* of an epoch without principles. To discharge our duty as presenters, we have here related the ideas of Chamberlain: let one guard however against taking them seriously, and from conceiving the better tendencies in racism in their light.

Coming to modern times, Chamberlain sees two powers in battle for dominion of the world; that of the epigones of the Teutonic race and that

---

turn against the regime in its failing, and in consequence was shot to death in his car by partisans. He came to be known as the "philosopher of Fascism," though Evola strongly contested this epithet (see Chapters 1 and 34 of *Recognitions*).

33   The Ghibellines were originally Italian supporters of Frederick Barbarossa, who subsequently sought to expand the Holy Roman Empire into the lands directly or indirectly controlled by the Pope, and thus to bring the Holy Roman Empire back into Rome, the point of its origin in the times of the Ancient Romans. The Ghibellines were opposed by the Guelfs, the supporters of the Pope, and the conflict between them became a centerpiece of Medieval politics, lasting some three hundred years, from the twelfth to the fifteenth century. Evola, as Dante before him, thought very well of the Ghibellines, and speaks often with disdain of those who opposed them.

of a new "ethnic chaos," which is associated in good measure with Judaism. The Jews, according to Chamberlain, are bastards, a mix between Semites and Syrians. "Whether or not there is truly a secret Jewish league which has consciously pursued the end of the material, spiritual, and moral destruction of the Indo-Europeans, and with them of their civilization, I do not know: I believe that the simple instinct of this elusive demon of human decadence [the expression "the demon of human decadence" for Judaism is Richard WAGNER's], an instinct cultivated for millennia, is sufficient for our needs."[34] As things stand, the alternative arises: either the Teutonic element will be able to reorganize itself and to impose itself, or else Europe, with the victory of ethnic chaos and of Judaism, will take the same descending road that already Hellas and Rome had taken.

The World War of 1914–1918 appeared to Chamberlain as the fratricidal battle between peoples that, like the Germans, the French, the English, the Russians, appear in his conception to be branches of the single problematic Arya nucleus, that is the Slavo-Celtico-Teutonic nucleus. In this battle, he moreover saw the reflection of spiritual antitheses, and a kind of insurrection of the peoples against the particular strength intrinsic to the ideal that Germany held in itself. "Germany does not ask aught other than the liberty to give whatever it can give, to be able to place itself indisputably at the head of all the peoples," wrote Chamberlain, "since only then will it be able to realize its divine destination." Amongst Germany's antagonists, the Russians and the French, for Chamberlain, did not represent clear ideal forces. The true antithesis was to be found in England, as the exponent of a mercantile imperialism which suffocates the world under the force of its economy. Until yesterday, Chamberlain dreamed of a Germany which with its strength and its victory would open the way to its superior civilizing right. In 1916, he wrote: "For whomever does not believe in the divine destiny of Germany, it would be best if such a one were to hang himself today, rather than tomorrow." But at the same time: "What can I say? I am afraid of becoming illogical and almost unfaithful: I could consider a defeat for the Germans only as a postponed victory. But I would say: the

---

34   I have been unable to source this quotation.

time, however, is not ripe, it is necessary to faithfully safeguard the sacred patrimony in the restricted limits of a fatherland."[35]

❧

In 1902, WOLTMANN came to found a *Review of Political Anthropology* which gathered the principal exponents of prewar racism, comprising LANGE, Chamberlain himself, VON EHRENFELS, and various others. In this group, we would like to indicate also Joseph Ludwig REIMER, a writer who can be considered as the direct disciple of Chamberlain, whose theses he brought to a greater degree of coherency in his book of 1903, a work entitled *A Pan-German Germany*.[36]

Here commences the distinction between *culture* and *civilization*. Culture has its roots in the very heart of race; it is the direct expression of race, and only subsequently might give rise to a civilization. To each race corresponds a unique culture, which is valid only for it, and which suffers from any cross with a foreign race. Culture, connected to blood, is non-transmissible. Civilization on the other hand, can be transmitted, since it is so to speak the exteriorization of culture, intended to create a given form of material existence for it in a given environment, although not beyond certain limits. Modern Japan, for example, has adopted a civilization which has no relation to its culture and which serves it for its material affirmation. It is however true that "culture and civilization act reciprocally on one another." There are peoples and races which to a high civilization have united an inferior culture (Carthage, etc.) and vice versa. It is the capacity of civilization to create for the material part of humanity the greatest possible life and power, independently of whatever constitutes the essence of the human being. Whence the man of one of the most refined and perfected civilizations might be a barbarian or a brute. Civilization is not essential, but secondary to man; in any case, it has

---

35 Evola evidently translated these citations from one of Chamberlain's German works — either *Kriegsaufsätze* or *Die Zuversicht*.

36 This work has yet to be translated. All quotations from Reimer are translated from Evola's Italian.

elevating force only if it draws its base directly from the culture of a race. Up to this point we find in Reimer however sensible points of view, which are precursor to ideas which have become common domain through the well-known book of Spengler: *The Decline of the West*. But immediately after the usual fixations reappear.

Indeed, for Reimer the correspondence between culture and civilization appears in an eminent way only in the German people. Here the harmony between culture and civilization is thought to be perfect. The current view amongst contemporary racists would seem however to be the contrary: Germany, up to the time of National Socialism, was subjected to a "civilization" alien to its culture, a civilization largely "Judaicized," internationalist and rationalist, which has undermined the qualities of race.

For Reimer, "race appears to us in history, so to speak, under two diverse forms: the one, which was developed in the remotest prehistorical times, constitutes the immutable and indestructible part, the very essence of race"; the other, variable, mobile, is often subject to a thousand contingencies, and furnishes the links which connect culture to civilization. "It is in culture that the originating foundation is to be discovered, the essence of race." Here too we find a judicious racism which, thought through to the end, would necessarily come to shift the center ever more from the biological to the spiritual plane and of the "races of the spirit." Which is to say, race might begin to mean something other than that which it expresses in the case of a dog or a horse.

Regarding the difference between the races, Reimer opposes the Teutonics to the non-Teutonics, the first corresponding, as in Chamberlain's conception, to the Slavo-Celtico-Teutonic group, and the second correspond in Europe to two types:

1)   To brown man, small and round of head (brachicephalic), hailing from the Alpine region and from the Sudetes, a type almost always rectified by crosses with Nordic elements;

2)   The brown dolichocephalic Mediterranean man, to be considered as
a derivative branch of *homo europaeus*; near to Nordic man more
than any other race.

Reimer passes on to consider the problem of the possibility of an empire
on a racist basis. Already here an ambiguity clearly reveals itself which
will become quite characteristic of contemporary tendencies: on one
hand a principle of difference is affirmed, of hierarchy and of authority
for whatever regards the superior race as opposed to the others. But on
the other hand, one does not hold to such a principle within the superior
race itself; with respect to this race the already marked intolerance for
everything aristocratic and imperial manifests itself, and one ends up in a
species of liberalism or democratic Caesarism. As if the Teutonics ought
to affirm the aristocratic principle before all others, but ought not tolerate
this principle for themselves.

In any case Reimer's premise is that an imperial idea needs to be
imposed "in the face of the chaotic development of the Germanic nations," but "an imperial idea, which must come into existence like that
of the Romans. A global empire which wishes to guarantee its duration
must not become universal in the Roman mold: it must not extend its
domain over nations and heterogeneous races for purely commercial and
economic races toward the end of subjugating them, absorbing them, and
confounding itself with them." How Reimer might have believed that it
was by such a path that the ancient *Imperium* of Rome was realized, is
not easy to comprehend. In any case, his idea is that that every imperial
race should disseminate its blood in conquered regions, maintaining itself
however pure; penetrating with its ramifications into each of the other
races, giving them its imprint, but not bringing these to fuse into it. In
the particular case, on one hand, a return to the primitive Teutonic race
and energetic care for its health and its organic development; on the other
hand, expansion. How this exigency might be realized practically is not
however altogether clear: if the Teutons must remain pure, and yet fertil-
ize the other races with their own blood, nothing else can be imagined
than polygamy and hypergamy. Enclosed in a kind of inaccessible caste,

the conquerors would have to have the possibility of giving the gift of their seed to the women of the conquered races, leaving these however in their present state. Moreover, today we have not been lacking in those who have rehabilitated on racist basis the famous *jus primae noctis*:[37] according to the proponents of this idea, this would not be the abuse of dissolute and immoral lords, but rather a means for diffusing aristocratic blood in inferior elements, thus ennobling them.

"To practically realize a global empire in Europe," states Reimer, "it is essential that a race really exists which is capable of culture, which, by the force of an external or internal necessity, is driven to conquest of the world." This is a principle against which nothing in general can be said: when, that is, one does not add that in Europe "it is recognized that this race is the Slavo-Celtico-Teutonic one, to which European culture is joined by bonds of origin." For Reimer, there are two imperialisms. The one, "feudal, reactionary and of divine right," is "anachronistic" and "must rapidly disappear." (Let it be noted that the author wrote this before the World War.) The other is a "purified imperialism" which has as its basis "democratic education," which is to be developed across various generations. Here we return anew to accusing Charlemagne of having, by assuming the Roman crown, ceased to be a king of Teutonic race, so that the "principle of universalism triumphed over that of empire founded by a race." The Medieval German empire was not, according to Reimer, anything other than the prolungation of universalist Roman imperialism, that is, the adoption by a part of the Teutons of the idea of a universal empire devoid of nationality; "and this legacy is the fount of our worst miseries." The Teutonic world emancipated itself from Rome, but "a new German empire unified on a non-universalistic basis could not realize itself other than at the twilight of the Habsburgs." Here Reimer does not hesitate to posit a Teutonic action in the revolt of Prussia against Austria, the which, as is known, was formally precisely the Catholic heir of the

---

37 Latin for "right of the first night," a right which was supposedly exercised by lords over women of lower classes (it is also called the *droit du seigneur*, the "right of the lord"), in some cases on their wedding night.

Holy Roman Empire. Reimer could well have seen a gift from Providence
in the World War of 1914–1918, which has had as its effect the disappearance both of the empire of the Habsburgs and of the remains of the
anachronistic "feudal" imperiality of Germany itself in the Hohenzolern.
Now, it is singular that precisely this end was consciously and notori-
ously sought, in that war, by Masonry and international Jewry.[38] Let this
give to a certain class of readers a sense of the suspect influences obeyed
by every racist myth which does not have, like that which we ourselves
defend, precise aristocratic-traditionalist premises, but reveals rather
"socializing" and modernizing tendencies.

---

38   [Note is Evola's. — Trans.] Regarding this, see that important work which we our-
     selves have translated: E. Malynski and L. de Poncins, *The Occult War (Arms and
     Phases of the Hebrew-Massonic attack against the European tradition)*.

CHAPTER V

The Theory of Heredity

Genetic racism. Theory of environment and theory of heredity.
Laws of Mendel. Hybridization and dehybridizaion.
Racist deductions.

ITH THE EXAMINATION of this group of writers we have already brought to light the fundamental concepts which inspired the racist ideological recovery of the postwar period. The development of such concepts in the new period, up to the advent of National Socialism, assumes these fundamental directions:

1) Above all one seeks to justify or to fortify from the scientific point of view the idea of race by means of positive and well-defined laws — the laws of heredity. And the development of the theory of MENDEL in the deductions of a "genetic" racism (FISCHER, LENZ).

2) In the second place one seeks to specify on anthropologico-descriptive basis the principle of the inequality of the races, by describing a certain number of primary ethnic types (GÜNTHER, VON EICKSTEDT, GIESELER), sometimes also psychological types (CLAUSS).

3) The racist theses unite ever more closely with anti-Judaism.[1]

4) The Arya myth, in the form of the myth of the primordial Nordic race, becomes the basis for reconstructions in the grand style of the highest prehistory (WIRTH).

5) The racist interpretation of the history of civilizations takes on ever more decisive and uniform traits (ROSENBERG, VON LEERS), and in certain current extremists the racist vision of life begins to manifest itself not only as anti-Catholicism, but also as anti-Christianity and neopaganism.

6) Finally, from theory one passes to practice, to positive action. The racist idea penetrates the field of law and exercises its influence. From being the private idea of a more or less marginal group of writers, racism becomes, through the new national revolutions, an idea of State, giving place to a new legislation, a whole group of measures for social hygiene and an ethnic selection founded on the idea of the Arya race.

Let us pass therefore, to the consideration of these various points.

So-called genetic racism has taken form from a determinate use of the discovery of the positive laws of heredity; this genetic racism is distinguished from the racism which we described at the beginning by the fact that, for the fundamental point of its definition of various racial types, it does not adopt the external characteristics of the individual, but, so to speak, those potentialities of which the external characteristics are but the manifestations, potentialities transmitted through heredity. Eugen FISCHER, one of the foremost exponents of genetic racism, defines race in this way: "It is a stock determined by groups of equal 'genes,' not by men externally similar in their forms: it is a hereditary group,"[2] thus conceiv-

---

1   Evola does not use the term antisemitism here; given his peculiar view of the Jews, I have thought it best to preserve these differences wherever they appear, despite sometimes having to use uncommon English words (i.e., anti-Judaism) in consequence.

2   Once again, the works in question have yet to be translated, and the original German is hard to come by. All Fischer's quotations are translated from Evola's Italian.

ing qualities of race, not as all those qualities which a given human group might present in a given moment in the better part of its individuals, but only as those qualities which are susceptible of hereditary transmission.

The concept of the "gene" comes from biology and from genetics: it is precisely the potential, persisting through generations, of generating a form or a type, and also of activating certain qualities — all of which forms, types, or qualities derive from the "gene" in accordance with precise laws, and not always uniformly. In various conditions, the same "gene" might manifest itself in different ways, as we will immediately see more clearly by considering the general laws of heredity. There follows from this a fundamental distinction in genetics which racism, and even political racism, has transposed and thus made its own: namely, the distinction between *genotype* and *phenotype*. Genotype is the fundamental and origi- nating type, connected to the specific nature of the "gene" or of a given group of "genes"; phenotype is instead the apparent, sensible, individual form which appears from that potential, a form which, as has been said, might vary. From which derives another most peculiar distinction; that between *idiovariation*, meaning mutations capable of etching the essence, the "gene" or genotype, and which therefore are accessible to hereditary transmission, and *paravariation*, meaning external and individual modi- fications connected to the phenotype, and which as such do not have the power to transmit themselves through heredity. Genetic racism therefore diminishes the importance of a merely descriptive research, and of a simple cataloging of characteristics and of traits: for it holds that, so far as race is concerned, only the individuation of "genes" and of the genotype is important and decisive — which is to say, only the originating hereditary and fundamental element of race.

It is a singular fact that genetic racism, for example that of Fischer, while on the one hand reinforces the concept of differences through views of this kind, making these differences profound, organic, hereditary, on the other hand winds up relativizing these differences through a monistic conception of origins, opposed to that which EMPEROR JULIAN had al- ready defended when he declared himself for polingenesis. This genetic racism in fact maintains that the genes were differentiated from out of a unique substance in an epoch which falls somewhere near the glacial period: strong selections, favored by constant environmental conditions, thus stabilized these differentiations, fixing in definitive form the various nature of the "genes," so that from that period the races, as well defined and distinct hereditary groups, came into existence, governed physically and in part also spiritually by the fundamental laws of genetics, and in particular by the Mendelian laws on heredity.

By way of introducing a brief exposition of these laws, so as to give the sense of the racio-political deductions that have been drawn from them so far, we will mention that they have been assumed by contemporaneous movements of national renovation, and first of all by German National Socialism, as a weapon in the battle against the theory of the influence of the environment — theory which these currents consider to be the scientistic auxiliary of Marxism and liberalism. In order to defend their dogma of the fundamental equality of all human beings, despite clear refutations of this idea inflicted by experience itself, both as regards the inequality of individuals and also of races, Marxism and liberalism put their hands on the theory of environment. According to this theory, every differentation should be traced back to the external influence exercised by the environment, be it natural, social, or historical. Thus, each difference is only exterior, accidental, and contingent, and might be removed through an appropriate modification of the conditions of the environment. The corollary of this view is humanitarianism: if there are inferior or unworthy beings, these are not such by nature, but only because they have been the "victims of their environment."

To the theory of the environment racism, National Socialism therefore opposes the theory of *heredity*, according to which the differences between the beings do not have external but internal cause — an essential, congenital cause, connected to heredity. External conditions can indeed either accommodate or obstruct the development of innate inherited dispositions; they can even bring it about that one or the other rises to the fore, "but no force of the environment, be it of material or of spiritual nature, is capable of mutating the more intimate essence of dispositions, and thus of the nature of man" (Walter GROSS).[3] Consequently, "the value of men, both in good and in evil, is no longer the consequence of a good or bad environment, but it is the expression of inherited qualities residing in the human blood, which come to them from their fathers and their mothers. We cannot transform such qualities, nor even arbitrarily awaken anew those which have been lost. According to our present consciousness, we should rather think that from the time that a people appears in history with its qualities, and these subsist up to the point that the line of blood is broken; at which point a part of the originating qualities is forever lost. The great majority of men are originally gifted with good qualities on average, a minority can elevate itself over these on account of its higher bodily, spiritual, and character qualities, and another minority rather has inferior and diseased dispositions. All this, let it be said yet again, does not derive from the diversity of the forces of the environment, from social conditions, etc., but from the force of destiny, which here manifests itself in the form of heredity." Whence comes a reinforcement in the first place of the principle that the inequality of the races is essential and not accidental; in the second place, the principle of the inequality of civilizations, of ideals, of values, etc.; in the third place, that "rather than the empty formula of equal rights for all, the National Socialist principle enters into play: to each his own — those rights, those duties, that influence, that responsibility which correspond to his particular innate gifts."

◆

Having thus presented the meaning that the theory of heredity has to-day, even politically, let us examine this theory more deeply. So far as its "official" character goes, we shall refer primarily to the exposition that Hermann BOEHM has recently made on it.

To begin with, the Augustinian abbot Johann Mendel[4] is considered the "father" of the theory of heredity, the man who formulated its laws

---

3   Evola gives no indication of the source of this quotation; Gross is not listed in his bibliography. I have translated from the Italian.

4   His full name was Gregor Johann Mendel (1822–1884).

above all on the basis of experiments and observations made in the animal and vegetable kingdoms. For so long as Mendel was alive, his research did not awaken any sympathy. Only at the end of the last century was it adopted by official science through the results obtained independently by the Dutchman DE VRIES, the German CORRENS, and the Austrian TSCHERMAK. Its assumption into racist ideology is yet more recent.

First point. Two principal factors contribute to the particular form that a given being possesses in a given moment: heredity and environment. The first objection that the new theory raises against the principle of environment is that the faculty and the mode of reaction to a given influence of the environment is not the same for all individuals, does not derive from without, but can only be explained by something that has its roots within, as an inherited, congenital trait. However, the action that the environment can exercise depends precisely on this congenital and specific mode of reaction. An exponent of thus intellectual current, Erwin BAUR, has expressed this idea thus: "That which one inherits is always and exclusively a specific mode of reaction to external conditions, and that which we perceive with our senses as the external characteristics of an individual is naught but the result of its reaction to the accidental constellation of all those external conditions, under the influence of which the individual is properly developed."[5]

Let us clarify this abstract statement through a few examples. Chinese primrose has two varieties, one with red flowers and the other with white flowers. In normal conditions, that is, between ten and twenty degrees, it produces red flowers, while at over thirty-five degrees and in damp conditions it produces white flowers instead. Is this a sign of the influence of the environment? Up to a certain point. Rather say, it is the displacement of the concept of heredity. The external characteristics of "color red" or "color white" are not inherited, so much as the capacity to *constantly* produce red flowers in normal environmental conditions and white flowers in hot greenhouses or in tropical climates. We should therefore consider as hereditary and determinant a very precise, even if not unambiguous,

---

5   This has been translated from the Italian.

way of *reacting*. The external aspect, contingent on the individual which finds itself in a certain environment, should therefore not lead us to draw conclusions regarding its congenital and inherited dispositions. We might be dealing with external modifications which say nothing regarding the essence and the forces of heredity. The conditions of the environment can only influence in the sense of bringing forth one or the other of the dispositions enclosed in the essence and conditioned by the genes, but they cannot influence this essence directly at all; there, heredity acts alone.

This is the first law of heredity: *the environment can produce only certain external variations* (paravariations or modifications). Such variations are contingent, transitory; they do not transform themselves into elements of a new heredity; they are lost. The Chinese primrose which, born in an overheated greenhouse, has always produced white flowers, not so soon as it is placed into nature, flowers anew in red. Suppose we take a primrose from the greenhouse, suppose we transplant some of its seeds again in the greenhouse, and then after a series of generations we take an exemplar of this white species and carry it into normal conditions: once again the white flowering will cease, it will produce again the red flowers of its "ancestor plant." The environment has therefore been able to effect nothing on an entire series of generations with respect to the innate mode of reaction of this plant, which is to constantly produce red flowers at 15° and white flowers at 35°.

It is thought that things proceed analogously in the animal kingdom. There exists a particular species of insect, the paramecia, which is unicellular and which reproduces by division of the nucleus and thus, from a single cell, divides into two equal parts. Its "children" would therefore have the same biological heredity. Now the size of this insect varies, oscillating between a maximum and a minimum, which are determined by the conditions of the environment. Put into two different environments, two offspring of one and the same parent assume one a larger and the other a lesser size. But if we permit these two insects to reproduce, we see that the descendants of the larger insect are not larger than the descendants of the insect which developed, by environmental pressures, to a reduced size. This is a new proof that the "modifications" or "paravariations," which is to say the forms conditioned by the environment, are not transmitted through heredity, but are transient, they are not etched into essence and descendance.

Genetic racism holds that this first law of the theory of heredity is valid also for man. It is admitted that a human race is not defined by a rigid anthropological type, but rather by a type which oscillates around an average value, that is, which has a maximum and a minimum of modification (just as the primrose had its two form-limits red and white). The environment can exercise its influence only within this interval. That influence is not ever strong enough to carry an organism past the maximum of variability, fixed by the intrinsic nature and by the capacity for adaptation of a given anthropological type and a given race. And even when entire generations of a given race are constrained to adapt to their environment, to assume the form that is the remotest extreme from their originating type, this modification is not transmitted, but if their descendants return to normal conditions, the type is once again manifested. Hence, with an image, we can say that the type behaves as an elastic substance which can be deformed within certain limits (beyond which it breaks) under an external agent, but so soon as the external action ceases it returns to its primitive form.

LAMARCK had formulated two laws on the basis of the theory of environment. According to the first, use develops faculty, and disuse atrophies it, up to the point of carrying it to its disappearance. The second law is that, if external (environmental) conditions persist, by force of which a function develops or atrophies, this function transmits itself or else disappears in descendance. The theory of heredity declares these two laws to be false, or at least incomplete. Example: one can withhold nutriments from a variety of a bean plant, such that it remains only barely alive. From the seeds of this undernourished plant sprout seedlings likewise ill, frail, underdeveloped, which remain in such a state even when they are brought to a soil which is rich in nutriments. It would seem, therefore, that the disability created by the environment in the mother-plant is transmitted through heredity.

But it is not so: we are not dealing with the transmission of an essential element, but of a resonance extending itself so far as the new plant, from the action exercised by the external on the mother-plant. Beneath this action, seeds are formed with insufficient nutrition for the germ of the new plant. But this posthumous influence of the environment little by little is extinguished. It suffices to take the seeds of the new plant, develop them, take new seeds, etc. Already at the third generation the plant recovers and vegetates in a normal way.

Certain curious investigations were made by Johannes LANGE on "criminal twins." This researcher had distinguished two forms of the process from which twins are born. In the first, the ovules are simultaneously fertilized, and so the twins are gifted differently. In the other, a single cell, fertilized in a given moment of its development divides itself into two parts, which go on to give place to two beings, and these two beings, that is the two twins, therefore have equal heredity, they are equally gifted.

On the basis of such a genetic theory, the advocates of the doctrine of heredity think they can nullify the force of one of the best-known arguments adopted by the advocates of the doctrine of the influence of the environment: the latter credited to environmental influence the fact, otherwise inexplicable to them, that twins sometimes present very different qualities, though they have the same heredity. Equally delinquent twins, for example, are not to be found save when their heredity is truly equal, that is when their birth could be related to the second of the two types of process. To FISCHER we owe further, vast and systematic research in this field, the study of twins constituting one of the *experimenta crucis*[6] of genetics.

As a corollary to the first law of heredity, racism draws this particular conclusion:

Education is not omnipotent. The purpose of any form of education must consist in bringing its object to the highest development, through the formation of a

6   Latin for "crucial experiments," meaning, an experiment capable of deciding, within the present context and limits of scientific knowledge, which of two or more theories or hypotheses is presently the superior one.

condition of life maximally favorable to good congenital and inherited qualities. Where the chord of heredity is not present to sound upon, even the most gifted artist cannot draw any note whatsoever, and the pedagogical action never but never can be efficacious.[7] (BOEHM)

Let us turn now to the laws of "hybridization," that is to the laws relative to the results of crossbreeding between parents of diverse species. These are known under the name of *laws of inheritance.*[8]

There exist two varieties of the "snap-dragon" plant, the first with red flowers and the other with flowers the color of mother of pearl. From a parent of the red species crossed with a parent of the mother-of-pearl species, flowers of an intermediary color are born, pink snap-dragons. This is the first law of Mendel on inheritance, the *law of segregation* (that is: in the hybrid product, the two different qualities are made uniform, they balance in an intermediary quality).

Let us turn now to the second generation; let us cross a snap-dragon of the hybrid mixed pink quality with another equally hybrid pink. *The result is not a species which repeats the unique species of the hybrid parents*, that is, the unique result is of the new cross is not flowers which are themselves also entirely pink, but there rather is found a "disassociation" (dehybridization) of qualities: in the overall number of the second hybrid generation, 50% of the flowers are indeed pink, but the remaining 50% are composed 25% of flowers which reproduce the pure red quality, and 25% of flowers which reproduce the pure mother-of-pearl quality. Hence the characteristics of the ancestors reappear, which in the hybrid parents seemed to have disappeared and instead were only latent. This is the second law of Mendel, the *law of independent assortment or of dehybridization.* The red ancestor is therefore reborn in 25% of the offspring of the second generation (we could say: in its grandchildren), the mother-of-pearl ancestor likewise in

---

7   Translated from the Italian.

8   Evola calls Mendel's laws of inheritance the "laws of mixed-variation," and he provides the following names for these laws: 1.) the "law of uniformity"; 2.) the "law of dissociation or hybridization"; and 3.) the "law of independence." These are not the names currently used in Italian biology, and I have translated them using the current terminology in English, so as not to confuse readers to no purpose.

25%, and only in the remaining 50% is the mixed or hybrid pink quality of the direct parents conserved.

But it is not conserved for long. Let us now crossbreed two exemplars of those which in the second generation remained hybrid. In this third generation, the same dissociation is reproduced: the mixed heredity is maintained only in 50% of the resulting flowers of the new cross, while in 25% of them once more the original red heredity is reborn of one ancestor and in the other 25% that of the original mother-of-pearl of the other ancestor. The hybrids tend therefore ever further to segregate: they lose themselves bit by bit along the way, so to speak, they are gradually eliminated in their descendants, even while the pure original heredities or qualities resurface. These qualities or heredities remain heterogeneous; they do not meld together, they do not disappear: when they cross, almost forcibly, they form parts of unstable amalgamations, from which the same liberate themselves, becoming themselves once again, in descendance. Heredity is destiny. It is not lost.

Let us then turn to a new case, that in which the force of the two originating species or heredities which are crossbred are not equal. A red snapdragon is united with another, not of the mother-of-pearl species, but of a third species, a *white* species. This third species proves weaker, and it does not have any power of influence on the cross. The hybrids which result therefore would seem not to be hybrids, because they are not pink, as in the precedent case, but rather they are themselves pure red. The white heredity would seem to have disappeared in the cross. The offspring absolutely resembles that parent with the stronger quality, and at this point it is not possible to distinguish it from that which is born from the cross of two parents of the red species, rather than a red parent and a white one. But so soon as we pass to the successive generation, which is to say so soon as we cross-breed two exemplars of this species which seem pure, though they are the result of a cross, we see that in the resulting flowers also in this case dissociation manifests itself, as well as the consequent resurfacing of the original heredity. The proportions are the same, only that here we must distinguish a red which is truly pure, a reincarnation of the original, from an apparent red proper to the first hybrid offspring. This second red appears in 50% of the flowers of the second generation carrying with it however a "contained" or latent and invisible white, which is ready to manifest itself in the successive cross; then there are 25% of integrally red flowers which do not dissociate any longer in successive generations, and finally a last 25% in which we can see the white heredity reemerge which seemed to have disappeared or to have been dominated. The dissociation of the presence of a stronger (or "dominant") parent is not eliminated: it remains only retarded. The weaker (or "recessive") heredity remains repressed, but sooner or later in development it will resurface. Heredity once again is destiny.

◆

Let us consider one final case. Let us cross a flower of the hybrid quality, not with another hybrid, as we have up to now considered in order to observe the process of dehybridization, but rather with a flower belonging to one of the pure original varieties. In the results of this cross, dissociation once more manifests, according to the following percentage: 50% of the elements resulting from the cross of the bastard with the pure race, so to speak, also remains composed of bastards, and 50% reproduce the quality of the parent of pure blood — which, however, behaves as in the preceding case, that is, as the carrier of a heredity of "dominant" type. The pure blood therefore has, with respect to the bastard, the part of a "dominant" with respect to a "recessive." However, according to the law relative to the preceding case, here too the dehybridization is retarded and not eliminated in the subsequent offspring of crosses between hybrid elements.

These are the laws of Mendel on heredity: experimental and deterministic laws, which that racism of scientistic mold maintains are valid for all living beings, and therefore also for man. Naturally, the racists forget to ask themselves if man must not be considered as something else, beyond being a "natural being" and a "living being." No doubt he is also such, given that he does not think, does not create, does not battle in some immaterial over-world; no doubt therefore, that so far as his biologically and physically conditioned aspect goes he is subject to certain laws which have in him a similar action to that which they have in a plant or in an insect. But the true problem is that of considering up to what point these laws interfere with laws of a superior nature in man, and feel the influence of these: feel, that is, the influence of laws properly human, relating to man insofar as he is man — personality, spirit — and not insofar as he is one among the many species of beings in nature. It is most singular that racism, which desires difference, here, in order to affirm itself "scientifically," ends in a leveling, that is, in putting on one and the same plane, dominated uniformly by the laws of heredity, men (and amongst men, superior races and inferior races), rabbits, plants, insects, etc. In our book *Doctrinal Synthesis of Race*, we have however studied the limits and the true sense that the law of heredity has in a complete theory of race referring to man as such.

Moreover, even the scientistic racists admit that the laws of Mendel, even in their biological aspect, are not so easy to observe within the various human species.[9] However the cause of this scarce visibility for them resides above all in the difficulty of specifying the various elements of human heredity and of following their developments in cross-breedings, given that we do not have at our disposal human exemplars of absolutely pure race, which one might combine together experimentally; still less can one follow the results of such combinations in a sufficient number of case sand of generations. In the second place, the difficulty resides, according to them, in the fact that man is not defined in his heredity, as the "snap-dragon," by a single typical quality, but by *many* qualities. In certain special cases, it is believed nonetheless that even in man the laws of inheritance have been verified with sufficient approximation: e.g., with regard to the color of eyes. It has been verified that a dark color of eyes acts as "dominant" with respect to the light color, which is "recessive" (as the red snap-dragon with respect to the white), whence certain known consequences (the first generation resulting from the union of a parent with

9   Italian: *le specie umane*, the *various* human species.

dark eyes with a parent with clear eyes has black eyes, in the subsequent offspring of a crossing between these children with black eyes however, the suffocated light color returns, etc.). It has been in any case ascertained that a series of diseases and disabilities are transmitted hereditarily, even if in the passive, dominated or "recessive" form, as in the case of eyes of fair color: these diseases and ills, in the children of the first generation, that is in the union of the ill person with a healthy one, might seem to disappear, though they subsist in the latent state and manifest themselves in a successive generation. As in cases of hereditary transmission of spiritual gifts. As cases of the hereditary transmission of spiritual gifts one often cites the Bach family, which showed musical gifts for five generations, the Bernoulli family by an analogous heredity of mathematical dispositions and then, above all, many cases of uninterrupted transmission of military capacity in aristocratic lines.

We come to a final case: the development of heredity in the case of a cross, not between two qualities alone (the color red and the color mother-of-pearl; eyes of light color and of dark color, etc.), but between *two groups* of quality. One case which has been experimentally examined regards the consequences of a cross between a white guinea pig with curly hair and a black guinea pig with straight hair. Here, curly hair and black color play the role of "dominant" qualities, and the hybrid product of the first combination of the two parents is a black and curly offspring, that is determined apparently only by the two aforementioned dominant qualities. But even here, continuing on to combine these hybrids amongst each other, the suppressed qualities of the parents resurface in the successive generations and, in general, it has been verified that the process of heredity follows the laws already known, remaining however distinct for each of the characteristics: that is, the development of heredity relative to color unfolds independently of that relative to the type of hair. This is the third law of inheritance, *the law of dominance*.

This law would also count for various inheritances — some spiritual, some corporeal — of the human species which come to coexist in those

beings which emerge from racial crossings: they would therefore transmit
themselves separately, without any necessary correspondence:

> Thus, it is an error to wish to draw hasty conclusions regarding the character of
> a person on the basis of his physical aspect. Such would be legitimate only for
> racially pure instances: but practically speaking, in central Europe, mixed as it
> is, there is nothing to be found of truly racially pure instances. In the veins of
> each man runs the blood of various races. For which, it cannot be said that an
> individual who is somatically of the Nordic race, thin, tall, blond, necessarily
> has Nordic qualities of soul and of spirit, and thus it is likewise possible that
> in a squat and small brachycephalic body there dwells a Nordic soul. However,
> taking a group of a hundred men who are somatically Nordic, and comparing
> them to a hundred men who are somatically of Oriental race, it is plausible
> that a Nordic race is to be found much more often in the first than amongst the
> second. (BOEHM)

The importance of this acknowledgment will not escape the reader, as
regards the formulation of a complete racism. From the point of view of
"selectionism," that is the practice of a purification of the race, if the laws
of inheritance are true and conserve all their value also for the human
species, it is evident that by impeding every further crossing of the hybrids
of a nation with the elements of another race, and doing so for a series of
generations, by the force of the laws of inheritance, the unions between
these hybrids would give place to a progressive dissociation of the mixed
qualities, by way of which the originating qualities of the pure state would
come in the end once more to the light of day: and so, isolating the carriers
of those qualities, which originally adulterated the pure Arya race, having
now come to betray themselves, and conserving or fortifying the dehy-
bridized Arya qualities, one would cause the reintegration of the race. It
is thus that Mendelism appears among the theoretical presuppositions of
the measures taken by National Socialism for the *Aufnordung*, that is for
the "Nordic" regeneration of the German people: while the other side of
this doctrine, relative to the fatal reemergence of that heredity interrupted
by a heterogeneous or diseased biological element, is assumed as the scientific basis for various hygienic measures and racial prophylactics, upon
which we will have more to say later. So far as the limits of the laws on

heredity go, it must be noted that even Mendelism and genetics recognize
the fact that non-accidental and extrinsic variations, as those referable to
the action of the environment (paravariation), but deep, incised in the
idioplasm, that is in the part of the cells of an organism on which depend
the nature and the heredity of the individual — Mendelism and genetics
recognize that variations of such a kind are not limited only to those
created by hybridism, that is, by the cross of parents of different races
(mixed-variation). They admit rather a third species of variation, called
"idiovariations," which are produced directly, without mingling or external action, in the essence of the race or of a given lineage of an individual
of that race, and which would be transmitted through heredity.

Regarding the cause and the essence of these idiovariations, of these
mutations that can appear without the introduction of environment or intermixing, the theory of heredity as of today knows next to nothing. These
mutations remain mysterious. However, some research such as that of DE
VRIES has recognized their fundamental importance in fully explaining
the differentiation of the species, against Darwinistic hypotheses (theory
of the environment). For the human species, it seems that we have been
able to establish that one of the causes that bring about an essential and
hereditary alteration in the germinal number is the action of alcohol and
also that of ultraviolet rays. But it is evident that such observations are
limited to details; they do not touch those parts of the human being which
are most important. *Once the concept of idiovariation has been admitted it
is always possible to suppose that within a race, either in the direction of as-
cendancy or in the direction of degeneration, or, in the end, in the direction
of a mere transformation, a cause might act which is no longer a physical,
biological cause.*

Thus, the determinism of heredity would be broken or, more precisely, it would work only to register and to regulate the development, the
conservation, the alteration and the dissipation of new qualities, which
themselves are not explained by this same determinism. Moreover, is it at
all possible to believe otherwise as regards that famous differentiation of

"genes" from a single substance in the glacial period, which, according to
FISCHER, gave rise to the multiple varieties of the human race?

To admit rather that one of the causes of idiovariation is the cross
of parents of extremely diverse race, means to destroy the distinction
between mixed-variation (variation by intermixing) and idiovaration,
and thus to prejudice the rigor of the laws of Mendel with imponderable
factors. Erwin BAUR, a well-known scholar of the problem of heredity,
has recognized this, together with MENGHIN, another eminent scientist.
This has not stopped the pure racists from going so far as to affirm that
the intermixing between heterogeneous races is the essential cause not
of hybridism (mixed-variation), but also of irreparable alterations of the
heredity of race, transmitted to descendance (idiovariation). So it is that
while they, in order to cut the feet out from under the critiques brought
against them by a philosophical or spiritual point of view, haughtily
entrench themselves in the domain of "science" or "known facts" — then
they take whatever they want from "science," and from the "positive facts,"
considering only those which accord with their more or less preconceived
ideas, substituting their own byword for what scientific prudence might
suggest. A complete and enlightened doctrine of race ought to conduct
itself in an entirely different manner.

In any case, the reader has been give an overview of the entirety of the
theories of heredity, of its laws, and of its problems, so as to become aware
of one of the components of that general atmosphere which has favored
racism as a modern myth.

CHAPTER VI

Racist Typology

The "primordial hunter" and the "primordial farmer."
Nordic man, Phalic man, Western man, Dinaric man, Alpine
man, Baltic man. The "psychoanthropology" of Clauss.
The religiosity of the Nordic race.

URNING TO THE TYPOLOGICAL individuation of the various races which has been developed since the end of the war, we will examine above all the classification of MERKENSCHLAGER, then we will explain that — of more anthropological type — of GÜNTHER, and finally we will give mention to the new "psychological Anthropology" cultivated by the school of CLAUSS.

According to Merkenschlager, the concept of race should be understood in a living way, as a "process," as something dynamic, not static and rigid. The static definition of race is: "Race is a group of men rendered unitary by common hereditary, corporeal characteristics and distinguished by these characteristics from every other group of the same kind." To this concept is opposed the idea that "the races are not ever anything absolute, but represent always and only a *state of equilibrium* between innate hereditary gifts and the environment." Proceeding from this idea, Merkenschlager defines race precisely as a "state of equilibrium" and defines as the "optimal race" that which "possesses forces capable of reestablishing such a state of equilibrium, each time that it is altered."

Taking this as his premise, Merkenschlager relates the difference between the races (for him this difference reduces to the opposition between two primordial racial types) to determinate geographical and geological situations, and for this purpose dates it back to the "glacial period," taking once again the road that the research of WILSER and then of FISCHER had already set off down. According to Merkenschlanger, the glacial period was not, as most maintain, a static and dead age. It was rather an age of great movements. Ice extended over the face of Europe, then slowly withdrew, then advanced anew, so that a minimum of five glacial periods can be counted with three intermediate periods. And in the environment produced by these grand climatic-geological alterations, for Merkenschlager, the first originating race took form, the type of the "primordial hunter" (*Urjäger*).

No other type could have had the possibility of existence then; amidst tundras, frozen steppes, winds, and tempests, an active, mobile, individualistic type necessarily had to take form, a type of hunters and migrants, with a cranial and corporeal structure suitable to the dynamic and exposed style of its life, to its nature, to its environment. This is the blond dolichocephalic, which almost without exception has been sculpted and transmitted by the glacial period: the races of Aurignac and Cro-magnon man (we will later speak of the prehistoric races to which these denominations correspond), up to the stage of the so-called "civilization of the reindeer," or the Magdalenians.

Toward the end of the Middle Stone Age (the Mesolithic Period) a new principle manifested itself: in the breast of the grand heroic heredity of the glacial epoch, the world of the "races of the palafittes"[1] makes its appearance, who concern themselves now with the earth, with everything capable of assuring them a stable life: thus cultivation, and no longer the

---

1   That is, the race of men who built their houses over bodies of water on stilts.

mobile distances of the hunt across Europe. This is the type of the "primordial farmer" (*Urbauer*) which arises in confrontation with that of the "primordial hunter," pressing into Europe from the Orient.

According to Merkenschlager, a silent battle ignited between these two types across long prehistoric epochs. The "primordial farmer" is characterized by pertinacity, by the attitude of observation. He is turned in upon himself, and to this attitude corresponds the round form of his cranium. With him the brown brachicephalic appears in Europe. This type already manifested itself sporadically starting from the first Stone Age, but collectively and in large zones of civilization it appears only in the Middle and Late Stone Age, parallel to new geographical and climactic conditions, which render agriculture ever more possible. The new race is strictly related to that which today is called Alpine, but improperly so, since the attitude for agriculture never could have developed in an originating location of alps, of high mountains. The expression the "race of the Jura" would be a happier one, because it was represented more in the plateaus of the Jura more than in the Alps.

Merkenschlager says that agriculture little by little conquered Europe. However tragic its history might have often been, its history was not heroic, not alike to the style of high tension of the glacial hunters. While the race of the hunters continued to develop a superior interpretation of life, fixed in grandiose symbols of stone (megalithic civilization), and while the influence of this civilization is observed throughout all coastal peoples, from northern Europe to Mediterranean Africa and Asia Minor, Central Europe does not show it: the new race had already achieved its mute and silent colonization.

On this basis, Merkenschlager establishes a classification of types. From the primordial hunter developed the technician, the inventor, the builder, the engineer, the soldier, the individualist. From the primordial farmer, on the other hand, developed the man that examines, the intuitive, the burgher, the humanist, the contemplative philosopher. The inventive European spirit is a heredity from the glacial age, while in the domain of Alpine man there is more "stability," more color, more sensitivity, a better capacity to surpass every crisis, more attachment. The primordial farmer had need of a sense of security precisely because he was tied to the earth and drew from the earth his living. Thus one can say that the originating cell of the bourgeois days back to 7000 years B.C.: the man of the palafittes is the man constrained to defend himself; he is no longer the man who has joy in movement and assault.

Recapitulating, Merkenschlager writes, "The glacial period had, therefore, differentiated the 'active' type (differentiation of the races); with the appearance of agriculture, the 'persevering' type became clear, and in the post-glacial period a powerful intermixing of all the European human substance (intermingling of races) took place, in the wake of which, in the zones of the Nordic climes, a blood manifested itself which was ever more alike to that of the glacial age, while in the zones of the continental climate the Alpine blood predominates. In function of various environments, now one and now the other of the two originating types manifested itself, but with new traits in each case (mutation of the races)."[2] This is the way in which Merkenschlager specifies the three fundamental concepts of differentiation, intermingling, and mutation.

The ages of metals, and above all the Bronze Age, present a renewal of the dolichocephalic races, which is to say, of the heroic-hunter civilization, as against the vehement expansion realized by the agricultural and sedentary type. Here enters the mixed type: the "Celtic" type, a Nordic-Alpine synthesis, manifests itself and begins to expand. "The Celtic element," says our author, "is the form in which the primordial hunter and the primordial farmer joined to compose a single people. But never has there existed a Celtic race, still less a Germanic one. The Celtic element has never had anything but the existence of an alloy. Even the Germanic element is an alloy in which there appears a greater quantity of hunter blood of the glacial age."

We will not follow Merkenschlager in the later developments of his themes. We will mention only that he is carried by his "dynamic" concept

---

2   Merkenschlager's work has not been translated, and the books cited by Evola are rare. I have translated all his quotations from the Italian.

of race a little outside of the usual conclusions of pure racism. For him, particular conditions of environment can favor the emergence now of one, now of the other of the latent or suppressed qualities of blood in the mixed European types. The fear of expanding "denordicization," felt by the better part of contemporary racists, is for our author devoid of foundation. Great spaces and great distances might rather act toward the direction of selection of the reintegration in a people, precisely because it would constrain the blood of the primordial hunter to remanifest itself. If conditions could in some way be reestablished similar to a new glacial era, with its tundras, its winters, and its extended frosts, the dehybridization and the selection of the mixed substance of the European blood would spontaneously and rapidly be produced. "The most precious heredity of the glacial era has need of movement," concludes Merkenschlager. Every recipe, every exterior action to augment or preserve this heredity, is condemned to failure. "The hygiene of the race cannot achieve anything serious, because the genius of race is higher than the material of race."

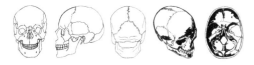

And now to Hans F. K. GÜNTHER. A professor of Social Anthropology at the University of Freiburg, he is among the best known and cited of the German racists. The anthropological classification which he formulated is more or less the predominant one, and has become a theory of common currency; that of other authors, for instance LENZ or VON EICKSTEDT, do not differentiate themselves from it other than in details or terminology.[3]

---

3   In the original 1937 edition, Evola continued the present paragraph with the follow-
    ing observations: "His views regarding the history of civilizations from the point
    of view of race are more or less considered as once 'acquired facts' for all National-
    Socialist authors and educators. In truth, the reader can observe that there is little
    here of originality with respect to what we have already learned from other racists,
    his predecessors, and especially from de Lapouge, to whom Günther at bottom might
    call himself, in more than a single respect, disciple. Indeed, there is often a worsen-
    ing, owed to a more scientistic and biologistic, and thus more materialistic, point of

For Günther, the notion of race belongs before all to natural science, even as other classificatory notions, such as for example that of family, genus, species, and subspecies. And as the natural sciences describe before all corporal characteristics of the type of the species, by the same route the science of race will proceed: purely measurable and definable data, whenever possible translatable into numbers, will constitute the certain part of its knowledge. After this scrutiny of positive character, that is after the visible image of race has been traced in the most precise way possible, one can give rein to research which for Günther is no less important, research regarding the psychological structures which seem to inhere in each of the single races. We already know that race for Günther signifies "a human group which is marked off from every other human group through its own proper combination of bodily and mental characteristics, and in turn produces only its like."[4] Günther however recognizes that a group of the kind, in the state of a closed unity, with a single faith, a single language, and a single nationality, constitutes in practice and in history an exceedingly rare case, and therefore, "the science of race finds itself in the painful situation of having to declare that overwhelming majority of Europeans are nothing other than bastards."[5] However, he does not doubt that certain types of race pure in origin have existed and that it is possible to reconstruct them with sufficiently positive non-hypothetical characteristics. His research was carried above all on the principle and typical races present in the European peoples.

These races are six in number: the *Nordic race*, the *Phalic race*, the *Western race* (Vestid), sometimes called also the *Mediterranean* or *Atlantic* (Fischer), the *Dinaric* race, the *Alpine* or *Ostic* and the *Baltic-Oriental* race. This, leaving aside the *Levantine race*, or that of *Asia Minor* (Armenoid) and the *Desertic* or *Orientaloid*. We summarize the descriptions according

view. Only in the latest of his writings, especially in that dedicated to the religiosity of the Nordic race, does Günther seem to have arisen to horizons which are somewhat wider." These comments were redacted in the 1942 edition.

4   Taken from *The Racial Elements of European History* (London: Methuen And Company, 1927), Chapter 1.

5   I could not find the source for this quotation.

to Günther here, completing them here and there with certain details taken from other authors (LENZ, GIESELER, VON EICKSTEDT, PETERS).

I — The Nordic Race

A) **PHYSICAL CHARACTERISTICS.** Tall (1.75 meters on average), slender, dolichocephalic (average cephalic index 74), thin visage with pronounced chin, fine straight or wavy hair which is fair or reddish, deep and clear eyes, light blue or gray, pink-white skin which is transparent and sensitive to the sun, straight or slightly sloping forehead. The cheekbones are pronounced, the nose long and thin, usually straight, sometimes slightly curved, delicate nostrils with high root, often directly united to the forehead ("Greek nose"). Its position and thus also its curvature in the Nordic race falls in the last upper third in the line of the profile, as compared to the Levantine race and often also the Dinaric race. The opening of the eyes is relatively large and the upper eyelid is not pronounced as in the Phalic type. When of tall stature, Nordic man has also developed legs, but not excessively so as in certain black and Jewish types; wide shoulders in men, thin and free neck, length of arms between 94% and 97% of full stature, which is to say, regular arm-length, neither short as in the Mongoloid, nor long as in the Negroid. The Nordic cranium, as however also the Dinaric, has a characteristic occipital prominence. Accented and energetic development of the jaw. The triple prominence of the forehead, the nose, and the chin gives the impression of an active and combative type. Thin lips and with decided form, without fleshiness. On the whole, a cold and dry type. The gaze has a certain keenness (*acies oculorum*,[6] CAESAR noted in the Germans) and when excited acquires a character of wild splendor (fair eyes of "terrible gaze").

B) **PSYCHIC CHARACTERISTICS.** Reflection, sincerity, and strength in action. From reflection proceeds a sentiment of justice, an inclination

---

6   Latin: "having keen eyes."

toward objectivity, to determination and also to individualism against every spirit of the masses; a mastery before phenomena. Realism and full fidelity for whom has earned his trust, objective judgement also when dealing with his worst adversary. Nordic man is little inclined toward "human warmth," he can go so far as a cutting cerebral coldness. He cares little for the pleasure of others, he possesses a high sense of responsibility and a strong moral conscience. He easily comprehends the idea of duty and he has a certain rigidity in affirming it before both others and before himself. The Nordic type cannot be called passionate, especially in the sense of a pronounced sensuality, which facilitates his distance, his detachment, and indeed his faculty of reflection, while the imaginative faculty is impoverished thereby. A measured nature, self-conscious and self-dominating had always been given as typical of aristocrats, in all the peoples of Indo-Germanic language. But such traits, according to Günther, are not found closed in an elite in the Nordic race, but rather more or less in all the present exemplars of the race. Uniting itself to a spirit of reality, the strength of action can become audacity, an impulse toward any undertaking. Whence comes a special spirit of competition and of emulation, with its own lucid passion substituting itself for that of the senses. The Nordic type is silent, the fidelity of his word, when he has given it reflectively, is firm, and the aptitude toward command which is properly his own makes his race rich with military commanders or, at least, gives it the characteristic of "a pronounced military pride and of excellent soldierly qualities."

Presently, the Nordic race according to Günther is to be found in fairly homogeneous groups in the North and the North-West of Europe, in the central and southern parts of Sweden and Norway, in Denmark, in Scotland and in Germany. In the whole of Central Europe, it appears in small groups and in Meridional and southwestern Europe is found only as the component of various ethnic mixtures.

II — The Phalic (or Dalic) Race

A) **PHYSICAL CHARACTERISTICS.** Dispersed here and there in north-western Europe, but also in the Canaries, this race is considered by many as the remains of a prehistoric people (Cro-magnon?) derived according to some from a Nordic lineage. Moreover, Phalic man has many traits in common with the Nordic type, in general he is rather taller, but of complexion much thicker and heavier. His cranium goes from dolichocephalic to brachycephalic. His visage has a pronounced chin and cheekbones, fair hair, fair skin, eyes that go from light blue to gray, often with a characteristic gaze in which one eye seems to aim higher than the other. Short and strong neck, often wide visage, hands and feet larger and thicker than in the Nordic and Western races, a shorter and straighter brow, with a frequent, characteristic swelling of the frontal bone above the brow (*torus supraorbitalis*) which confers to the eyes a special hollowness.

The opening of his eyes is smaller, his nose is large and short with a flattened tip, the opening of his mouth is ample and his lips thin and compressed. Strong occiput, but straighter. Movements are somewhat slow and as if clumsy. In the normal position of rest, Phalic man stands stolidly on both his feet, as is typical amongst sailors.

B) **PSYCHIC CHARACTERISTICS.** To a certain degree, these reflect the heavy and burly characteristics presented by his body in comparison with that of the Nordic. Attachment to his own soil, rather than an impulse toward distant horizons, is proper to the Phalic type — attachment to his own goods and to his own traditions. Often, he is yet more faithful than the Nord, but poorer in interiority. Still less than the Nordic type has he any proclivity toward contact with other men; he is a rather closed and pertinacious type. More measured than audacious, lover more of liberty than of domination, more ingenuous, less inventive, better suited to building. Among the various arts, architecture is nearest to him, more than music or eloquence. He is very conscientious and every bit as stubborn; he carries out that which he has decided inexorably and meticulously. He is not talented in command, but under a good commander becomes an excellent element. In the religious field, he brings more an attitude of moderate sentiment than the will which the Nord brings. He is predominately a farmer and property owner.

In this race — the "heavy blond race" — Günther claims that there is trace of something primordial; one almost thinks of the "giants of prehistory." The intermixing of this type with the Nordic type has often given optimal results (Bismarck, Hindenburg). Lenz called the Phalic Race "Atlantic," and in his opinion "precisely when Atlantic solidity couples with Nordic audacity, do figures of megalithic proportions arise." Mixed with the Mediterranean type, groups of Phalic race of smaller stature are to be found also in Italy, in Lombardy, in the central Apennines (Umbria, Maiella).

III — The Western Race

A) PHYSICAL CHARACTERISTICS. This race is of small stature (1.61 meters average for a male), however of slender, well-proportioned dolichocephalic type; visage with a little-pronounced and rounder chin, cheekbones less pronounced than in the man of Nord race, a lower brow, but often straighter and with rounder temples. Thin, delicate nose, often meatier than the Nord's, with high root. Straight and also lightly curly hair, tending from chestnut to black. The eyes have this same color; light brown skin and, under the effect of the sun, dark brown. This type, though generally well-proportioned and often slender ("short slender"), can easily tend toward heaviness. According to Günther, the physiognomy of the Western type is more delicate, less virile. While the Nordic Race tends toward audacious and clean facial features, the Western Race has a more cordial and almost feminine aspect; the width of the shoulders and of the chest is limited; the neck is slender; hands, feet, and fingers give an impression of nobility and of lightness. Lively gaze, now mobile, now contemplative. The opening of the mouth is rather large, the lips are often accentuated, shapely, with the upper lip better defined than the lower. Legs with a characteristic development of the calf. The growth of this race is accomplished quite rapidly, and likewise, both sexual maturity and also aging occur more rapidly. Western children often seem as knowing as adults, in the same way that adult Nords seem to be children. In the general proportions of its members, this type is roughly the same as the Nordic. Both of these, according various authors, derived from a single stock.

B) **PSYCHOLOGICAL CHARACTERISTICS.**[7] The principal characteristics of this type are: passion and spiritual mobility. All the psychic powers are turned more externally than in the Nord, and therefore, a particular expression and propensity toward eloquence, toward affection, toward gesture. The sentiments find a rapid exteriorization, the intellect is vivacious; it grasps immediately, but it is little capable of clear judgement. In reaction, this race obeys sentiment more than reason. The Western type loves all that which has color, life, mobility. Its temperament is rather variable, it little knows patience and perseverance; it can pass rapidly from one extreme to the other, its impressions easily seize it. Its rhetorical gifts are noteworthy, but at the same time, it easily grows drunk on simple words. It is more inclined to feel the joy of the world, while Nordic man is more inclined to feel its problematical quality. If this last is more likely to posit himself as his own judge, Western man is rather likely to posit himself as his own defender. A pronounced attitude of cordiality, courtesy, amiability, and cheerfulness is characteristic of Western man. The expression of Western man often degenerates into a posture. More, a pronounced sensuality, a vivacious interest for sexual things characterizes the Western type. "Wishing to appear as something, rather than wishing to be something" is supposedly characteristic of Western man.

---

7   Evola uses the word "Psychic" for all groups except the present, for which he uses the word "Psychological." This is evidently intentional; in the 1937 edition he used "Psychic" only for the *first* group.

While in the Nordic Race the strength of imagination is scarce, in the Western Race it is particularly well developed, mobile; more plastic, less dreamy, and less regulated than that of the Nords. Günther writes that "if de Lapouge could ascribe to Nordic man the spirit of Protestantism, attempting to establish a broad relation between the categories of the races and those of the religions in Europe, it might be said that Protestantism is rather far from Western man, who loves exciting elocution, vivacious colors and spectacles."

Günther puts this race into relation with that which DENIKER denominates the "Iberic-insular" and litoral or "Atlantic-Mediterranean" species, which SERGI calls the Mediterranean variety of the Euro-African species. It is found in the coastal zones of the Mediterranean, and today predominately in Spain, in Portugal, in Italy, in the Mediterranean islands. In small groups it appears in the Balkanic peninsula, then also in France and even in England. In Germany it is present above all in the area of the Rhine, in a state of mixture, but in negligible numbers.

IV — Dinaric Race

A) PHYSICAL CHARACTERISTICS. A tall and strong type (average male height 1.74 m), with, at most, less pronounced dolichocephalia. The strongly modeled occiput is very characteristic, which protrudes almost as a rectilinear prolongation of the spinal cord. High straight forehead, similar to the Nordic. Thick nose, protruding, and often curved, aquiline or vulturous. Rather developed chin, but not protruding. A crease proceeding from the nostrils to the angles of the mouth is characteristic. The lower lip has a notable fleshy development ("Habsburg lip"), the profile descends then in a straight line up to the point that the extremity of the chin sticks out. Well-developed chest, well-proportioned, but somewhat shorter, arms, while the legs are long as in the Nordic and Phalic type. Straight or slightly waving dark-chestnut hair. Eyes of the same color, rather sunken, with a propensity toward heavy bags. Rather brown skin. Both the body and the face appear fleshier than in the Western or Nord type. Accentuated development of the beard, which grows often up to the superior part of the cheek. In women, there is a propensity toward a hint of mustaches. This type demonstrates particular solidity and physical resistance.

B) PSYCHIC CHARACTERISTICS. Courage, love of fatherland, strong allegiance to the earth, sense of honor, united to a certain receptivity, excellent soldierly qualities, perseverance. The Dinaric type loves nature and loves style and order in his house. He lives in the present more than the Nord race; in comparison with this race, he is simpler, sometimes coarser, less dynamic. His undertakings have narrower horizons. His audacity is of a predominately physical character. His expressivity is rather scarce. He has an inclination to describe, to a certain degree also to the theatrical. The Dinaric type is readily jovial, he has a special inclination toward wittiness and incisive speech. A certain exaggeration characterizes his initial presentation of himself. His sociality is rather loud, but his type maintains always a certain rectitude. He is often gifted as a tradesman and merchant. Moreover, the Dinaric race appears particularly gifted in music, from popular songs to true and proper art. In a series of well-known musicians, Paganini, Chopin, Berlioz, Haydn, Mozart, von Weber, Liszt, Wagner, etc., Dinaric traces are supposedly visible, either pure or mixed. For Günther, the Dinaric race for its spiritual qualities comes directly after the Phalico-Nordic race in the hierarchy of European races. The zone of the Dinaric Alps, from Yugoslavia up to lower Austria, presents the greatest percentage of types of this race. In the South, in the Balkans, it gradually proceeds to confuse itself with the populations of Asia Minor, with which it has various characteristics in common. In the West and toward the North, beyond the central Alps up to France, this race has strands which reach into Northern Germany and even England.

Günther conceives the Dinaric race as a ramification of the so-called "Levantine" (Armenoid) race, or at least as a race which is very alike to it. Among the Armenians types are indeed to be found which are similar to that just described, and many think there is a unitary race, which in the Caucasus has taken the same form as in Serbia and in certain Austrian alpine valleys. It is curious to note that while Dinaric man is placed in terms of his quality immediately after the Nord, though observing his affinity with the Levantine type: despite this likeness with the Levantine type in racial bodily characteristics, Günther along with many other racists, finds himself brought to ascertaining the bitterest antithesis of spirit between the Nords and the Levantines (who are associated with the Jews).

V — The Alpine (Ostic) Race

A) PHYSICAL CHARACTERISTICS. Short stature (average 1.65 meters), round head (brachycephalic), with rounded chin, hardly pronounced at all; short, snubbish nose, often fleshy, with a rather flat nasal root. Compared with the Western type, the type of the Alpine Race is stockier and heavier, larger, fleshier: while the legs of the first are excessively long in proportion to the body. This type gives the overall impression of a "compressed" stature. Short neck, at the back often "bull necked." Narrow and often rounded shoulders. Given his height, his arms are longer than in the Dinaric type. Brown eyes with round or almond-shaped opening, protuberant, with rather fleshy and flat lids, and cheeks almost always full. Small and round forehead, rounded temples as well, following the round form of the cranium. Lips are almost always thick and round. Hard, thick hair, either black or dark-brown. The beard, on the other hand, is less developed than in the Nordic race and often grows thin. Skin, of yellow-brown tone, seems thicker than in the other European races, and compared to them, even in the young types, almost as if dead: one would say that the blood does not reach the surface. This type is less susceptible to the sun.

B) PSYCHIC CHARACTERISTICS. The man of the Alpine race is prudent, sedentary, rather closed and diffident toward strangers, diligent and industrious so soon as he clearly sees a goal, rather astute and avid with money. Rare leaps of sentiment and scarce impulse toward pure action. He stays by himself; whatever his social position, he manifests the characteristics of the petty bourgeois, he loves the *pathos* of a tiny closed world. Only with difficulty does he know the interior contrasts of the Nordic man or the cheer of the Western man. Everywhere he seeks to unite the useful with the pleasant. The man of the Alpine race loves uniformity, he does not feel the urge to depart his particular horizon and to acquire significance by reconnecting himself to some whole. He has a pronounced collectivist sense, but one that is restricted to his little group. He is not a warrior type and only reluctantly becomes a soldier: when constrained to this above all by the need to defend himself, and if well directed, he can manifest qualities which are not inferior to those of the Dinaric or Nordic soldier. The instinctive-passionate life in him is more tenacious and moderated, but less controlled than in the Nordic type, less rich in leaps than in the Dinaric, blunter than in the Western.

Günther calls this type *Ostic* (*ostisch*), however in a specific sense, without direct reference to Asia. It is better however to use the expression "Alpine" race or "Dark-Oriental" for this race. It is variously dispersed throughout Europe, and it is found in Poland, in the Carpathian zone and in the Balkans, but also in Silesia and in the Ukraine, in Holland, Denmark, and Norway. The Ostic and Oriental type in the proper sense, the Asiatic type, corresponds rather to that which these theories designate above all with the term "Mongoloid."

VI — The Baltic-Oriental Race

A) PHYSICAL CHARACTERISTICS. This race has various traits in common with the previous race. It too is short (average 1.64 meters) and
compressed, short and relatively thick of head, with a wide face and a
barely pronounced chin, developed cheekbones and ample and thick
jaws. The nose is rather thick and blunt, flattened at the root, often
bulging in the lower part. The breadth of the shoulders is greater
than in the Oriental type. Short and stocky neck, hands and fingers
are short. The body is not however as fleshy as in the Oriental type,
the bone structure is notable. The eyes are fair — gray-blue and sea-
blue — and seem to be smallish; they are cut often to seem oblique,
so far as to recall something of the Mongolian type. The skin is fair,
but without that transparency which confers the Nordic pinkish
undertone, rather tending toward gray, and little sensitive to the sun.
Hard, almost rigid hair of a clear color, which could be called blond,
though it lacks the golden or reddish hue of the Nordic type, tending rather toward ash-blond. In many cases, noteworthy muscular
development. The growth of this race is somewhat late, while aging
is rather swift.

B) PSYCHIC CHARACTERISTICS. A relatively closed and irresolute type.
The men of this type have the sense about them of men who seem
to be little content. Strong, but also confused, fantasy, more musical than plastic — and capable of intensely living the images of the
mind. Precisely for his interior dissatisfaction, the Baltic-Oriental
type is particularly inclined to the supernatural and to superstition.
His social sentiment is collectivist like that of the Alpine man, with a
certain added undertone between the fanatic and the mystic. He has
an innate need to communicate, to penetrate into the interior life
of the others, as well as to undress his own soul exhibitionistically.
One can call him a "born psychologist." His conception of sexual
life is rather unrefined, animal instincts are not rare. This type bows
before the State and before any dominating force, supporting it with

a kind of fatalism, and this gift of tolerance can manifest itself also in his daily work. A certain servile spirit is proper to him. It is characteristic of the Baltic-Oriental type to oscillate between the most corrosive rationalistic coldness and a disorderly, impetuous mysticism. The ease with which one sentiment in him can give place to its opposite is also characteristic of him: from unbridled choler he can pass over to abandon and pardon, from pride to humility, from altruism to egotism, from the rawest sincerity to shrewdness and deceit. This type shows a special disposition for music. Altogether his characteristics very much recall those imagined of the "Slavic" type, and also those of the best known Dostoevskian characters; in DOSTOEVSKY, Günther moreover recognizes a type with a strong Baltic-Oriental component.

Beyond these six races, mention is often made of the "Levantine Race" (*vorderasiatische*) and of the "Orientaloid Race," whose description we will however postpone, for when we discuss that made by CLAUSS. Amongst the non-European races, which often for intermingling have brought mutations within the aforementioned races, Günther records the "race of Central Asia" (Mongoloid), the "Sudetic" race, also called the "Pre-Slavic, referring to peoples which in prehistory resided in the lands later occupied by the Slavs; finally, the "Negroid Race" or "Afro-Mediterranean."

Regarding the six races described above, the problem appears as to whether they must be considered as original, or else derived from common ethnic stocks. Günther opines that on one hand the Nordic Race, the Phalic, and the Western, and on the other hand the Alpine Race and the Baltic-Oriental, can be traced back to two distinct and unitary origins.

Regarding the Nordic Race, he does not adhere to the myth of its polar origin, nor attempts to force the secret of higher prehistory. The cradle of the Nordic Race for him was the region of the high Danube. From there, two prehistorical currents of Indo-Germans flowed, the one which emigrated to Asia, the other which diffused itself throughout Europe. This bipartition corresponds to the philological differentiation of the Indo-Germanic languages in languages of the *centum* group and of the *satem* group (*centum* and *satem* are two different inflections of pronunciation for the word that in the Indo-Germanic languages expressed the number "hundred"). The *centum* group corresponds to the European Nordic Indo-Germans, the *satem* group to the Indo-Germans which diffused themselves throughout Asia.

The Nordic, the Phalic, and the Western races above all were creators of civilization in Europe, according to Günther. The Alpine Race seems to have penetrated into Europe through a species of infiltration, perhaps along the Alps. The Dinaric Race must have been the latest comer into Europe, having for its original fatherland Asia Minor. Europe, in general, had two currents of civilization: the most ancient from West toward East and toward the South in the Neolithic period (Nordico-occidental races); then, toward the first Bronze Age, a counter-current from East toward West.

From the point of view of the theory of race in general, Günther completely assumes the idea of persistence and of autonomy of racial characteristics, an idea more or less derived from Mendelism and from genetic racism. "Mixed races," for him, do not exist as such. He excludes, that is, that from the cross of two or more races an effectively new race might arise. The product of any cross will be simple a composite, in which the heredities of the component races will be conserved, more or less dominant or dominated, but never carried beyond that limit of variability which inheres in the originating types. "Even when the races are crossed many times, so as not to permit the subsistence of any pure type of the one race or the other, even in this case and even after long periods of time, no mixed race results. One will still have a people which demonstrates a confused compenetration of all characteristics: in the same man the stature proper to one race will unite with the cranial form of the other, the principal color of skin of one to that of the eyes of another,"[8] and so forth, the same thing extending to the psychic characteristics themselves. A cross might therefore create new combinations, without the ancient heredity disappearing. A selection and an elimination can moreover take place:

---

8   I was unable to find the source for this.

special circumstances could — on the whole — facilitate the presence and the predominance of a certain group of characteristics and suppress others, so much so that for as long as such circumstances persist, a relatively stable special combination will be maintained, which can give birth to the impression of a new type. Save that, when those circumstances depart, the other suppressed characteristics reemerge, the apparently new type decomposes and comes once more to manifest the characteristics of all the races which gave place to the mixture. In any case, each race has its own determinate ideal of beauty, which is adulterated in any cross, so that the ethical principles which likewise correspond to each blood likewise are adulterated.

On this basis, Günther thinks it absurd that, by means of a general intermingling, one might reach in Europe a kind of unique European race. Indeed, he holds it to be impossible that one could come to such with respect even to the German people. "The greater part of the Germans," he says, "not only do not derive from parents of different yet pure races, but are the result of elements already mixed." From such an intermixing nothing creative could come. For Günther, there is no doubt that the Nordic blood holds in itself every superiority. Repeating the formula which we have ever seen return, beginning as far back as GOBINEAU, he writes: "When we survey the fall in each case of the great empires and creative cultures from India to the West, this much is always clearly to be seen: that every 'fall' of a people of Indo-European speech is brought about through the running dry of the blood of the creative, the Nordic race. From which it follows logically that the purity of race and the richness of the progeny of Nordic men in a Nordically oriented people constitutes the most precious of its goods."[9] For which, regarding Germany, "coherent, sincere, and creative development of values of the German life is only possible on the basis of blood and of the spirit of the Nordic race." He

---

9   The first sentence is taken from *Elements*, Chapter VIII, Part Three, toward the end. The second sentence, however, does not appear in this version of *Elements*; I have translated it from Evola's Italian. The next quotation also does not appear here. It is possible that Evola has taken these quotations from another work, and that the sentence I have taken from Günther is merely very similar.

sees a grave menace for European civilization in the fact that presently
natality decreases from South toward North, from East toward West, so
far as to favor the eruption of new currents of non-Nordic blood from
the southern and oriental regions into the northern ones, which are
moreover already undercut racially, both from the physical and from the
moral point of view, by the deleterious conditions of modern civilization.
"The task of bringing about a Nordic revival seems to arise very obviously
from the history of the (Indo-European) peoples under Nordic leader-
ship, as the most natural ideal to set against the 'decline' which to-day
is also threatening the peoples of Germanic speech. [...] This being the
situation, the problem is how to put a stop to denordization, and how to
find means to bring about a Nordic revival. How are Nordics and those
partly Nordic to attain to earlier marriages and larger families?"[10] Thus:
"Once this question is seen by thoughtful men in the peoples of Germanic
speech to be the one vital question for these peoples, then they will have
to strive to implant in the predominantly Nordic people of all classes a
spirit of racial responsibility, and to summon their whole nation to a community of aims."[11] From here, the recovery of the selectionistic theories
of DE LAPOUGE and the passage to the defensive measures and to "racial
hygiene" which have been adopted, before all, by National Socialism.

Further on we will speak of the "religiosity of the Nordic Race," which
Günther himself reconstructs. For now, for reasons of continuity, we must
occupy ourselves with a new type of racism, that spiritual-typological

---

10   *Elements*, Chapter XII, toward the end of the book. I have taken the quotation from
     Günther which is nearest to Evola's citation, but Evola was probably translating from
     a different work here. His Italian reads, "Past the menace of such a twilight, a new
     ascent can be realized only if the Nordic blood, to which we owe the historical great-
     ness of all the Indo-Germanic nations, fortifies itself anew, and if the Nordic man
     anew becomes numerous, prolific, dominating."

11   *Ibid.* Here again, Evola might well be drawing from a different source. Here is the
     translation of his Italian: "We are in need of a vision of the world characterized be-
     fore all by a will to reawaken a sense of responsibility for all that which regards the
     blood."

kind created by Ludwig F. CLAUSS, to see what this new order of research adds to our comprehension of the six races already described.

Clauss wishes to elevate the theory of race from the level of a "medico-physiological" science to that of a special science of human interiority: he does not content himself with the various hereditary physical and psychological characteristics, but wishes to penetrate into the spiritual essence of the various races, the *soul* to which each of them corresponds. These souls translate into a definite "style" of internal experience, a comportment and a use, both of corporeal form and of psychological gifts — comportment and use which differ for each race.

The road by which this new form of racism develops itself is essentially "physiognomic": the study of the expression of the visage everything expressive which the figure presents ought to serve to rise up intuitively to style, and thus, also to the idea of the race. "The difference between the races," writes Clauss, "is not a difference of quality, but of style."[12] Race is defined by a hereditary *style* common to a given group. "Not the possession of this or that quality or this or that gift defines the race of a soul, but rather the style that manifests through these qualities or gifts present in the individual." For which, Clauss believes that to know the essence of the difference between the races, it is vain to lay out statistics and to compile tables of dominant characteristics: more than the *number* of single cases here, what is decisive here is the *choice* of that which might count as the most complete example, and as the purest representation of a given type. The body, for Clauss, receives its significance from the soul, to which it serves as a means of expression. One must find those types in which this expressive correspondence is most perfect, in which the internal style manifests itself with the greatest degree of purity.

The new theory, maintaining thus the existence of race of soul, strengthens the principle of the inequality of the races: this difference exists also on a level must deeper than that of simple biological or psychological heredity. The races of soul condition, beyond the style of individuals, the various manifestations of the civilization of a people. Whence Clauss

---

12 All quotations from Clauss have been translated from the Italian.

writes: "If scientific consciousness can exercise an influence on history, the task that psychoanthropology has in this respect is the following: to define the frontiers which no national community, no community of blood and culture can exceed or remove without destroying itself. The research of the frontiers of the soul today constitutes therefore a historical task."

Taking this as his premise, the following six human times are distinguished: the "creative man" (*Leistungsmensch*), corresponding to the Nordic race; the "steadfast man" (*Verharrungsmensch*), corresponding to the Phalic (or Dalic or Atlantic) race; the "expressionistic man" (*Darbietungsmensch*), corresponding to the Mediterranean-Western race;

the "man of revelation" (*Offenbarungsmensch*), corresponding to the Desertic (Orientaloid) race; the "man of redemption" (*Erlösungsmensch*), corresponding to the Levantine or Armenoid race; the *"man who flees"* (*Enthebungsmensch*), corresponding to the Alpine race.

The "man who produces" or "creative man" is that man who in his expression, even if it be immobile, manifests a kind of readiness for attack: not necessarily in a warrior sense, but in general, as a stance of formative possession in the surrounding world. He conceives of the world as something which counterposes itself to him, which presses him to the attack with his investigation, his action, his production. Other races too "produce" or create, but this does not define the principal trait of their nature, it does not constitute the plane whereupon they feel entirely themselves. The soul of this type is beyond all characterized by dominating its own expressive capacities, and using them only in a measured way, appropriately to their aim. The Nordic soul speaks — essentially — by keeping silent. Accompanying this is an innate interior dominion, whence this type, whatever might be its social condition, has something of the "lord" and the "free man" about it. Gifts of intellect, of objectivity, of force of action, of responsibility receive their orientation from this base-attitude. "In acting by his own responsibility, in the best and most appropriate way, the Nordic man manifests himself: even repose can signify nothing else for him but a gathering of strength for new deeds."

Turning to the second type, the term *Verharrung* signifies both tenacity and arrest, stasis. It characterizes the style of the "Phalic race," a heavy race, bound to the earth, closed and at the same time persistent, laborious, such that once it has taken an attitude, it does not let itself be moved from that attitude even in the face of a better one: such that, having assumed a principle or a goal, it maintains itself faithful to it up to the point irrationality, for which he is not capable of development, of movement, and of novelty. In general, Clauss here recognizes the typical form of the spirit of the peasant, which from the plane of rural life can arrive at the meaning of a general mode of comporting itself in every form of life, both material and spiritual. The Germanic type for him is composed of a mixture between the Phalic type and the Nordic type.

The "Mediterranean-Western race" on the other hand presents a type in which expressing itself, exhibiting itself, assuming meaning in function of environment, constitute the fundamental attitude. The preoccupation with one's own way of appearing before others is perhaps the only preoccupation which this type deeply experiences. His life unfolds as if in a tribunal: he is a continual representative before a society of spectators, without which his sense of life grows wan. This does not mean that he exhausts everything in games, vanity and superficiality, but that for this kind of man solitude remains devoid of sense, continence in expression means suffocation, the sense of distance remains something unnatural. In general, we are dealing with a human type whose best gifts have no worth for the type itself, but only their recognition.

The "Desertic race" is the race of "revelation." It is the style of life of the nomad, in which the unpredictable, the instantaneous reigns, that which manifests itself in a sudden revelation that masters the entire being, and by the entire being is accepted. It is the type which knows nothing of itself, which might be now a child at play, now a prophet, now a dangerous beast of prey. The way in which the Desertic type lives his world might be called the "style of chance." The experience of each instant has value to him as if it were cast from the hands of God: and as a believer he accepts this experience with humility. Considered from the point of view of another

race, this type appears therefore passive and devoid of interior dominion. The Nordic dominates himself, he places himself before himself as
before an object and he submits himself to his own judgement. Even the
Mediterranean has a certain internal mastery — according to Clauss: that
of the conductor of an orchestra occupied with the execution of his music
before an audience. All of that is utterly alien to the Desertic type: to him,
to penetrate into the intimate logic of various happenings seems almost
a sacrilege. The symbol of the wind, which blows where it will, and one
knows not whence it comes nor whither it goes, encloses the final significance of his life. The mobile Semitic tongues according to Clauss had
their origin in the Desertic race, and the living residues of these tongues
are found today in those languages spoken today by the Bedouin stock of
north and central Arabia.

The "Levantine Race" is the race of "redemption." Here a contradictory
human type finds expression, a type affected by an internal scission and
by an internal dualism. On one hand, it cultivates spiritual ideas, religious
norms, while on the other hand it posits the flesh as the non-sacred, as
the enemy of spirit, as the fount of sin. The flesh must be overcome; this
is the sense of its life. But the flesh resists and maintains its threatening
strength — indeed, the more it is combated by the spirit, the stronger it
becomes. Whence a continuous oscillation, an interior deviation which
has two outcomes: the first is that of the ascetic, the priest or the saint as
the type which has been "redeemed" from the flesh after painful mortification of the self; the second is that proper to the type which, precisely
because the goad of redemption has vainly hounded him his entire life,
precipitates desperately into matter, abandoning himself to a boundless
yearning for matter and for material potency. These last feel themselves
to be the slaves of the flesh, and for this do not want to see anything but
slaves around them. They dominate out of hatred and transform their
entire lives into a vendetta against each creature which they see living in
sincerity and spontaneity. All the values proper to their type practically
capsize into their opposites: rather than mortification there is desecration,
rather than the type redeemed from the flesh, there is the cult of the flesh,

rather than the spiritualization of the flesh, there is the carnalization of the spirit. While the first solution — that of the ascetic — gives rise to the Christian ideal, the second characterizes the *Jewish* spirit and type.

The Nordic type, according to the style that gave form to the first Apollonian Hellas, is opposed to both the one and the other: for him, there is neither "flesh" nor "spirit," these are one thing only, and their unity exists in the state of innocence. While the ideal type in the vision of the other races is the Hero, in those races where the Levantine type predominates, it is represented by the Priest.

Finally, the type of "flight," corresponding to the Alpine Race. It is characterized by a general discontent, by a dissatisfaction not for this or for that, but for restless terrestrial existence in general. He never feels at home, but rather feels himself to be in a world which is hostile toward him and full of sharp corners. To defend himself is to withdraw; his way however is not detachment and isolation, but rather sentiment, the *pathos* of intimacy and of feeling together, even as a happy working community aimed at realizing a calm and sheltered well-being. From this, an almost maternal inclination to protect, to care for, to accommodate, and also to apply himself to small, fine things. At its boundary, one finds the type of him whose internal tranquility is no longer disturbed by anything at all, who tolerates with equanimity any injustice, contingency, and suffering. "The battle of Jacob with God and for God would be an impossibility," says Clauss, "since every battle is devoid of sense and of value at the level of evasion. The figure of the dying Socrates, which the *Phaedo* describes, is the most perfect example of the true type of the man of evasion."

We have mentioned this "psychoanthropological" classification to complete the predominately anthropological classification sketched by Günther. For Clauss, no generic mode exists, common to all men, of living, but rather a "creative" or "expressive" or "revelatory" mode, etc. etc., of living, and thus also a specific way of exercising every activity: to be warriors, merchants, researchers, etc. The correlation in this research between these modes or types with the races in the proper sense, even now, appears little sound and only approximate. Moreover, Clauss admits

that these various *styles* interweave and are simultaneously present in the
same individual, and that they appear now one and now another in the
various aspects of his life. Thus for Clauss, given the present intermixing
of the types even with respect to "races of soul," race in regard to a modern
people is the object less of observation than of a *decision*: one must decide,
in the sense of choosing and electing that which demonstrates itself most
creative in the tradition of that people, amongst all that people's various
racial-spiritual influences: to see to it then that this influence or "race of
the soul" gains the upper hand over all the others.

Günther seems in the end to have undergone the influence of the
Claussian current, whence in his last works the spiritual aspect of the
races comes strongly to the fore. In various books, he sought to individu-
ate the presence, the efficiency, and the destiny of the Indo-Germanic or
Nordic element, both in ancient Oriental civilizations, and in the Greek
and Roman civilizations: and here it is evident that the hunt for all the
testimonials regarding blue eyes, blond hair, tall stature, etc., could not
suffice for this end, and the consideration of the Nordic element also
under the light of culture and spirituality had to be imposed: for the
richest and most certain testimonials that remain from those civilizations
above all come from this field. The finest result of such an amplification
of Günther's horizons is a little book[13] meant to define the religiosity of
the "Nordic" type. The reference here is to the Indo-Germanics, that
is to the peoples of Indo-Germanic language which Günther believes
descended from a Nordic ethnic nucleus dating back to the Bronze Age
and constituted as the dominating class and the bringer of civilizations in
various peoples. He begins by saying that in order to gain knowledge of
the Indo-Germanic spirituality it is wrong to base oneself above all on the
beliefs of the Teutons, since in them the Nordic spirit was already adulterated with Druidism and then by religious conceptions of a Mediterranean
type, either Jewish or Levantine. A much solider basis is offered rather
by the spirituality of early India, of early Persia, and of early Greece, then
that of the Italics and of the first Romans. In all this, the Indo-Germanic

---

13   [Note is Evola's. — Trans.] H. F. K. Günther, *Frömmigkeit nordischer Artung*, Jena 1934.

spirit presents itself in a much purer state, given that one knows how to separate from it certain elements of magic and popular superstition which are united in it as expressions of certain inferior ethnic elements, those that had been subjugated by the Indo-Germanics. The first characteristic of the Indo-Germanic spirituality was according to Günther an absence of fear both before their gods, and before death. This spirituality does not even know man as a "creature," less still as a "servant of God." The world appears to it as an order in which both gods and men have their place, their function, their destiny. Thus, not humility before the gods, no sense of distance, but of friendship, if not of affinity, of consanguinity and of similarity. Indo-Germanic religiosity is a religiosity of the here and not of the hereafter. A "taste of destiny" is proper to it, which does not carry one to any aspiration toward "redemption," nor toward the concept of "sin," but to a tragic sentiment of life, to a will to conserve and to affirm one's own nature despite everything. According to Günther, he Indo-Germanics were inclined to think of destiny as a power superior to the very gods — an affirmation which is rather arbitrary. The Indo-Germanic knows nothing of a dualism between soul and body: he is rather wont to conceive the body as an expression of the soul and not as the dirty prison shutting in a soul reaching toward transcendence; thus, respect and estimation of the body. The world for him is *cosmos*, divine order, structure interpenetrated by an immanent *ratio*. He believes in a law of life — the cult of the ancestors — and the strengthening of life, which culminates in the idea of a "greatness of soul." The idea of death does not govern — as it does in other forms of religiosity — his faith. It has for him but slight weight. The idea of "redemption" is likewise extraneous to him: the divine order, of which he feels himself to be a part, is not an evil, and adverse forces are only to be battled and to vanquish. Consequently, even the concept of the "Redeemer" is lacking, as a mediator between God and men. According to his racial nature, the Indo-Germanic has ever created a road directly to the divine, and for this in the civilizations he has created, so long as these conserve themselves as strong and pure, the priestly caste, as a mediating caste, either has been absent or has had only a limited prestige. Measure, spiritual equilibrium in the face of every frenzy, every ecstasy, every haphazard leap proper to other types of religiosity — this measure, this equilibrium, are Indo-Germanic virtues. The life of the Indo-Germanic is justified in itself and Günther goes so far as to say that "faith cannot be an Indo-Germanic virtue, but a value for men of the Oriental race, that is the Desertic race." With which, to be consistent, Luther himself would be the first to have to exile himself from the pure Nordic world: nor would one be wrong to affirm such — though for somewhat different reasons.

Another characteristic of the religiosity of the Indo-Germanic race, according to Günther, is the absence of fanaticism, the spirit of tolerance for the gods of other nations: then the absence of dogmas, thus also of Churches. "It is also a fact that Indo-European religious communities have never become churches. The churchifying of a belief is again an assertion of the spirit of the Oriental (desert lands) race or of the joint effect of Oriental and Hither-Asiatic race spirit."[14] On such a basis one might speak of a mystico-anti-ecclesiastic tendency of the Germanic soul, but only provided that one conceives a mysticism ever accompanied by a love for form and by a creative will toward form, and always distant from any drunken and haphazard thrust, be is sensual or super-sensual, toward the indefinite, the boundless, the amorphous. One might therefore speak of a "realistic mysticism" (*Wirklichkeitsmystik*), and one that is not evasive, of a mystic vision always accompanied by dignity and by nobility of soul. From here a totalitarian ideal which includes discipline and the deployment of the strength both of spirit and of body, even as that concept of *humanitas* as "human completion" or "nobility of race" which was found in the aristocratic-republican epoch of Rome. Whence an ideal of heroic realization of self, a religiosity such as a worthy and virile soul might conceive.

The Nordic stock of creators of civilization were, according to Günther the carriers of such a spirit in the cycle of the various Oriental and Western nations of Indo-Germanic language. Already here we see how racism

---

14   Taken from *The Religious Attitude of the Indo-Europeans* (London: Clair Press, 1967), Chapter 5.

goes toward constructing an ideal not devoid of a certain nobility, one which results in a true "vision of the world," whose most characteristic traits enter in decided contrast with those of Christianity, be it Catholic or Protestant — that is, of the religions which up until yesterday were believed to be specifically Western, and which racism now considers as an originating contaminating contribution from the Desertic races or the Semitico-Levantine races of the lower Orient.

Beyond the Claussian study of the soul, a study which poses the problem of the race of spirit, in general terms, toward the end of specifying a general morphology of the varieties of religious experience and of the attitude of the men of the divers races with respect to a transcendent world — such a study remains to this day a task, which a superior form of racism must discharge. Perhaps it will be permitted in this connection to recall the contribution that we ourselves have made in our *Doctrinal Synthesis of Race*, in which we have sketched the first general theory of "race of spirit," taking our bearings from various intuitions of J.J. BACHOFEN. On that occasion, we also sought to separate the valid from the arbitrary contained in the views on the "Nordic" nature, such as those of Günther, which we have here explicated.

CHAPTER VII

The Arctic Myth

Exploration of the origins. The civilization of the reindeer.
The Nordic-Atlantic race. Sanguineo-serologic research.
Primordial solar monotheism.

SWALD MENGHIN, dean of the University of Vienna, wrote these characteristic words: "More than any other discipline, the science of prehistory has carried itself and yet more must carry itself to the center of the spiritual battle of our times. I do not believe I am wrong in affirming that, along with physics, general prehistory will be the science which will guide the next generations." Germany in the most recent years has lived this impulse toward the origins in a very characteristic way. The origins are presented under a special metaphysical light. One comes again to intuit that the primordial times lived meanings and spiritual symbols in a yet pure state, meanings and symbols which were subsequently lost, obfuscated, or adulterated. Prehistorical research, carried from a plane of disanimate scientistic-archaeological or anthropological positivism to a plane of spiritual synthesis, promises therefore to open new horizons for the true story of civilization.

We have already seen in more than one case the influence of racism on prehistoric research. Given that present humanity appears more or less as an ethnic chaos, to give foundation to the theory of pure and originating races, it was necessarily to return to prehistoric times and to seek to force the mystery of prehistoric humanity. Here however up until recently a synthesis in the grand style was lacking. Those of WILSER or of MERKENSCHLAGER were naught but attempts above all limited to anthropology. The schemes on type of GOBINEAU, no matter how brilliant, were already old, incapable of comprehending the later developments of knowledge regarding the ancient civilizations. On the other hand, precisely due to that development, the concept of the "Nordic Race" began to become problematic. Once the characteristics of this race as a European race had been fixed in relation to the characteristics of a type of culture and spirituality, little by little one was forced to ascertain analogous characteristics also elsewhere, a little bit throughout all the world. Already we have seen how GÜNTHER was constrained to admit that to see the characteristics of the Nordic spirit in the most authentic state, it was necessary to refer to other civilizations and traditions rather than those which were considered Nordic *par excellence*, that is of the Germanic Europeans. In terms of symbols, a characteristic example for such a state of affairs is offered to us by the *hooked cross*. The hooked cross for a certain period was considered as the symbol proper to the Arya-Teutonic races. Save that from the entirety of successive research it appeared that this symbol is to be found in Korea, in California, in Central Asia, in Africa, and even amongst certain Semitic peoples; in short, in a whole group of places which lie absolutely beyond those places which up until yesterday one maintained the Arya colonies and migrations had reached. A similar difficulty presents itself in other fields, with the threat of rendering indeterminate and arbitrary all that which the racists had sought to build as the monopoly of the Nordic-Arya race. A new myth was needed to sustain the Nordic idea, a myth all the more audacious for being rich, complex, and articulated; such a myth was now matter for the consciousness to dominate and to organize, according to an explanatory principle. Such a myth was forged by the Dutchman Herman WIRTH with the reclamation of the "Arctic" theory which we have already seen rising up in WILSER, and with the "reconstruction" of the origin, of the history, and of the civilization of the "Nordic-Atlantic race." The theory of Wirth should be considered as a daring *coup de main*, whose intimate directive impulse takes inspiration from extra-scientific intuitions, the which then seek justification through an exceedingly laborious philological, anthropo-geological, mythological, and symbological armament. The solidity of such an armament is quite relative, and the seriousness of Wirth as a scientist has moreover recently been compromised in a rather grave way by the *Uralinda Kronik* affair, an exceedingly antique presumably Saxon narrative which Wirth set himself to deciphering and to valorizing enthusiastically, when it then came to light that it was a vulgar mystification.[1] But as the contingent equilibrium and the discontinuity of the blocks of ice in a winter river say nothing against the continuity of the current which transports them, so all that which is scientifically inexact, arbitrary, fantastic, and a-systematic in the work of Wirth should not hide the force of the "myth" which animates and directs the whole, its deepest significance and its character of necessity before the problems we have indicated.

In connection to Fabre D'OLIVET, we have already noted that the "Arctic" hypothesis, in itself, is more than but one of the many hypotheses of modern researchers: it corresponds rather to a consciousness of the "traditional" order which has been conserved in certain "esoteric" circles. It has value therefore quite independently of the efforts of those who, as Wirth, and have had some obscure intuition of it, have made to justify it with modern "scientific" notions; and above all, it has value independently

---

1   The *Oera Linda Chronicle* purports to be a compilation of old and ancient historical or mythological Frisian writings (one part of it is supposed to be the copy of a text dating back to 2194 BC). Wirth oversaw the publication of this text into German in 1933. It is worth noting that there are some scholars who support the authenticity of this book, among them James Nienhuis and Jan Ott. Ott in particular presents some very good arguments for at least taking the text more seriously than has been done in late years.

from the attempts of certain racists, and of Wirth himself, to use it *ad usum delphini*,[2] that is, for more or less contingent political ends.

In order to bring the theory of Wirth "into focus," it is useful to review what can be positively asserted regarding the ancient races, traces of which remain on our continent. The most ancient remains are those related to the "Neanderthal" race, so named for the place in which the vestiges of this human type were found for the first time in 1856, near Düsseldorf. This is a race which dates back to the end of the glacial period, for which it was called also the race of the "glacial" or "Mousterian man," and, for its antiquity, *homo primigenius*. Other remains have been found in Spain, France, Belgium, Croatia, Bosnia, Palestine, and also in Africa, in Rhodesia, etc. In their entirety, these relate to an extraordinarily long period, perhaps as long as some hundred-thousand years. The Neanderthal race is of a repugnant morphological brutality, such as cannot be found even amongst the most primitive Australian aborigines: it is a bestial and simian type, and the possibility has now been ruled out that *homo sapiens*, that is the lineage of current humanity, might have developed from this type, which seems to have gone mysteriously extinct at the beginning of the Stone Age.

A second type of human of likewise inferior character, but of more recent existence, is represented by the so-called "Grimaldi race" or the race "of Menton," for the site of its first findings. We are dealing with a short, distinctly Negroid type, a type that very probably emerged from Africa when there yet existed land-crossings between Africa and Europe, which today have been submerged.

A third type of human, with already superior morphological characteristics, is constituted by the "Aurignac race." Its relevant traces are found from Bohemia up to Serbia, and present a slender man, already of medium or tall stature, with an almost always dolichocephalic cranium, free at this point of the simian prognathism of Neanderthalic man. This race

---

2   Latin: "for the use of the Dauphin," that is, for the use of the authorities, meaning generally that the material in question has been expurgated or altered to serve political ends.

must have supplanted the glacial race, but not so rapidly that it did not live side by side with that race for a series of generations, and thus mixed to a certain extent with that race. In any case, Aurignac man already appears to the anthropologists as the type from which present man might have developed — according to some (RECHE), above all the Mediterranean-Western man, according to others (KLOATSCH and WIRTH), the Nordic race, and according to yet others, both of these races.

Yet more recent, nobler, and nearer to us, is the "Cro-magnon race." Its traces from the Franco-Cantabrian peninsula proceed as far as Belgium, Holland, Northern Germany, Denmark, and Sweden. The civilization relative to it has been located in Altamira (Northern Spain) or in certain of the Canary Islands, because in this location exceedingly noteworthy traces have been found, especially in pictographs and petroglyphs: it has also been called the "civilization of the rein-deer," as this animal figures in a very characteristic way in these traces. The anthropological type which corresponds to it is already of tall stature (1.80 meters), slender, with a tall and straight brow, and an almost dolichocephalic cranium. The fragments of its civilization which have reached us demonstrate inventive spirit, artistic sensitivity, dynamism. MERKENSCHLAGER — as will be remembered — referred to this type with his "primordial hunter." Toward the end of the latest period of the Glacial Age, the Cro-magnon race must have made itself the dominating race in central Europe, subjecting or repelling the aboriginal races which existed there, not without sometimes crossing with them. But then the traces of the "civilization of the reindeer" suddenly disappear. In the findings, there is a lacuna; the traces which chronologically follow those of Cro-magnon are separated by an interval of thousands of years and are of a different species; we are dealing here with a civilization of agricultural type. The interval goes from the last period of the Paleolithic until the first period of the Neolithic. It seems therefore that Cro-magnon emigrated toward an unknown destination. Since the last traces of their civilization are found toward the North, the hypothesis has been advanced by some that, to escape from rising temperatures in Central and Western Europe, this race emigrated in the direction of Sweden. Wilser already had advanced this hypothesis, believing that the Nordic race had developed from the stock of Cro-magnon emigrated into the Scandinavian island at the end of the Paleolithic.

In these terms, the panorama of prehistoric anthropology approximately presents itself. WIRTH's theory and that of his disciples intervenes in the following way.

First of all, it speaks of two primordial races. We are dealing above all with the "Negroid" race, derived from an exceedingly ancient continent, in large part vanished, which dates back to the Carboniferous period, and extended from South America, across central and southern Africa, up to Australia (the "Gondwanaland"). The other race is the yellow-brown "Finnish-Asiatic" race, which according to the theory was conserved above all in the Mongoloid race. According to Wirth, amongst the peoples derived from the various crosses of these two primordial races, at a given moment other races made their appearance — destroying and subjugating the other two — races belonging to a third and likewise primordial type, or derived from it, which were absolutely superior to the first two types both from a physical and from a spiritual point of view: these are the "primordial Nordic races," or "pre-Nordic" or "Arctic" races.

The two prehistoric types we have already considered above — Aurignac man and Cro-magnon man — are for Wirth *already derived types*: derived that is from a cross of the Pre-Nordic race with the aboriginal European races, the Negroids and Finns. Wirth finds two ways of avoiding the difficulty presented by the fact that there are no remains nor fossils of this Pre-Nord race together with that of Cro-magnon and Aurignac man, save — as one should indeed think — in yet more ancient findings. First, Wirth attributes to this Pre-Nordic race the practise of not burying their cadavers, but of exposing them (a practise which he rediscovers amongst the eldest prescriptions of the Arya of Persia): for which the crania, the bones, etc., of this race, could not conserve themselves to our day from such ancient times, but only from relatively more recent times, those corresponding to the period of the Middle Paleolithic, in which period indeed crania of pure Nordic type are to be found. In the second place, the Wirth situates the originating fatherland of the pure Nordic race in lands which have today vanished: above all, in a polar land, and then, in an Atlantic land, in the legendary Atlantis of PLATO.

The Arctic region by this view was therefore the originating fatherland of the primordial Nordic race. From the geological point of view, in fact, it appears that present-day Greenland once extended so far as to connect Europe to America. Under the glaciers which cover the remains of this antique Arctic continent, vast leavings of carbon fossils have been discovered. This means that where today there is ice, in other times there existed a luxuriant vegetation, and the examination of carbon fossils has verified that it derives from trees that do not have the sign of the years in their cores, which is to say, trees whose development was not interrupted by invernal rest. In that continent, not only was there not the present-day freeze, but there existed a moderate, continuous climate, permitting an uninterrupted development of vegetation, such as today one finds in the tropics. The freeze did not manifest itself save at a given moment, by way of a repositioning of the terrestrial axis, which some geologists today admit — a repositioning which turned the North Pole from the direction of west toward north-east. In the traditions of the ancient Iranians, the Celts, and the Germans, one finds moreover mythologized memories of a terrible frost or winter which for this reason precipitated onto the Arctic region, constraining the "Pre-Nordic race" to emigrate. We ourselves have amply spoken on these matters, along with a series of concordant testimonials from a variety of origins, in the second part of our *Revolt Against the Modern World*.

Moreover, Wirth, in order to maintain the Arctic thesis, has also sought to use a very modern order of research, so-called *sanguineo-serologic* research, or research on "blood groups." This research, by extracting blood from various human types, has seen that there are distinct possible behaviors both of blood corpuscles, and of serum, the which is more or less likely to agglutinate the blood corpuscles of another type of blood with which it has been mixed. On this basis, four principal serologic groups are distinguishable, which then are related to definite ethnic groups. It has been seen that the first serologic group is mainly represented toward the Arctic region, not only in in Iceland, but also amongst the North-American Indians (decreasing toward the south), in England and even in Italy. The second serologic group takes Sweden as its center, and develops in various European countries. The third group takes India for its center, while the last group, which seems refractory to any mixture whatsoever, is scarcely and sporadically represented in various parts of the world, and seems to correspond to the remains of an exceedingly ancient vanished race. Wirth puts into relation the first serologic group with the primordial Nordic race: he considers the second group as proper to a race differentiating itself from the Nordic race, for idiovaration (that is for an internal mutation, perhaps connected to climactic and environmental circumstances) and the third group, as proper to a race developing from intermixing (inheritance). The Arctic zone was that which still today — from Greenland to America — conserves traces of the purest race, and Wirth indeed believed he had found blond dolichocephalic types with blue eyes of an almost "Arya" aspect in the Eskimos of eastern Greenland. As the freeze suddenly took hold, the Pre-Nordic race found a route to the South, toward the Atlantic, as the single route of escape free of glaciers. At this point, Wirth accepts the hypothesis of the existence of Atlantis, and maintains that in Atlantis the center of civilization of the Nordic race shifted, radiating outward from there both to the Orient toward the coasts of Europe, and toward the Occident, toward the American coasts. The race of Cro-magnon and Aurignac man were, by this theory, therefore formed by the intermixing of groups of Nordic-Atlantics with the races that already dwelt in Europe, and the Solutrean Paleolithic civilization (from 17,000 to 12,000 B.C.) and the Magdalenian (from 12,000 to 7,000 B.C.) was derived from that. The "civilization of the reindeer" was therefore a civilization of Nordic origin, and its affinity with the civilization which has conserved itself up to the most recent times in Sweden and in the Arctic regions, would not indicate a presumed emigration to those areas of the Cro-magnons, but would indicate their common origin with other ethnic stocks descended later precisely into northern Europe, perhaps directly from the Arctic. After the period of the Magdalenian people, the emigration of the Cro-magnon and the development of their power of civilization until the Megalithic Age assumed rather a totally different direction.

Here the most hazarded part of Wirth's research enters the stage. We have already spoken of the lacuna existing between the hunter civilization of Cro-magnon and the traces of the agricultural civilization which succeeded it after many millennia. Wirth believes he can bridge the gap by giving voice — where the anthropological evidence ceases — to the language of symbols, and on the basis of symbols, according to their correspondences and variations, associated to whatever might furnish the folklore, the legend, the alphabets and the most ancient inscriptions, that which survives in certain practises or traditions of savages, etc. — on the basis of all this, he believes that he can also identify the itinerary followed by the Nordic and Nordic-Atlantic race across the entire world. In brief, this is what he proposes: the Nordic-Atlantic race possessed a series of symbols, which Wirth calls "sacred series," the which fix the various points of the course of the sun over the year in correspondence with the twelve zodiacal signs, commencing from the point which, for a reason we will speak on later, appeared to him of greatest significance: the winter solstice. This series according to him corresponded to a unitary linear primordial alphabet, with its phonetic roots, and moreover would have had sacred value, the value of a calendar, etc. Now we know from astronomy that, because of the inclination of the terrestrial axis, from time to time, and more precisely every two-thousand years there would be a different radiation of the disposition of the "sacred series." On this basis, Wirth first of all follows a passage of the Nordic-Atlantic civilization in all those places in which he believes he has rediscovered traces corresponding to the signs of a "sacred series"; in the second place, from the different disposition of these symbols or signs, associated to concordant confirmations reached by the most various of methods, he draws an orientation for stabilizing the chronology of the various emigrations. The oldest trace of the "sacred series" is according to Wirth found in incisions on the rock of the Arctic-American zone, that is of the domain where in serologic terms even today are found the largest percentages of "pure race individuals" of the first group, the domain which has for its dominating sign that corresponding to the constellation of Leo. But the winter solstice fell under that constellation between 16,000 and 14,000 B.C., and such would therefore be the age of that civilization. There follows a redaction of the sacred series dominated by the sign of Cancer, which refers to a group of traces farther in the South, corresponding both in Europe and in America between 14,000 and 12,000 years B.C. This correspondence would be explained through the derivation from a unique center of civilization, which would have been precisely Atlantis. But arriving at the year 9,000 B.C. These correspondences mysteriously cease, the symbols disperse, there is no longer trace of unity. According to ancient traditions, in this period Atlantis was destroyed by a telluric-oceanic cataclysm.

After which, we have yet to speak of the ways which, according to Wirth, the colonizing Nordic-Atlantic emigration would have proceeded in its movement from North-East to South-West. After the cycle of the Franco-Cantabrian civilization of the Madgalenians or the Cro-magnon civilization of the reindeer, the radiation of the Nordic-Atlantic race evidently followed these directions: before all across the Rhine and along the Danube so far as the Black Sea. Moreover, it is already known that many have been inclined to see the origin of the Indo-Germanic peoples, which later established themselves in Asia, in the Danubian region. A second more recent direction takes the road to the Mediterranean, from Spain toward the Balearics, Sardinia, Malta, and Crete; and in Troy, in the most ancient archaeological strata of this city, there are traces of a civilization created by the encounter of this migration with the precedent. From Crete, this colonization developed as far as Cyprus and Palestine — and here the race of the Philistines enters the stage, dogged enemies of the Jews and subsequently their dominators, a race constituted, according to Wirth, by the Nordic-Atlantics. Finally, a third itinerary, referenced by Wirth, of a southern variety, the South-Atlantics, through the strait of Gibraltar carried along the chain of the Atlas Mountains and Libya up to Egypt, giving place to the first Pharaonic dynasties. As the principal testimonials of this emigration, Wirth adduces the traces of the so-called megalithic civilization: *dolmen, menhir, cromlech*, etc., which is to say mighty arrangements of stones obedient to symbolic or ritual intentions in which our author believes he often rediscovers the themes of the winter solstice and the sacred series. Wirth thinks he can relate the name of *Mo-uru*, interpreted as "Land of the Mother" or "of the Waters," to the originating center of the Atlantid civilization. From this name, or from the inversion of the two syllables, he draws a designation recurring amongst the emanations of the Nordic-Atlantic race: *Am-uri* and *Ma-uri*. Thus, the name of the Mauri subsists in certain populations of Morocco. *Am-uri* is found in the Briton-Brythonic designation of the Armoricans and the Amorite amongst certain populations which were the enemies of the Jews in Canaan. But that is not all. According to Wirth, the South-Atlantics took yet another way, along the coast of Africa, creating various civilizations in its litoral regions, and, bordering that land, they arrived as far as the Persian Gulf, rising through the outlet, then not yet reunited, of the Tigris and the Euphrates. Here they constituted the *Sumerian* civilization, whose linear writing is supposed to visibly reflect solar Atlantic ideograms. In part by a route through Central Asia, in part by another route along the coast, they arrived at China itself, and here we are referred to recent findings of an exceedingly ancient civilization of a type which was indeed much similar to that of the Sumerians and the Egyptians, and which ought to be associated with the remains of a language which seems not only of Indo-Germanic kind, but also of the *centum* and not the *satem* group, that is of the group proper to the Indo-Germanics of Europe, and not to those of Asia. Finally, Wirth goes so far as to suppose, rather fantastically, an emigration of this legendary race so far as Australia, referring to the *Ma-ori*, the last descendants of this archaic South-Atlantic colony, which in their anthropological type, in their symbols, in their language, display even today a neat difference with respect to the savage aboriginal stock of Negroids and Mongoloids.

This is the first cycle of civilization, contained in the Stone Age, of the North- and South-Atlantic civilization. A second cycle is found much later, toward the Bronze Age. Relating also to ancient Briton and Irish legends, Wirth speaks of a last Nordic-Atlantic wave flowing into Ireland and there known as the divine race of the *Tuatha* or *Tuatha dé Danann*, in part established on that island, in part pressed toward the Orient, so far as to touch Doggerland, the Frisio-Saxon islands then still united to the continent. Here, according to Wirth, a new center was constituted, which corresponds to the name of *Polsete*, which should be related to a region on the coast of the North Sea, which vanished not in a catastrophe like that of Atlantis, but from the progressive advance of the sea in that area. The Teutons and more properly the races to which Tacitus gave the name of *Ingovenes*, were themselves nothing other than these *Tuatha*, that is these Nordic-Atlantics who had settled on the coast of the North Sea, and there partially intermixed with the aboriginal race of the Finnish-Asiatic type. The runes — the sacred Ancient Nordic linear script — were the last form directly derived from the ideograms of the solar "sacred series," and Wirth does not hesitate to establish relationships, which he takes to be illuminating, between the runes and the other ideograms or types of linear script of prehistory — Sumerian, American, Egyptian, Chinese, Swedish, Phoenician, etc.

Wirth attempted to reconstruct not only the history of the Nordic-Atlantic race, but likewise its religion. This religion according to him was already superior, monotheistic, much distinct from the animism and the demonism of the Negroid and Finnish-Asiatic European aboriginals, without dogmas, of a great purity and potential universality. At its base was a species of natural revelation, that is, a perception of the law of the spirit directly suggested by nature. With the sudden coming of the Arctic freeze, winter was prolonged for six months, whence the annual return of the sun must have been experienced by that people almost as a liberation, a resurrection of life. This is precisely the point of the winter solstice: the solar light appeared as a divine manifestation bringing new life, the year was the theater of this manifestation; and the winter solstice — as the

lowest point of the ecliptic, in which light seemed definitively to die, sink-
ing into the earth or in the waters, but rather from there to rise again in
splendor — was the decisive point of this cosmic-religious experience. As
has been said, the sacred series for Wirth precisely fixed the various phases
of this symbolic annual occurrence in the Nordic-Atlantic civilization,
summarized, in general, by a circle inscribed with a cross. The primordial
religion of 15,000 B.C. was thus solar, and was permeated by the sense of a
universal law of "eternal return," of death and rebirth. Just as light, so also
the life of men has its "year," its perennial dying and being reborn. The
Christian Christmas, the birth of the Savior on precisely a date which falls
in the period in which all peoples celebrated the winter solstice, was for
Wirth a distant fragmentary echo of this prehistoric religion. In general,
Christianity took its origin from the tradition conserved amongst an
Atlantic group of Galilea, a country rich in traces of the megalithic solar
civilization. The most salient episodes of the life of Jesus up to his crucifix-
ion, which takes up the theme of the Year-God, giver of life, nailed to the
cross of the year, were for Wirth pure symbols from the Nordic-Atlantic
tradition. Thus, Wirth speaks of a primordial Nordic monotheism, and
of a "cosmic Nordic Christianity," which would date back thousands of
years before Christ, as a precursor indeed of Protestantism (which has
only contributed to the "re-Nordicization" of that tradition) and naturally
having nothing to do with the Jews.

Here a connection arises with ideas already touched by CHAMBERLAIN
and WOLTMANN, and moreover, an imaginary bridge is posited between a
presumed tradition of high prehistory and the themes so dear to German
Romanticism and to the modern "Faustian" religion of life — the themes
of death and arising again and of eternal renovation. However, so far as
this last goes, the divergence of views between Wirth and other racists,
such as GÜNTHER himself, is visible enough. The concept of "dying and
rising again" which for Wirth acts as the keystone to the Nordic religiosity,
Günther would probably lay upon a Semitic-Levantine spirit; and no less
a perceptible divergence stands in the fact that while Wirth avers that the
symbol of a priestess or divine mother was in the foreground amongst

the Nordic-Atlantics, which according to him even called their land the "Land of the Mother" — *mo-uru* — Günther and various others more sensibly relate such conceptions to the southern races, and at most to the Celts, which were a race already distance from the pure Nordic race, and more like to the Mediterranean races.

In any case, from these arbitrary personal adaptations of Wirth, one must distinguish between the value and the significance of the Arctic thesis (or, as we prefer to call it, the *Hyperborean* thesis) in itself, because the plane to which it belongs is altogether another, and has altogether another dignity than these reconstructions of contemporary researchers — reconstructions which are moreover not devoid of interest as symptoms and as obscure presentiments of truth. VON LEERS writes that the preceding epoch of liberalism and of scientism was characterized by three fundamental ideas: 1) the equality of human kind; 2) Nordic barbarity and the origin of every civilization in the Orient; 3) the Jewish origin of montheism. These three ideas in the racist cycle which brings us to Wirth are demolished and overturned: 1) humanity is differentiated into very distinct races; 2) civilization did not come from the Orient, but from the North; 3) not the Jews, but the Nordics knew, and infinitely earlier, a superior religion of monotheistic type.

CHAPTER VIII

The Racist Conception
of History

Rosenberg's new myth of the blood. The Nordic race in Oriental
civilization. The Nordic race in Greco-Roman civilization.
Anti-Christian and Neo-Pagan racism. The myth of the new
"National German Church."

ET US NOW TURN TO the latest developments of racism, in the
sense of a "vision of the world" and of a racist vision of history, which have occurred in the very inner circles of National
Socialism. In this connection, we must consider above all the ideas of
Alfred ROSENBERG, which have an almost official character: however
much Rosenberg has declared that his ideas should not be identified as
a "credo" of the National Socialist Party, nonetheless his influence in
Germany is noteworthy, especially in the organizations which aim toward
the politico-spiritual formation of the new generation.

Rosenberg draws his principal inspiration from the theories of
CHAMBERLAIN, accenting them however in the "Nordist" sense, which

is to say by substituting, for the Chamberlainian concept of the racial Celto-Slavo-Teutonic unity, that of the pure Nordic race; and by giving to the whole a yet more evident anti-Catholic coloration, and establishing points of contact between the general interpretation of history and the new German myth. The influence of Chamberlain is associated then with that of WIRTH and, to a certain degree, that of BACHOFEN. J.J. Bachofen was a Swiss, a contemporary of Nietzsche's, and today has been particularly revaluated in Germany. As a philologist, archaeologist, and mythologist, at the base of his often ingenious reconstructions, Bachofen posits the antithesis between two types of civilization and of religiosity, the one of the solar type, celestial and virile, connected to social systems erected on pure paternal right, the other of telluric type (adoration of the forces of the earth), feminine (adoration of the Mothers of life), connected to promiscuous and more or less communist social systems erected on matriarchies. The relation of these two types of civilization, the one to the Nordic races and the other to the Southern races, had more or less already been carried out by various researchers and historians who took their bearings by the school of MÜLLER. Rosenberg takes up these orientations from Bachofen, and equally from the theory of the origins of Rome and of the anti-Roman character of the Etruscan civilization.

In one of his speeches to the Bavarian students, Rosenberg did not hesitate to declare that the discovery of the racist soul in the history of civilizations constitutes a revolution of no less import than that of COPERNICUS. To which are associated the following characteristic words of his principal book, *The Myth of the Twentieth Century*: "Today a new faith is awakening — the Myth of the blood; the belief that to defend the blood is also to defend the divine nature of man in general. It is a belief, effulgent with the brightest knowledge, that Nordic blood represents that MYSTERIVM which has overcome and replaced the older sacraments."[1] Every race has its soul and every soul has its race. There exist no disembodied

---

1   Taken from *The Myth of the Twentieth Century* (Noontide Press, 1982), Book I, Chapter I. All further quotations by Rosenberg are taken from the same source, unless otherwise noted.

and universal values. Blood and spirit are — for Rosenberg — only two different aspects of one unique and indissoluble reality: "Race is the outward
image of a definite soul."[2] "[T]oday an entire generation is beginning to
have a presentiment that values are only created and preserved where the
law of blood still determines the ideas and actions of men, whether consciously or unconsciously."[3] The history of every race is therefore natural,
and at the same time mystical. Behind every religious form, moral or
artistic, there are living nations conditioned by race. In the intermixing of
the blood all candid values are in the end riven apart, the individualities
of peoples disappear into ethnic chaos, and an amalgam which vegetates
and does not create, or which becomes materially or spiritually the tribu-
tary of the strongest will of a new pure race. History then, for Rosenberg,
obeys no predestined plan, toward the realization of which each people
is assigned its various tasks. The history of the Hindus, of the Persians, of
the Greeks, etc., was not therefore the preparation nor the prelude of our
epoch, and still less was it a preliminary attempt which culminated in the
Christianization of all the races, all the nations, but it discloses rather a
dramatic battle between the various races and between the various souls
of the races.

Moreover, in the events of this battle, referred back more or less to the
events of the Nordic race in the various civilizations which preceded us,
Rosenberg sees the coming of that light which brings out also the linea-
ments of the visage of this race itself, so as to gradually determine the
content of the racist myth, the myth which is to serve as the basis of the
twentieth century. From here proceeds precisely the latest development
of history on a racist basis, but, also, a species of vicious circle. Indeed,
to grasp the profoundest sense of the history of civilizations, one refers
to the idea of race — and on the other hand, to define the content of this
idea, one refers to the history of civilizations. The fact is that elements of
every kind converge in these constructions: "results" of this or that scientific research associated to intuitions, disparate elements giving the air of

---

2   *Myth*, Book III, Chapter III.

3   *Myth*, Book I, Chapter I.

fortifying one another, but which are in reality chosen and regulated by a preexisting central idea.

So far as prehistory goes, Rosenberg more or less assumes the ideas of Wirth regarding the migrations of the Nordic-Atlantic race in America, Europe, and Asia, and regarding its originating fatherland. In Rosenberg, therefore the same obscure sensation of a primordial truth manifests itself.

Hindu civilization was created by Nordic stock which descended into that country around 2,000 B.C. These are the *Ârya*, which subjected the aboriginal peoples, creating simultaneously a barrier of racial defense against them, by means of a caste system. We are already familiar with this idea, derived from the fact that in Sanskrit, to speak of caste one speaks of color, so that the inferior castes are often called "dark" and "enemy," while the superior castes are called "fair" and "divine." In the first testimony that one finds for the Hindus or for one of their branches around 1,400 B.C., they are called *hari*, that is "blonds" or "redheads," and the Hindu tradition speaks of the most ancient national deity, Indra, who with his "white friends" conquers the country, repulsing from their thrones, from place to place, the "black men." These are described as being "without nose" — which is to be understood as snub-nosed — while the *Ârya* are thought of as great, white, fair, and beautifully nosed (GÜNTHER). The first Hindu period was a period of expansion and at the same time of battle against the magical cults and the low ecstaticism of the indigenous peoples. But these inferior forms reacted against the Arya spirituality, they insinuated themselves into it, they adulterated it. If the originating sensation that the conquerors possessed against the I was that of born lords, of an immortal soul in the fullness of which one feels oneself to be cosmic, the successive pantheism, the degeneration of this sentiment into that of a unity of all things and thus of the equality of all beings, already signified — for Rosenberg — the decadence of the Arya race. Another sign of decadence was the prestige which the priestly caste assumed over that warrior caste. That which presents itself in this period as mysticism is less a product of the heroic and aristocratic spirituality of the Arya warrior caste, descendant from the ancient Indo-Germans, so much as a species of sublimation of animism and of the magical conceptions of the aboriginals.

The interpretation which Günther puts on Buddhism is characteristic of a certain racist mentality and of a spiritual sensibility which is certainly not so very developed. The term *yoga*, which in Sanskrit designates spiritual discipline, "connected to the Latin *jugum*, has amongst the Anglo-Saxons the value of *self-control*, and appeared among the Hellens as *enkrateia* and *sophrosyne* and still again in Stoicism, as *apatheia*, amongst the Romans as the bluntly Roman *temperantia* and *disciplina*, which is eminently recognizable still in late Roman stoicism: *nihil admirari*. The same value appears in Medieval chivalry as *mesura* and in the German language as *diu mâsze*: regarding the heroes of Spanish legend, who are described as typical Nordics, it is said of the blond *Cid Campeador* that he appeared 'so very measured' — *tan mesurado*. The Nordic trait of self-discipline, of restraint and of cold measure, instead transforms itself and almost falsifies itself in the most recent period of certain Germanic peoples which have already been de-Nordicized, giving place to the idea of a mortification of the senses and to ascesis."[4] The ancient Indo-German affirmed life. Under the influence of pre-Aryan forms, one associated ascesis to the ancient Hindu concept of *yoga*, which derived from the style of restraint and of self-discipline proper to the Nordic race — ascesis being the idea that with exercises and various practices, even corporeal, one might reach liberation from the world, which is to say a supernatural strengthening of the will. The most noteworthy transformation in such a direction is found precisely in Buddhism, in which the vital originating Nordic impetus, brought into an environment which was no longer adequate, an environment which

---

4   I was unable to find the source for this quotation. Günther, however, makes a very similar point in *The Religious Attitude of the Indo-Europeans* (Chapter 5), thus: "Measure (balance), yoga (Latin: *iugum*, German: *Joch*, English: *yoke*), *metron*, *temperantia*, are as above, distinctive features of the Nordic race soul and of the original Indo-European religiosity: *eusebeia* synonymous with *sophrosyne*; Sanskrit: *upeksha*, Pali: *upekha*; likewise in the religiosity of the Stoics (*apatheia*) and of the Epicureans (*ataraxia*)." Thereafter follows a very interesting discussion of the Indo-European view of inebriation.

thus was felt to be an environment of "pain," so to speak introverts itself, it renders itself into an instrument of evasion and of liberation from life, from pain. "Beginning with the diffusion of Buddhism, the State of the Aryas' descendants loses ever more its power. Beginning from the Nauda and Mauria dynasty, that is from the fourth century B.C., dominators of inferior caste appear, ethical life is adulterated, the sensualistic element is developed. For Aryan or Nordic India, one can therefore calculate a millennium of life, more or less from 1,400 to 400."[5]

The incomprehension for and the depreciation of aesthetic values in the face of warrior values, at bottom of a merely secular and naturalistic type, which the interpretations above demonstrate, and which had already taken their start from the Nietzschean philosophy of "life," bring Rosenberg and with him various others to esteem the Persian civilization more than the Hindu. Even the Persian civilization was according to Rosenberg created by Arya races, which indeed in their traditions remember even their originating Arctic fatherland and the freeze which forced them to emigrate. The doctrine of Zarathustra fortified the style of life of these races once they dispersed and lost a unique central authority — the doctrine of Zarathustra, which did not lose itself in "contemplations or ascesis hostile to the world," but which makes of the divinity Ahura Mazda the divine protector of Aryanism; it gives as a religious vision the heroic battle for this God against the God of Shadows and his emissaries, which often bear the traits of non-Arya populations; it gives a whole series of norms as an ethics, in which the preoccupation with a purity of life, of body and of blood, has a conspicuous place. "From the time that the White Land (which is to say the arctic fatherland) disappears," writes von Leers, "the Arya spirit has never found a nobler doctrine than that of Zarathustra. From the original knowledge of the grand order of the world, here the vocation of the man of the high race is drawn — the vocation to disseminate the truth, and to battle the lie, the chivalric vocation of the light-bearer. The 'splendor of the Arya land,' the 'lance of Persian man,' with the great King Cyrus, Darius, with the 'noble knight,' *artha*

---

5   Translated from the Italian.

kshatriya, whom we know as Artaxerxes, and with the luminous dynasties of Persepolis, extended itself throughout Asia Minor."[6] For Günther, the well-known idea of a divine order in the world stands out particularly in the doctrine of Zarathustra:

> The broad vision of the Indo-Europeans — a vision of man summoned to spiritual freedom, to *theoria*, or beholding (gazing) as perfected by the classical art of the Hellenes — such a vision comprehends the whole world, and all divine government and all responsible human life in it, as part of a divine order. The Indians called it *rita*, over which Mitra and Varuna (Uranos in Greek mythology) stand guard — 'the guardians of *rita*'; the Persians called it *ascha* or *urto* (salvation, right, order); the Hellenes, *kosmos*; the Italici, *ratio*; the Teutons, *orlog*, or *Midgard*. Hermann Lommel, in *Zarathustra und seine Lehre* (Universitas, Year XII, 1957), speaks of a 'lawful order of world events', which the Iranians are said to have represented. Such an idea, the idea of a world order in which both Gods and men are arranged, permeates the teaching of the Stoics, and when Cicero (*de legibus*, I, 45; *de finibus*, IV, 34) praises virtue (*virtus*) as the perfection of reason, which rules the entire world (*natura*), then he once more expressed the idea of universal ordered life.[7] (GÜNTHER)

But this impulse to give order and form to that which is formless, translated into an impulse toward empire, appears to these authors predetermined by that destiny which already GOBINEAU had recognized. "With the expansion of the Persian strength over non-Persian domains the de-Nordification of the Persian element had already been prepared."[8] The usual causes: intermixing of the blood, decadence of the peasantry, the destructive action of large urban areas, the introduction of spurious and exotic cults. Following the familiar line of thought, racism here comes to see in the new religion of Mithras (Mithracism) a sign of the decadence of the ancient religion of Zarathustra; Mithras appears as a god of the "imperialistic" period — wherefore even in Rome he had the significance of a

---

6   All von Leers quotations have been translated from Evola's Italian, as the originals are inaccessible.

7   *The Religious Attitude of the Indo-Europeans*, Chapter 4.

8   Translated from Evola's Italian.

fautor imperi[9]—and for this reason, he is seen less as an Arya god than as a god of all the populations of the empire, whose cult ends by assuming non-Arya traits. If Mithras preserves the "Nordic" characteristics of custodian of justice, of purity and of veracity, as well as having the aspect of the warrior God, at the same time he presents the mystical anti-Nordic characteristics of a "savior," something which already smacks of dualism and of the scission between soul and body proper to the Levantine race. Before the Romans, the kings of the Sassanid dynasty presented themselves as the renovators of Zarathustra's doctrine, and when the last of them fell under the Islamic onslaught, the last believers of the ancient Arya religion of light, the Parsi, sought refuge in the direction of India, bringing with them the last remains of the Arya tradition. Rosenberg writes, "Cut into the rock walls of Begistun on the order of a great Persian emperor are the words: 'I, Darius, the great king, king of kings, of Aryan race...' Today, the Iranian mule driver passes, uncomprehendingly, by this wall; a sign to the multitude that personality is born and dies with the race."[10]

In Greece, meanwhile, the same destiny more or less repeated itself. Together with KRETSCHMER, Günther distinguishes three strata in the Greek people: "above all a non-Indo-Germanic stratum, then a proto-Indo-Germanic stratum related to the cycle of Minoan and Cretan civilization; finally, a recent Indo-Teutonic stratum, constituted by the Hellenes descended from the North, of Nordic type. This emigration of Hellenes in its turn consists of three waves: the 'Ionian' wave, then the 'Achaean' wave, and finally the 'Dorian' wave, which appeared when the previous Indo-Germans had already largely been de-Nordicized."[11] The race which the Hellenes found in the conquered territories had the name of Pelasgians: in part, they were crushed and destroyed, in part enslaved. HERODOTUS recounts an epoch of his people during which no slaves existed. Only the

---

9   Latin, "defender of the empire."

10 *Myth*, Book I, Chapter I.

11 I have been unable to find the source for this quotation, or for the next. Günther discusses the Greeks and their ethnic components in Chapter VIII, Part Two of *Elements*.

Hellenic emigration created a caste system with the division into the free and the non-free, which had the ethnic meaning of the subordination of a non-Nordic population, enslaved before a class of rulers, predominately of Nordic type. The gods of the *Iliad* and of the *Odyssey* are blond; Athena has blue eyes and Demeter is blond. Aphrodite is golden-blond, and amongst the heroes, Achilleus, Menelaos, and Meleager are blond. Hector on the other hand, as a foreigner and enemy, is described as black. Apollo, Rhadamanthos, and Aurora are blond; Poseidon on the other hand has dark eyes and hair and "precisely this god of the sea is not a Hellenic god, but a pre-Hellenic god: in his characteristics he takes us back to the semi-bestial figure of the world of the demons and of the gods of the ancient Mediterranean." The fact that the iris in Greece had the name precisely of *iris*, sends us once more to the clear color of the eyes that amongst the Hellenes must have been normal. And Günther proceeds along this road, searching for Nordic characteristics in the most representative traditions and art of the Hellenes. The battle of Hyperborean Apollo against the demon Python symbolizes, in his view, the conflict between the Nordic civilization of the light and the demonic civilization of the aborigines. The constitution of Sparta reflects the same spirit of the Indo-Arya caste system. The three classes of the *spartiati*, the *perioikoi*, and the *eiloti* are interpreted racistically in the way we have already stated: the first is constituted by the rulers of Dorian lineage; the second, subordinate though constituted by free men, is related to the descendants of the pre-Dorians, that is of the already de-Nordicized Achaeans; the third, servile class gathered elements of a predominately Western and Oriental-Levantine race. Analogous considerations are carried out for Athens. The mixing of the castes, and thus of the races, was originally forbidden; a wife had to be herself free and of the same state as her husband. Rosenberg meanwhile adopts the already mentioned ideas of BACHOFEN, with the following modification. If Bachofen had distinguished two strata in the whole of Greek culture, religion, and ethics, the one dominated by the feminine-maternal principle and the other by the heroic-virile principle, he had conceived the second as a superior form, evolved from the first in the breast of one and the same people. Rosenberg on the other hand denies this concept of development relating to two strata and to two different races; the establishment of Olympic civilization and paternal right in the place of the matriarchy and of the ancient Mediterranean demonism, and of the heroic spirit in the place of the naturalistic and promiscuous spirit, are taken by him as so many victories of the Nordic-Hellenic races over the Mediterranean, southern, Pelasgian, Phoenician, Levantine ones. For him, Dionysianism, Pythagorism, Orphic mysticism and the mystery traditions in general are similarly exotic extra-Hellenic phenomena — all alterations of Nordic-Dorian Hellas.

In the view of these authors, the decadence of the Nordic spirit of race came to Greece through the destruction wreaked by fratricidal wars, through the prevailing of economic and mercantile interests, sensualism, demographic decadence, which little by little brought the emancipation of inferior ethnic elements and a general intermixing. The interior liberty of the ancient Hellenes, their sense of responsibility, stood for Rosenberg in continual tension with the obtuse and impure spirit of Asia Minor. And Greek democracy for him did not signify the sovereignty of the people, but the sovereignty of Asia Minor over a Hellenic stock which was exhausted in its blood and in its men. Moreover, as regards Apollo — that is the symbol of the Dorian-Nordic religion of light — both Rosenberg and Bachofen agree: "In spite of the sacrifice of the Greeks, therefore, Apollo may be credited with the first great victory of Nordic Europeans, for after him there emerged from the Hyperborean fastnesses new bearers of the same values of freedom of soul and spirit, of organic shaping and questing creativity. For a long time the Roman sword repelled the reinforced near eastern spectre. More rigorously and consciously, Rome nurtured the patriarchal principle. It thereby strengthened the idea of the state as such and of marriage as the prerequisite of national and racial preservation. Finally, in time, Germania (in a new form) became the representative of the god of the heavens."[12]

---

12 *Myth*, Book I, Chapter I. It's worth noting that in the Italian, Evola translates the German as "solar god" in the place of "god of the heavens" at the end of this quotation.

Whereupon we find ourselves brought to consider the racist interpretation of our very own Roman civilization.

According to racism, even Rome was founded by a wave of peoples which crashed upon it long before the Teutons and the Gauls, in the fertile valley south of the Alps, shattering the Etruscan dominion, the domain of this "mysterious and foreign (Levantine) people," joining itself most probably to a yet pure Mediterranean stock, and ever demonstrating a steady Nordic character, since the dominating element in it, the agricultural and heroic element joined "nimbleness of intellect with the iron energy."[13] Here too Rosenberg takes up the ideas of Bachofen on the genesis and the essence of the Roman civilization, opposing this civilization to the previous Etruscan and in general Italic civilization. But in contrast to Bachofen, here, too, he introduces the ethnic criterion: the demonic-naturalistic spirit for him yet once again manifested itself in the pre-Roman element, a priestly and disordered spirit of the ancient southern-Mediterranean races, while in the Roman civilization, one of a virile and aristocratic type, similar to the Dorian civilization, arose once again. Save for that, while ethnically the Hellenic type is Nordic with a Dinaric component, the Roman type according to Rosenberg was Nordic with a stronger Oriental and Phalic component. The Indo-Germanization of Italy did not have however the extension that it had enjoyed in Greece, because the Romans managed to subdue the great kingdom of the Etruscans only in the fourth century B.C. And Rosenberg here does not tire of bringing attention to the frightful depictions of the afterlife proper to the Etruscans (in Dante's *Inferno* — in his opinion — be it ever portrayed ever so grandiosely, Etruscan antiquity lives once more), their superstitious ritualism, their obscene demonism of Levantine type. Though the Romans politically destroyed the Etruscan element, in various forms of their civilization they succumbed to it: the Etruscan haruspex conserved his power, and it was he who opened the doors of Rome to Asia Minor, calling to his aid the Great Mother, the goddess Cybil, with her eunuch priests, at the moment of the Carthaginian threat. For Rosenberg, the Etruscan heredity gathered

---

13 *Myth*, Book I, Chapter I.

from Rome, and thence from Catholicism, corresponds to its anti-Nordic element *par excellence.*

Günther gives to the ancient Roman social constitution the usual racist interpretation: the patricians corresponded to the descendants of the conquerors of Nordic blood, the plebs and *clientes* to the descendants of the aboriginal populations which were predominately Western, and — in the North — even Alpine-Western. To patricians and plebs corresponded to two distinct forms of marriage, and originally, to preserve the purity of the blood, *connubium* was forbidden between the one class and the other: the patrician caste was to remain pure. The ill-born were killed in the Spartan way (racial hygiene). *Virtus et gravitas* characterized the ancient, true Roman, a *nobilitas* and an innate dignity, traits which were extremely similar to those of the Nordic type. The Senate for the entirety of the first century B.C. appears to be "Nordic."

> It an enlightened audacity, a mastered bearing, a convinced and measured speech, a meditated deliberation, a cold sense of dominion. In the senatorial families, first in the patriciate, then in the *nobilitas*, arose the ideal of the true Roman, which sought to realize itself — that human model of Nordic nature, in a formation which was particularly Roman. Here moral values of the Nordic type held sway: *virtus* as virility, *fortitudo, sapientia, disciplina, gravitas*, and *pietas*, ethical values which, when they were recognized, created Rome, and, when they were offended, tore it to pieces.[14] (GÜNTHER)

But in against the Senate, the nobility, the firm conception of right and the ethical significance of the Roman State, there ever subsisted in Rome the priest, the Etruscan haruspex, the impure plebeian religiosity, which little by little was nourished and sustained by foreign cults.

Already from the time of the Republic the noble name of *Flavus*, blond, was widespread, and VIRGIL made the creators of the kingdoms of Latium, Turnus, Camillus, and Lavinia blonde; OVID describes not only divinities like Apollo, Ceres, Venus, and Minerva as blonde, but also Romulus and Lucretia. Likewise, JUVENAL, CATULLUS, TIBULLUS, SENECA, STATIUS, and CLAUDIAN speak of blonde gods, heroes, and heroines, and

---

14   I have been unable to source this quotation.

Günther also for Rome undertakes this by now oft-mentioned research of all the testimonials which might report a Nordic type, or a type with strong Nordic imprint, up to CAESER and AUGUSTUS.

It is almost superfluous to say what conception Rosenberg and the other racists have regarding the successive imperial period. It is Chamberlain's old motif. The Rome which becomes a global empire is the Rome which destroys race, which founders in ethnic chaos, which "Punicizes," which declines. The wars which gave power to Rome destroyed its patriciate and its healthy agricultural class. The laws of caste deteriorate. Birthrates decline among the aristocracy. Merchants and *nouveau riche* rise to every office, rushing from all parts of the globe, trafficking and developing unchecked capitalistic and devastating instincts. Bastard emperors and even emperors of color take up the scepter. Religious decomposition results in syncretism, in the definitive and unconditional introduction of eastern cults, in the flight to philosophical consolations. Finally, an anguish and a diseased need of liberation pervades that ethnic chaos, the cosmopolitan plebs of the orientalized empire. From the East rises Christianity, which conquers the masses; with CONSTANTINE it becomes the religion of state, and its fanaticism destroys the last philosophers of those schools of the late Empire, in which the residues of a knowledge which once had been Nordic were yet preserved. Priestly dominion and despotism — the watermarks of the sub-race — win along the entire front. VON LEERS concludes these considerations in this way:

> At the end of classic antiquity we find a terrible cemetery of the Nordic race: Romanism and Hellenism have collapsed; their last representatives in Asia Minor, in northern Africa, and in Spain are in great part wiped away by desertic Islam; the Teutonic-Oriental peoples are destroyed and dissolved; the Persians are the servants of the Arabs; the Arya of India are momentarily under the dominion of the Huns. The only remaining Nordic peoples are the Western Teutonics, certain Teutonics of the South such as the Bavarians, the Lombards, slowly degenerating in northern Italy, and finally the Slavs, who pressed as far as Elba, and who are almost without a history.

Here we approach the anti-Christian and above all anti-Catholic theses of Rosenberg. JESUS himself is considered by Rosenberg to be a "great

personality": recognition to which however is associated the revaloriza-
tion of an old rumor: Jesus was not of pure Jewish origin, having for
his mother an adulterated Syrian, and for his father a Roman legionary
seducer. But the temperament of the Jewish, Levantine, and African
discharged itself onto the doctrine of Jesus, and Christianity, despite the
aristocratic element yet present in the Gospel of JOHN, is bastardized
and orientalized; then, above all through the fault of PAUL, it was made
universalist, abstract, stuffed with sensualizing mysteriosophy and with
a demonology of Etruscan and Pelasgian type. By way of its racial decomposition, Rome meanwhile become "a synonym of Africa and Syria,"
the simple personality of Jesus was overwhelmed and the universalistic
ideal of the late empire fused itself with the idea of a universal church,
indifferent to race. Thus arose the Church of Rome, and Rosenberg bases
his accusation against Catholicism on the following points:

1) On the aforementioned Syrian-Semitic element whose burden it has
   assumed, on the doctrine of love and of humility, incompatible with
   the Nordic doctrine of honor and warrior pride. Apart from the fact
   that in the drama of many "heresies," in the secular battle between
   Papacy and Teutonism, in a more or less conscious form, there is
   concealed a battle between "love" and "honor," as the principles
   of two irreconcilable ethics: "the Church wanted, paradoxical as it
   might seem, to dominate by means of love; the Nordic European
   wanted rather a free life in honor, or else a death in the name of
   honor."[15]

2) On the anti-racist universalism which we have already indicated,
   professed by Catholicism, which makes reference to the purely rationalistic (Scholastic) philosophy of Rome — this abstract philosophy,
   mechanically logistic, which nonetheless in Catholicism celebrates
   the most singular wedding with superstitious credences of low
   magico-sacramental type, mysteriosophic and exorcistic. Catholic

---

15   This is probably taken from another book that Evola uses to cite Rosenberg, *Blut und
     Ehre* (*Blood and Honor*). It has here been translated from Evola's Italian.

universalism and rationalism induce various racists to associate the idea of Rome with the Jewish idea, thence to international democracy and so forth, all of which constitute at the end of the day, according to them, a single front against the values of the blood, and against every cultural and religious truth founded on blood, toward the end of a leveling and an international uprooting.

3) On the general conception which Catholicism — as in general Christianity — has of the human being and of his supernatural destination. Rosenberg's racism, considering body and soul as two inseparable parts of a single reality conditioned by race, ends up more or less by negating that the soul can have an absolutely detached existence in the afterlife, and negates also that therefore it is essentially in function of the afterlife that man ought to orient himself on earth. He seems to incline toward believing that the soul of individuals survives and subsists essentially in the mystic forces of lineage and of descendance, almost as in certain aspects — which are not however even its superior aspects — in the ancient cult of the Lares and of the gods of the hearth.

4) On the Catholic doctrine regarding sin and grace, and regarding human existence as a "gift of God," on the precepts of the "cadaverous obedience" which culminate in the Jesuitic morality; on dogmatism and priestly absolutism; all things which are repugnant to the Nordic sense of independence, of liberty, of responsibility, and of honor, not to speak of the Nordic aspiration toward a direct and clear experience of the divine. "The doctrine of original sin," writes Rosenberg, "would have been incomprehensible to a people whose racial identity was unadulterated. In such a people there dwells a secure confidence in itself and in its will, which it regards as Destiny." The feeling of guilt is already "a sure symptom of racial bastardy."[16]

5) The entire Catholic doctrine of sacraments and of rites, of transubstantiation and of indulgences, of redemption through vicarious

---

16 *Myth*, Book I, Chapter I.

sacrifice, of the terrifying sanctions of the afterlife, and all like matters, would nauseate the Nordic sense even more. In all of this Rosenberg sees the world of the lowest Syrian-African or Etruscan magic rise again, and in this connection he does not hesitate to liken the Catholic vision of life to that of the savages, gathered together like objects, without regard to personality, communistically, around their omnipotent shamans. He writes:

> Philosophically considered, the dogmas of absolution and indulgence, together with an enormous quantity of others, form the doctrine of the monks. Up to those of consecrated oil and miraculous reliquiae, stand on the level of a vision of a world whose type is that of the medicine man[17] or the shaman of the savages. [...] Whoever described the attempt to realize politically on earth the magico-demonic conception of the world of the shaman or the medicine man, would write the question of the dogma and of the Church of Rome. [...] A complete victory [of the Roman Church] would come to signify the dominion of a priestly caste over a mass of billions of men, who without race and without will, in a community ordered communistically, consider their existence as a gift from God, mediated by that omnipotent shaman [the Pope].

However in this connection it is fitting to note the strange fact that while Rosenberg accuses "Roman" philosophy of rationalism, yet he himself demonstrates a much worse rationalistic — not to say even Enlightenment — attitude through such an objective and spiritual incomprehension of the profoundest, most objective and spiritual meaning proper to rite and sacrament. Rosenberg winds up finally in an apologia — intoned in a Chamberlainian key — for science and for modern technology, supposed creations of the Nordic spirit, born from the overcoming of religious superstitions of Etruscan-Levantine type, going so far as to write: "He who has never felt the power of forcefully overcoming time and space, he who has not felt, in the midst of machines and ironworks, in the midst of the interworking of a thousand wheels, the pulsebeat of material conquest of the world, he has not understood this

---

17   "Medicine man" is in English in the original.

one side of the Germanic European soul, and he will not understand the other mystical side."[18]

Beginning from the fall of ancient aristocratico-pagan Rome, Romanity for Rosenberg signifies naught other than priestly absolutism and Catholic universalism. Following from this is an evaluation of Luther and of the Reformation, which however is here not as enthusiastic as in so many other racists. Protestantism for Rosenberg has a double face: it is positive insofar as — in the form of anti-Catholicism — it has contributed to the battle of the liberty of Rome, to the formation of the national German life and of the free personality, "opening the road to everything which today we can call the work of our civilization and to our highest science."[19] But Protestantism is negative insofar as it substituted Jerusalem for Rome, insofar as it unearthed and brought to the foreground the sacred texts of the Jewish tradition, the Old Testament, this collection of "pimps and cattle dealer stories,"[20] and insofar as it idolatrously held itself to the sacred texts: something which, given his premises, was equivalent to falling from the pan into the fire; also because Rosenberg at the end does Catholicism the honor of recognizing the merit of having conserved — though adapting them to its own ends — certain cosmic symbols of the primordial Nordic-solar tradition, the tradition of which Wirth speaks, the cosmic Christianity of 15,000 years B.C., transmitted to the Galileans by the Atlantians. For Rosenberg, the great sin of Protestantism was therefore taking up the Bible, and having made of it the book of the German people, rather than widening the battle of independence for Rome and of Nordic reintegration on the basis of the message and the spiritual conquests relative to German mystics, such as MEISTER ECKHART.

While in the terrestrial aspect of the Nordic spirit, Rosenberg, as has been said, valorizes science and technology, in its metaphysical aspect he refers precisely to the Medieval mystic Meister Eckhart (1260–1328) and in him heralds the precursor of a new racist and Nordist religion. Meister

18   *Myth*, Book I, Chapter III.

19   I have been unable to find the source of this quotation.

20   *Myth*, Book III, Chapter V.

Eckhart is a model of the "aristocratic mystic," he is the one who spoke of the "noble soul" and who proclaimed: "That which is noblest in man is his blood." Eckhart was the one who conceived the I as a principle which causes itself, born from eternity, an impregnable fortress, such that, were it not to exist, not even God could exist; finally, Eckhart is the one who proclaimed: "Man must be free and a master of all his works, undestroyed and unconstrained"[21] and taught an austere path toward conquering the heavens, a way cleared of magic, of dogmatism, of obedience to the letter, and even of devout sentimentalism and humanitarian abandons. "In the last analysis," says Rosenberg, "honor and freedom are not external qualities but spiritual essences independent of time and space."[22] These values, innate to the Nordic blood, find expression according to him as much in mysticism of the type now mentioned, as in the style of the Nordic Viking, of the Teutonic cavalier, of the Prussian official, of German soldier and peasant. "The ideas of blood and honor are for us the principle and the end of all our thinking and acting."[23] By such a route, one arrives at formulating the project of a future "German National Church," bearer of a spirituality of the kind: spirituality to be found amidst the ancient myths of the Nordic-Aryan paganism which, adopted as symbols, in the education of new generations, must substitute the "little Jewish stories of the Old Testament." Odin, the god of the *Edda*, "as the eternal mirrored image of the primal spiritual powers of Nordic man lives today just as he did

---

21 The translation for this quotation is taken from *Myth*, Book I, Chapter III. A variant is: "Man should be free, lord of all his deeds, undestroyed and uncompelled." The quotation comes from Meister Eckhart's *Talks of Instruction*, 22. Eckhart von Hochheim (c. 1260-c. 1328) was a renowned German mystic who during the course of his Christian vocation was nominated a Prior at a Dominican convent and *twice* called to be *magister*, or teacher, in Paris (an honor which he shared at that time with Thomas Aquinas alone), before finally being accused and tried as a heretic. He was found guilty on several counts, though not before he passed away. Several of his Latin writings have come down to us, and through these he has enjoyed an abiding influence; his importance is indicated by the fact that he is almost universally remembered as *Meister* Eckhart.

22 *Myth*, Book I, Chapter III.

23 I do not know the source of this quotation.

over 5,000 years ago."[24] Christianity little by little must be supplanted by a heroic religion: more sacred than crosses must be the monuments of the heroes fallen on the field of battle, in the holocaust of life, in the mystery of their blood. In the villages and in the cities of the new Germany, the statues of the Prussian solder, substituted for those of the Saints and Madonnas, will be the destinations of new pilgrimages, since German martyrdom in the World War did not come from a political conspiracy, but was "the martyrdom of a new faith." Rosenberg writes: "Here the German must reach back to his magnificent heritage of mysticism so he can conquer and experience again the greatness of soul of a Meister Eckehart, and so that this man and the field grey hero under the steel helmet become for us one and the same experience and Myth."[25] And he concludes: "The longing to give the Nordic race soul its form as German church under the sign of the folkish Myth, that is for me the greatest task of our century."[26] "Catholicism, protestantism, Jewry and Naturalism must be cleared from the field before beginning a new world outlook, so that they are no longer thought of, just as the night lamp is no longer thought of when the morning sun shines over the mountains."[27]

The fact that we have stated that Rosenberg is even now an influential personality in Nazi Germany should not make one suppose that in Germany itself such ideas are widely held in all their extremism. The attempts to build a new Nordic-Teutonic Church commencing from the racist vision of the world have been reduced to little enough. From the ethical point of view, some have posited the following in the place of the commandments of the Old Testament: "Honor the divinity; honor your ancestors and your descendants (*pagan cult of the forebears*); honor the great men of your people (*the cult of the heroes*); honor your father and your mother; keep yourself pure; be faithful to your race; do not steal; be truthful; aid the noble man." The commandment to "not kill" has therefore

24 *Myth*, Book III, Chapter VII.

25 *Myth*, Book III, Chapter V.

26 *Myth*, Book III, Chapter V.

27 *Myth*, Book III, Chapter I.

been eliminated, and that of love of the neighbor has been substituted by the precept of solidarity only with the "noble men." Moreover, the German special corps of the so-called SS (*Schutz-Staffeln*) has attempted to make for itself an ethics of the kind, and to construct itself as a species of "Nordically" oriented "order" and "guard" in National Socialism. Even in its badges the runes of Pre-Christian Nordic Teutonism have been taken up once more, and the very insignia of this important corps, organized by Heinrich HIMMLER, the stylized double S, have clearly been understood as the so-called prehistoric "runes of victory" — *Siegrunen*. Even in the so-called *Ordensburgen*, new German centers meant to gather, select, and systematically and totalitarianically form elements which, racially and spiritually qualified, are destined to form the portraits of the future ruling political class — even in these centers, ideas of Rosenbergian intonation play a not inconsiderable role, and here too they act in an ethical sense. In the sense of philosophy and of spirit, on the other hand, those who have sought to seriously take up once more the idea of a new anti-Christian religion have ended up in mere dilettante exercises: such is the case for HAUER, VON REVENTLOW, LUDENDORFF, and LÖPMANN — to which, as a truly typical case on account of certain of his deviations, we can add Ernst BERGMANN, whose book on the German National Church has been placed on the Index together with that of Rosenberg, but whose interpretation of history, if adopted coherently, appears to be precisely at the antipodes of that which the readers have seen prevail up to this point. Bergmann would justify his views not with abstract and rationalistic hypotheses, but with positive facts; through biological and zoological observations on what occurs amongst the animals, indeed amongst the insects, he thinks he can obtain the firmest basis to define that which, with regard to man, should be considered normal. In brief, the amazing result of this research is that anywhere the feminine-maternal principle is not recognized as the center, and the masculine does not have a subordinate place before it, there is aberration; and therefore history, weft with revolts, emancipations, and usurpations of the masculine and of masculine civilization against the authority of woman, is altogether an anomaly, the wild nightmare of hysterics, to which it is time to bring an end. The feminizing elements which we have encountered in the conception of the religion of the Nordic-Atlantic race according to Wirth here take on a crazed tendency. It is true that Bergmann, who now proclaims: "Enough of Rome, enough of Jerusalem, let us return to the pure religion of the fatherland: our sacred thing is our fatherland, our eternity is our people, our God is that which we would like to dream"— is the same man who, in the German Church, would be sure to provide, beside the "dear and delightful and most blessed mother," the "masculine figure of the hero of light." Nonetheless this demonstrates well enough the furious oscillating of the new ideology, which in reality gathers every kind of confused aspiration, suggestion, hazarded impatience.

The great defect here is the preoccupation with politics, the concern with creating "myths" and watchwords without an adequate preparation and a clear and calm awareness above all for that which regards the true traditions of the origins. This is not at all devoid of dangers, because the disrepute which might strike the distortion and counterfeiting of certain views can easily extend itself to things which are in themselves valid, with the result of precluding the comprehension of that which ought to be adopted toward a truly constructive action. And thus, also with regard to the famous "paganism" of contemporary racism we have thought it well to proceed with a critical examination, so as to eliminate dangerous equivocations. The reader will find this examination in our *Synthesis of Doctrine on Race*. In general, from that which we have here considered from out of a duty to information, the reader must not believe that the unique conclusion to the problem of the "new vision of the world" is a species of idolatry of the nation racially conceived, and the idea that only through the nation one might invoke God, and that only the blood—as more or less today everyone conceives it—is a mystic sacrament. It is rather possible to reach horizons which are of a quite different breadth, and to exorcise every return of a spirit which covers itself with deceptive robes, and which is rightly called, at bottom, even Jacobin and Gallic.

Before closing this chapter, we would like to mention another false turn of certain extremist German racist circles — a false turn against which one must likewise guard, if one believes firmly in the positive part that an adequately formulated racist myth might have in our battle against the decadence of the latest civilization.

The circles to which we have just alluded[28] stand adverse not only to the Church, but with it also the very Ghibelline imperial tradition, the very "Holy Roman Empire of the German Nation." The tradition of the man of Nordico-Teutonic race according to these thinkers was not continued in Charlemagne, but rather in the lineage of the pagan Saxons eradicated by this emperor, and then in the Princes of the Reformation, in revolt against the imperial authority. Von Leers sees in the anti-aristocratic and communistic revolt of the German peasants "the last Nordic revolution of the Medieval" suffocated in blood, and Rosenberg, who likewise sees in this event an insurrection against the Roman servitude in the triple form of Church, State, and Right, adds that in the twentieth century this "spiritual" revolt will be lit anew for the definitive victory. In a yet more pressing way, these ideas are sustained by Walter DARRÉ, whose last work on the *Peasantry as Fount of the Life of the Nordic Race* has had a diffusion and a success in Germany which we would like to attribute to extrinsic causes. Already in a preceding work Darré came more or less to contest the Nordic character of the most characteristic and most traditional constitution of the Medieval Ghibelline, the feudal regime, and to trace its origin to anti-Teutonic customs, alien to the Nordic feeling of liberty, proper to the court of the Franks and then to Charlamagne. In his most recent book, Darré passes over to sustaining the following point of view, truly "revolutionary" in the face of what have been up to now the dearest ideas of racism and pan-Germanism: the truly Nordic type is not that of conqueror, but that of the *peasant*: an armed peasant, if you please, ready to defend himself, but a peasant nonetheless. According to Darré, even the dukes amongst the Teutons were ever peasants. The Nordic race is no longer the "active race" of the glacial age, the race of the "primordial

---

28   In the first edition, Evola attributes these beliefs specifically to Rosenberg.

hunter" eager for distances and adventurous undertakings, but rather a sedentary race, a race meant essentially to cultivate its own earth, maintaining itself by this earth, attached and faithful to it. According to Darré, the Teutons have never in history been presented as pure conquerors, that is as conquerors by nature and not by necessity: at most they have desired and conquered the land necessary to their existence. The Indo-Germans even conserve this character and supported this character on a firm agricultural stratum, and, when they were racially well preserved, they developed and were great. They began to lose their strength, their nationality, and their characteristics of race so soon as they neglected the peasant element, in order to give themselves to the life of the city-dweller and to the insane mirage of imperialism.

Here a theme we have already noted presents itself, but with a new, tendentious, and, we were almost about to say, demagogic accent, with which racism descends in level little by little, threatening to come to a point in which the doctrine of "Nordic" liberty and honor will only with difficulty be distinguishable from the more or less anti-traditionalistic and plebeian "social" demands of the modern world. Moreover, in 1933, a book which was if nothing else courageous, written by one Carl Dyrssen and entitled *The Message of the Orient*, already enunciated the logical consequence of such an order of ideas: National Socialism, if it does not want to be but a laughable revolution, must take sides against "Western" thought, which would be the liberal, capitalistic, feudal world, more or less safeguarded by the Church and today more organized than overcome by Italian Fascism. The spirit of the revolt of the peasants should be taken up by a new Germany; it is necessary to recognize the farmer-socialist tradition as a Teutonic tradition, and on that basis, to recognize that Germany is essentially related to the Orient, that is the Slavic-Bolshevik element: with the Bolshevik — which is a regime borne precisely by free agricultural-soldierly representatives — it must make a common cause against the "West," it must see in Bolshevik atheism itself only a "defect of adolescence," the expression of a repulsion for every "Roman" form of religiosity, which preludes a purification and a liberation of the religious sentiment very similar to that already prepared by the Lutheran reform.

There is barely any need to observe that Germany officially, in its foreign policy, has guarded itself against adhering to extravagances of the kind. Such enunciations are nonetheless significant and merit being recalled toward a prophylactic and pedagogic end, so to speak: these are extremist racist tendencies which are equivalent — as we have observed — to so many false starts.

CHAPTER IX

Racism and Antisemitism

The Jewish question. The ethnic problem. The genesis of destructive Judaism. The "Law" and the revolution. Jewish hatred. The modern forms of the appearance of Judaism. The Jewish problem is not a religious problem. The *Protocols of the Elders of Zion* and their meaning.

ALREADY IN THE PRECEDING PART of this book we have often encountered antisemitic elements. These elements in contemporary racism take on an ever more decisive character, so far as giving rise today to an equivocation, according to which racism and antisemitism are thought to be one and the same thing, and the quality of being "Aryan" would be simply the possession of whomever does not have Jewish blood or the blood of races of color. Despite the fact that certain poorly meditated forms of racism have gone to justify such confusions, it must yet be kept firm that antisemitism and, in particular, anti-Judaism, are consequential aspects, and so to speak, applications of the theory of race: they draw from it their principles, but they do not utterly identify themselves with it.

In this chapter, we propose a summary of the principal points of the Jewish question and of the polemic related to it. We will refer to the opinions of certain foreign antisemitic racists but we will also bring our attention to the points of view reached by Italian anti-Judaism, above all in the currents which take as their head Giovanni PREZIOSI and his journal *La Vita Italiana*, since these points of view — to whose clarification we ourselves, moreover, have contributed — often offer a character of greater completeness.

Let us begin, before anything else, by entering the Jewish question from the ethnic and properly racial point of view. According to racism, the Jews do not constitute a race in the proper sense, but only a "people," a people of mixed breeds (FRITSCH, GÜNTHER, etc.). The Semites in general, to which the Jews belong, were already by GOBINEAU considered as a mixed race derived from a cross between the white race and the black. Today there is the tendency to see in it a mixture between the Desertic and Orientaloid race and the Levantine or Armenoid race: in the specific case of the Jews, this intermixing was supposedly complicated by other ethnic components, which vary according to the stock, of both ancient races (the Amoritic, Arya) and extant races (for example the Mediterranean race and the Alpine race). Moreover, the Bible spoke of seven peoples who contributed to the formation of the blood and the "seed" of the Jews, not to speak of Hamitic (Egyptian) and Philistines infiltrations, and others. In the period of the dispersion and the Diaspora and of the last prophecy, yet other debris from the Mediterranean ethnic and spiritual decadence contributed to Judaism.

But if things stand in this way, if that which is Israel is not a race but a mixture of races, it will be asked to what Israel owes its incontestable unity, what it is that has drawn from this mixture a clearly recognizable type, which has had the strength to endure throughout centuries amidst the most unfavorable conditions, and whose sense of solidarity and fidelity to its blood is so vital, that the Jewish people practically has been amongst the most "racist" of all of history.

The reason for this unity must not be sought in race in the strict sense, but rather in the *formative force exercised by an idea and by a tradition*. It is a Jew, James DARMESTETER, who wrote: "The Jew has been formed, not to say fabricated, by his books and by his rites. As Adam issued from the hands of Jehova, so he [the Jew] issued from the hands of his rabbis."[1] It is the "Law," the *Torah*, which has created the Jewish type and Jewish unity: this "Law" in the Jew substitutes the fatherland, the country, the nation, even blood itself: this "Law" has reacted upon an original chaotic racial debris and mixture, it has imposed a form on this mixture, it has elaborated instincts and attitudes of a special type which through the centuries has become hereditary.

We have said "through the centuries," because the antisemites have justly noted the error of those who believe that after the Old Testament and with the succession of Christianity, the influence of the Jewish law has been, so to speak, neutralized and almost arrested. The contrary is true. The Ancient Law, or *Torah*, which already had been completed with the *Mišnâh* (repetition, the law repeated), that is with an equally Mosaic tradition transmitted first orally and then, toward the third century, fixed in writing, found its later development in the Rabbinic literature gathered in the *Gĕmârâ'*, which means precisely "accomplishment," and in that which is more commonly called the *Talmud*: moreover, in the developments proper to the *Kabbalah* and the formulations of the so-called *Shulchân 'ârûkh*. All of this should be taken as a whole, as a perfect continuity across the ages, before and after Christianity, up to our present day. And indeed, the Talmudic, post-Christian formulations of the Jewish Law are those that have further reinforced and characterized the Jewish way of being and instinct, above all with respect to their relations with non-Jews.

The Aryan and racist front considers Judaism as a destructive force for every other race or civilization. Let us examine the elements that justify such an idea — or rather, more precisely, the routes through which the effectively destructive character of Judaism manifests itself. The

1   Evola provides no indication of the source of this quotation; it has been translated here directly from the Italian.

predominant point of view of antisemitism is that, just as the germinal force of a plant does not make itself fully manifest save when it splits apart and begins to act on the material around it, so Judaism would not have begun so universally to manifest truly deleterious influences had it not been for the crisis of the ancient national Jewish tradition, with the political collapse and the dispersion into the world of the "chosen" people.

In the first place, we must consider the influences which ethnic elements, in themselves chaotic, spurious and constrained by the Law, must exercise at that point at which these are dissolved and pass into the free state. Guénon has justly observed that the relations between the Jew and the Jewish tradition are different from those which belong to other races. For the non-Jew who departs from his tradition as a religious law, there are yet a series of supports: there is the soil, there is blood, there is the fatherland. But in Judaism the Law takes the place of all these. At the point, therefore, that the Jew disbands, he becomes automatically a disintegrating force. Thus, it is that he who is raceless becomes anti-race; he who is without nation becomes the anti-nation. Mommsen wrote: "Even in the ancient world, Judaism was an active ferment of cosmopolitanism and national decomposition." Wolf saw in the Jewish element an ungraspable, elusive, nationless substance within every nation, and considered it the very principle of anti-race, anti-tradition, anti-culture: not the antithesis of a determinate culture, but of every culture insofar as it is racially and nationally determined. The Desertic or Orientaloid component in the Jewish composite strengthens this influence: with the spirit of nomads, of Desertic people connected to no land, the Jews have injected into the various peoples — beginning with the Roman — the virus of denaturalization, or universalism, of internationalism of culture. It is an incessant action of corrosion of everything which is differentiated, qualitative, connected to the blood and to a tradition. It is that which in modern times in the political field began to manifest itself also as Judaizing demo-Massonic ideology with related humanitarian-social and internationalistic myths.

The second element: the destructive influences of Judaism are tied also to the part that the *race of the Levantine or Armenoid man* plays, according to the psychology of that race made by Günther but above all by CLAUSS, who, as we have seen, has characterized that race as being the race of the "man of redemption." To the man of redemption, the anti-Aryan dualism between flesh and spirit is proper. Here the body is not conceived as the expressive instrument of the spirit, but precisely as "flesh," as sinful materiality from which one must be "redeemed." But this confused impulse toward "redemption" can fail: then this type of man, relapsing, plunges into materiality, revels and becomes drunk of it as if to forget himself and, moreover, acts toward the contamination of everything which tended toward that which he has not reached, every superior value: he revels in every crisis whence he sees the reflection of his own crisis, he takes pleasure wherever it is shown, or wherever he himself shows, that the devious and crass materiality into which he has relapsed is alone real and omnipotent—for then it serves as a kind of alibi, of justification. It is by this second aspect that the Jewish element, as we will shortly see, ever manifests itself through an action, be it conscious or unconscious, of contamination and degradation of every higher value.

As for the third point, we must consider the special efficiency that the fundamental motifs of this same Law have had in the place of the formation of instincts and of base-attitudes, and precisely in this way we must consider the secularized and materialized form of these same themes and of these instincts, which act automatically in the scattered and persecuted Jews. As has been observed, the central theme of the ancient Law is that Israel is the "chosen people," destined for dominion over all the peoples, the lands, and the riches of the world, so much so that all kingdoms will have to obey it. These are the themes of Mosaism: "And you shall lend to many nations, but you shall not borrow. And the LORD will make you the head and not the tail, and you shall only go up and not down" (Deuteronomy 28:12–13); "You must destroy all the peoples the LORD your God gives over to you. Do not look on them with pity and do not serve their gods, for that will be a snare to you" (Deuteronomy 7:16)—but these are also the themes of the successive prophetic literature: "Then the sovereignty, power and greatness of all the kingdoms under heaven will be handed over to the holy people of the Most High. His kingdom will be an everlasting kingdom, and all rulers will worship and obey him" (Daniel 7:27); "Foreigners will rebuild your walls, and their kings will serve you" (Isaiah 60:10); "And you will be called priests of the LORD, you will be named ministers of our God. You will feed on the wealth of nations, and in their riches you will boast" (*idem* 61:6), etc.

Think now of the sentiments which must have fatally given rise to this certainty, this *idée fixe* of "selection" and of universal dominion, at the moment that Israel ceased to exist as a political power, at which moment precisely, with the triumph of Christianity, this people, which continued to feel itself chosen, was identified with the last of peoples, to a damned and deicide lineage meriting every persecution, condemned by just penalty to servitude. The "potential" determined by this idea of the Law then necessarily was translated into a profound and boundless hatred for every non-Jew, and would concretize itself in a serpentine praxi, so to speak. It is this which the later, Talmudic development of the Ancient Law clearly shows us. Here are a few Talmudic passages recalled for our purposes by Preziosi and DE VRIES DE HEEKELINGEN: "What is the meaning of Har Sinai, that is Mount Sinai? It is the mountain from which *Sina* descended, that is, hatred against the peoples of the world." "You Israelites are called men, while the other nations of the world are not to be called men, but beasts." "The progeny of a foreigner [that is, of a non-Jew] is as the progeny of animals." "The best among the non-Jews, kill him." "Make them die closing their mouths so that they do not scream." "What is a prostitute? Any woman who is not Jewish." And so forth and so on. The expressions contained in a prayer, which every Orthodox Jew should recite daily, in the *Shemoné Esré*, are: "That the apostates lose very hope, that the Nazarenes and the Mimim [the Christians] perish at a blow, are erased from the book of life and have no contact amongst the just."

Now, we must consider a more modern period, in which the religious justification of these sentiments has disappeared, though its effectiveness has survived in terms of an instinct, an innate attitude. And the same could be said regarding that which must have proceeded from this original persuasion, that between Israel and the other peoples, there is nothing in common, whence it is absurd to adopt the same criteria of conduct with respect to the Jews and the "Gentiles," who are inferior beings which by right have worth only as beasts to exploit. The Talmudic precepts, in this connection, are clear: they establish two morals, the one that applies to one's neighbor, that is, to the Jews, the other which serves in the relations with the *Goyim*, with the non-Jews. And all that which is crime or unworthy action according to the first morality ceases to be so for the second. Thus it is that the *Talmud* and the *Shulchân 'ârûkh* authorize cheating the non-Jew; they do not consider as adultery that which is committed with a non-Jewess; they not only make a right of loaning with usury, but almost a duty; they prescribe, in any trial moved by non-Jews against Jews, that the Jews involved do not testify or else give false witness; they adopt the premise that "the patrimony and the goods of the non-Jews are to be considered ownerless, so that whoever first arrives has the right to them," stipulating only that if several Jews succeed with the deception, they are held to justly distribute the proceeds; they exhort to loan money, without ever borrowing it; they break their promises, and so forth. The antisemitic polemic has gathered an entire series of maxims of the kind, with precise indication of their origin and their "orthodox" character. As for the rest, if in the *Talmud* one also reads: "A Goy who studies the *Talmud* and a Jew that helps him in such study must be put the both of them to death"; if it is specified that "to communicate anything of our Law to a non-Jew is equivalent to the slaughter of all the Jews, because if the non-Jews knew what we teach with respect to them they would certain exterminate us" — if one reads such words, on has a precise confirmation of the full consciousness that the Jews have of the double morality contained in their orthodox texts.

But here one will object that we are treating of ancient texts, which have fallen practically into disuse. This is an error. As has been said, these ideas, these precepts have for centuries acted formatively in the intimate Jewish substance: they have left their indelible traces. The original religious and messianic justification may have been lost for this will to dominate, this hatred, and, finally, this Talmudic double-morality: but the complex of instincts has not been lost with it, nor the attitudes to which they have given rise on a "secularized" and practical plane. It manifests simply as a spontaneous mode of being, as a hereditary quality of "race" which has come to have, so to speak, its own existence. This is why the *religious element does not enter at all into the Jewish question*, which question modern racism has imposed. DÜHRING had occasion to write that "the Jewish question would exist even were all the Jews to abandon their religion and to pass into the breast of our dominant Churches." This is precisely the view of modern antisemitism, which agrees, moreover, with the view of the better part of the Jews, but contradicts that of the older antisemitism of Catholic derivation. "A Japanese or a Negro remains Japanese or Negro after having been converted or baptized. Thus a baptized Jew remains a Jew. [...] Whether they convert in good faith or not, baptized Jews continue to be Jews, to consider themselves Jews and to be considered as Jews by their old fellow believers" (DE HEEKELINGEN).

We read in a Talmudic text: "Wherever the Jews establish themselves, they must make themselves masters; and until they do not attain complete dominion, they must consider themselves exiles and prisoners. In order that they arrive at a governance of the people, until they do not rule entirely, they must not cease to cry: What torment! What indignity!" Here again we find a theme of the Law, likewise derived from the ancient Promise, that, once its original religious justification was obfuscated, had to leave as a trace a revolutionary instinct, which could act as an agent for itself, without any precise point of reference, as the ferment for a continual agitation and subversion. It is thus that we see the Jews widely represented in all the subversive and revolutionary modern movements, without exception, and in a characteristic way in Socialism and in Communism, whose greatest exponents are all Israelites: Karl MARX, Rosa LUXENBURG, KAUTSKY, TROTZKY, etc. So far as the structure of the state to be destroyed goes, this is of little importance. "In a monarchy, the Jews will be republicans; in a conservative republic, they will be socialists; in a socialist republic, they will be communists. It is all the same to them, so long as they can destroy whatever exists. They will remain antisocial as long as society conserves a vestige of non-Jewish basis." Once again, it is an instinct, something which subsists automatically as heredity, having as a remote and unconscious origin the idea that every system is unjust, illegitimate and usurpatory which is not that of the promised dominion of the "chosen people."

In modern Judaism, beside the column of revolutionaries, we see another movement acting, which seems to be contrary, in high capitalism and international finance. It is another derivation of the traditional Jewish themes. It must be recalled that the "Reign" of the Jewish Promise was not at all conceived in mystical or superterrestrial terms, but as that rule which would have gathered all the riches of the earth. "For I have plans to prosper you" and "you will lend to many nations but will borrow from none " are already Biblical maxims:[2] add to this the inclination of Semite and above all Desertic peoples to conceive riches essentially as mobile riches — as mobile as their very lives, that is, as gold — and little by little one will come to understand the inclinations which, materializing themselves and "secularizing" themselves ever more, have given rise to typically Jewish forms of capitalism, up to the omnipotence of an economy without spirit and a finance without fatherland: in these modernizing forms the ancient Jewish will to rule comes to revel, but directly and for the destruction and dejection of values which this omnipotence brings with it. According to HALFELD, even the divinification of money and of riches, the transformation of the temple into the bank, the puritan glorification of success and of profit, the preacher-impresario, the businessman and usurer with God on his lips, the humanitarian and pacifistic ideology at the service of materialistic praxi, etc. are all Jewish traits — for which we happily recall the saying of SOMBART, that America is in all its parts a Jewish country and that Americanism is nothing but the "Jewish spirit distilled"; or that of Günther, that the exponents and the diffusors of the so-called modern spirit have been predominately Jews; and finally, that of Wolf, according to whom the intimate connection between the Anglo-Saxons

---

2   See Jeremiah 29:11 and Deuteronomy 15:6.

and the Masons under the Jewish sign constitutes the keystone to Western history of the latest times. Moreover, Karl Marx himself wrote, "What is the secular basis of Judaism? *Practical* need, *self-interest*. What is the worldly religion of the Jew? *Huckstering*. What is his worldly God? *Money*. […] The Jew has emancipated himself in a Jewish manner, not only because he has acquired financial power, but also because, through him and also apart from him, *money* has become a world power and the practical Jewish spirit has become the practical spirit of the Christian nations. The Jews have emancipated themselves insofar as the Christians have become Jews. […] The god of the Jews has become secularized and has become the god of the world. The bill of exchange is the real god of the Jew."[3]

To the power of *gold*, in the action of modern Judaism, that of *intelligence* as a revolutionary force plays the counterpart. Here we intend to allude to a ferment of subversion which does not limit itself any longer to the social field, but acts properly on the spiritual and cultural plane in the most various forms, drawing from the aforementioned inclination of the carnalized "man of redemption." It is incontestable that in the field of culture, of literature, of art, of science itself, the Jewish "contributions" both by routes direct and indirect, converge ever in this effect: to falsify, to mock, to demonstrate illusory and unjust whatever for the Aryan people had the value of ideal, tendentiously bringing to the foreground whatever of the sensual, inferior, dirty, and bestial hides itself, or resists, in human nature. To sully every sacredness, to make every point of stability and every certainty oscillate, to instill a sense of spiritual dismay such as to favor abandonment to the lower forces — in this the Jewish action manifests itself, an action, moreover, essentially instinctive, natural, proceeding from the essence, from the "internal race," as to fire it is natural to burn and to an acid to corrode. The relativism of the Jew EINSTEIN, which has given the profane to believe that science itself has confirmed the impossibility of any solid point of reference, while on the other hand it gave the final blow to a concrete type of physical knowledge, substituting for it a purely "formal" system of mathematical and algebraic entities; BERGSON,

---

3   Taken from an 1844 essay entitled *The Jewish Question* by Karl Marx.

with his theory which exalts life in its immediacy, in its irreducibility to intellectual certainties, in its incoercibility, in its antithesis with respect to everything of the classical world of "being"; FREUD, ADLER and the other Jewish psychoanalysts, who have set themselves to discovering the turbid world of the subconscious and to demonstrating the omnipotence of this subconscious — as the locus of atavistic and savage instincts, of the primordial *libido* and the famous "complexes" — over every faculty and inclination of the waking I; the so-called Jewish sociological school, which has interpreted religions and mythologies no longer on the basis of a transcendent element but simply in the light of "social" and purely human constructions; the Jew LOMBROSO, who, beyond establishing aberrant relations between genius and abnormality, has conceived of the delinquent as the residual and yet pure exponent of a "race," which would be precisely the race from which we have developed; Max NORDAU, who intended to reveal the "conventional lies of our civilization," precisely as a series of Jewish novelists, beginning with WASSERMANN, who have specialized in uncovering the injustices and the inadequacies at the idea-basis of modern life; the historical materialism of Karl Marx, which as the unique creative force of history presents us with brutal economic process, giving to everything else the value of mere "superstructure" (whence this judgement of FRANCK: "The Marxist doctrine does not correspond to reality, but to the spirit and needs of Judaism, which does not consider anything other than problems of materiality and of money and mocks every ideal and every spiritual form. It is a leveling force hurled against every value of race and of blood"); the action of the so-called specialists in the sexual question, the great majority of them Jewish, beginning from the well-known Magnus HIRSCHFELD, who wished to make of *eros* a true obsession and to attract, by means of pseudo-scientific publications and divulgations, attention to all of the most abnormal and degenerate forms of sexuality; the "discovery" of the mentality of "primitives" on the part of the Jews LÉVY-BRUHL and DURKHEIM; to which the action of a whole dense rank of Jews in the field of exceedingly modern art acts as counterpart, in which the formless, the primitivistic, the element tied to pure sensation once more come to have the upper hand — and so forth. These are specific and easily multiplied examples of an action with a thousand faces but with a single effect: to disintegrate, to degrade, to subvert. It is *Schadenfreude* — the enjoyment in demoralizing, in spoiling, in dirtying, in sensualizing, in opening the doors to the "subterranean" parts of the human soul, that this might unleash itself and satisfy itself — it is the characteristic *Schadenfreude* of the Levantine-Jewish soul, the soul of the "man of redemption."

The extremist antisemites do not tend to consider this convergence of effects as accidental. The prevalent and wiser point of view is, however, that in all of this we are not dealing with a precise intention, nor a plan, but precisely an instinct, a mode of being which manifests itself naturally and spontaneously. The convergence realizes itself by "syntony," by the affinity of the instinct and of inspiration. With respect to these Jews one might thus not even speak of a true responsibility: the Jew cannot do otherwise, even as an acid cannot do other than corrode. It is his way of being, determined by the aforementioned atavistic and racial causes. For which, it is less a matter of hating him than of taking precise technical measures for limiting and neutralizing his action, before it leads to harm.

Antisemitism moreover sees the ancient Jewish solidarity persist in modernized forms, cemented by the double morality, so much so that — as Fritsch says — the Jewish community has less the characteristics of a religious community than of a social conspiracy: and the Arya States, ignoring that double morality and not defending themselves, inconsiderately conceding to the Jews equal rights as if these followed their same morality, put themselves virtually into a position of inferiority, reducing themselves, often without being aware of it, to the hands of the "guest people," of the international and antinational foreign race. Coming to awareness of this fact, there is a need to act along two routes: the first moral, the other political.

There can be no rapport — it is said — between the "Arya" and a race "devoid of the sentiment of honor and loyalty," which acts with two principal forces: deception and money. The "Arya" social concept is:

The sincere and conscious man places his pride in being worthy of the right to exist through loyal action and right productivity. He would rather perish than obtain advantage by dishonorable means. The rigorous idea of honor and of unconditional justice toward other men constitutes the presupposition of every heroic life and has its root in a profound element of the soul: the sentiment of shame. A people that renounces the sentiment of honor and of shame is unworthy to be called human: it is a sub-humanity.[4] (FRITSCH)

It is thus absurd — it is concluded — to insist on equal laws for Jews and for "Arya." Certain prophylactic-defensive measures are imposed. To give liberty to the Jews — according to these premises — would signify to permit them to play it. And it is for this that the liberalistic, individualistic, and democratic ideology has had, for evident reasons, Jews as its fervid proponents.

From here, the passage to the properly political action — that is, to measures which various States, assuming the theses of anti-Judaic racism, have adopted to take from the Jewish element those places of command of the political, economic, and intellectual life to which they have climbed *en masse* in the most recent period, with an advancement in the grand style. The antisemitic polemic has brought to light the fact that in commerce, in trade, in positions of command and also independent positions, the Jewish element was effectively predominant, while it decreased bit by bit as one descended to subordinate occupations, amongst the workers and the farmers, wherein the Jewish percentage became almost negligible compared to the number of non-Jews. In all, this antisemitism has seen a phenomenon of parasitism not devoid of relations to the hereditary Jewish instinct to "suck the milk of the peoples and suckle at the teats of kings," to "devour the peoples that the Lord will give," according to the ancient expressions of the Law. The Jew does not make, does not produce, but speculates and traffics on that which others make, and enriches itself at the expense of these and dominates. The Jew sets his sights directly on the intellectual occupations and positions of command, and while from

---

4   This is taken from one of Fritsch's untranslated works — either *Handbuch der Judenfrage* (The Manual of the Jewish Question) or *Der falsche Gott* (The False God). I have translated all Fritsch quotations from Evola's Italian.

there he undertakes an activity which is often suspicious and perverting, he leaves to the others, to the "Arya," the inferior forms of work.

From this, therefore, the well-known political measures intended to ban the Jew from public offices and to limit his representation in certain professions. The *Manual of the Jewish Question*, edited by Fritsch, closes with these characteristic sentences:

> The Jew is dangerous not only economically, but also spiritually and morally. By the Rabbinic law the Jew is bound to a particular State, which embraces all the Jews of the world. It is therefore impossible for him to sincerely be the member of another State. Each people which holds fast to the principle of its own liberty and its own honor and intends to protect itself against an impairment of its law and future moral degeneration can no longer tolerate the Jews in its breast. Where then must they go? This is *their business*. Certainly, not where they would drive farmers and artisans away from their houses and their goods. Apart from that, they possess enough money to purchase an entire part of the world for themselves — be it in Australia, in Africa. There they will be able to live undisturbed, according to their customs, and demonstrate to the world that with their strength they know how to create a civilization. To us, the abolition of the emancipation of the Jews is necessary.

And de Heekelingen:

> We do not at all reproach the Jews for working toward the greatness of their race. We even admire the tenacity with which they have pursued the realization of this end. That which we do not understand however is the blindness of so many non-Jews who do not demonstrate the same enthusiasm and the same tenacity to defend their most sacred interests.

With the considerations already undertaken above, the essentially "racial" side, beyond the political and social side, of the Jewish problem has been brought to clarity: it is racial, not in its reference to a pure race, but rather to instincts which have become, so to speak, an organic inheritance capable of assuming various forms of manifestation, but never of disappearing altogether.

Now we must say something on a book which has raised every kind of argument and which has had a fundamental part in the anti-Judaic polemic: we are speaking of the famous *Protocols of the Elders of Zion*. Since we have already treated of this book in the introduction of its latest Italian translation, edited by *Vita Italiana*, here we limit ourselves to a generic overview, because one cannot speak of the Jewish question without some clarity on this matter.

These *Protocols* issued, in their present form, in 1904 in Russia, edited by a certain Sergi NILUS, who presented them as a document which had been robbed from a mysterious Jewish-Masonic organization. In reality, it has been ascertained that parts of this text had already been previously divulged and published, and even Bismarck, it would seem, knew something of them. The central ideas of the *Protocols* are as follows:

a)   The various events and various ideologies which have brought traditional, Arya, and Christian Europe to its sunset are not accidental, but follow a precise plan of destruction;

b)   This plan of destruction heads an occult organization, which has elaborated all its details, studying at the same time, on the basis of knowledge of precise laws that tie causes to effects, the routes for its progressive realization;

c)   This organization acts in great part by intermediaries, who often do not know they are its instruments. Its action develops itself on three planes. First of all, there is the ideological: certain ideologies are disseminated, in which one does not at all believe, which are considered by the "Elders of Zion" to be foolishness, but which serve them machiavellistically, to disseminate subversion, to disintegrate society and the States: liberalism, rationalism, internationalism, democracy, etc. In the second place, it assures that the principal centers of fabrication of the so-called "public opinion," that is, the great international press, is under its control. In the third place, it aims to control the better part of the gold of the world, through international finance.

Acting with these three powerful instruments, one aims to disseminate everywhere the ferment of subversion, to spiritually and socially uproot all beings, to reduce them to a materialized mush without fatherland, without tradition, without interior force, without personality. True wars of revolution (which were supposed to have as their point of departure Russia — and note well that the *Protocols* have been in public domain at least since 1904) and carefully caused wars would conduct the crisis of Western man to such a point, that at the end he will be a passive thing in the hands of invisible dominators. At which point these will reveal themselves and assume universal power. At their head, there will be a king of the Jewish race.

This being the content of the *Protocols*, that which everyone immediately asks himself is if they are "true," "authentic." This question is senseless, for the simple reason that — as Guénon has justly observed — "no truly and seriously secret organization, whatever might be its nature, leaves behind it written documents." It is therefore not the case to speak of "authenticity," but rather of "veridicality." The document in question must be examined in its truth value according to the same criterion of "truth" of modern science, that is of the "working hypothesis" which serves to orient an inductive process that confirms it, a collection of facts that in virtue of this hypothesis come to show an intimate connection and a unitary law.

Now, from such a point of view, it can be said without doubt that even if the *Protocols* were not true, it is as if they were, for these two reasons:

1) Because the facts which emerged after their publication confirm them. Hugo WAST writes: "The *Protocols* might be false; but they realize themselves marvelously"; and Henry FORD: "The only statement I care to make about the Protocols is that they fit in with what is going on. They are sixteen years old and they have fitted the world situation up to this time. They fit it now."[5]

2) Because the fundamental ideas by which they are inspired are the same as those of international Jewry, for which even if the *Protocols* had been invented, the author simply wrote down that which every

---

5   The Ford quotation is taken from an interview with *New York World*, February 17th, 1921.

Jew faithful to his tradition and to the deep will of Israel, and conscious of his instincts, would have written.

Regarding both the first and the second point, the Italian edition of the *Protocols* which we have already cited gathers an ample and convincing demonstration. Having thus sketched the problem, the very question of "plagiarism," which provoked a thorny trial in Berne, appears to be, at bottom, frivolous.[6] Beyond any doubt, in the *Protocols* we find elements drawn from preexistent works, in particular excerpts of an operetta written in 1865 by a revolutionary Mason named JOLY. But here we are certainly not in the field of literature, in which to take something from someone else brings discredit. Even a strategist might make use of things first expounded by others, even conserving the literal formulation, if these are susceptible to being ordered in his plans, without their significance suffering from it.

Much more serious and conclusive is rather the verification of an entire series of antecedents to the *Protocols*, antecedents which date back even to distant times, and which in more or less "fictionalized" or mythological forms reproduce the obscure presentiment of this double morality:

a)   That all the principal happenings of history are not accidental, but have an inner logic and obey a certain intention;

b)   That there exists an occult center of the world.

The characteristic of the *Protocols* is found in a special formulation of these two general motifs: precisely, that the happenings of the modern subversion obey a certain intention and have a direction — and, in consequence, the occult center of the world has a shady character, it is a center of maleficent forces, consecrated to the destruction of traditional Europe. This particular formulation is the effect of a species of overturning and counterfeiting of a preexistent tradition, which is in itself neither Jewish

---

6   The trial in question began at the end of October in the year 1934. The court declared the texts to be forgeries; and though the court concluded that it did not have the authority to ban their sale, it was also quick to express its regret at this fact.

nor Masonic; of which, the reader can convince himself by perusing the last part of our book *The Mystery of the Grail*.[7]

In any case — it will be asked — at the center of this destructive plan proclaimed by the *Protocols* and demonstrated, often with an impressive precision, by successive events, are there really to be found the Jews? Even in the *Protocols* sometimes the reference goes to the Jews, and at other times to the Masons, which is not entirely the same thing. So far as we are concerned, in this connection we believe it is prudent to use only the expression: *secret directors of global subversion*. It is indisputable that numerous Jewish elements have been used by these masked Rulers, because, through their instincts and the deformation of their traditional ideas the Jews appear to be the most suitable and qualified tools. But it is not prudent to generalize beyond certain limits. It is necessary, moreover, to realize another point: that one cannot make of the Jews alone the unique and sufficient causes of the entire global subversion — as certain extremists would like — without ending up in a humiliating recognition of inferiority. Would the Jews have been therefore stronger than an "organized" Arya humanity, one in the fullness of its strength and its proper energy? This is nonsense. The Jewish action was possible only because the non-Jewish humanity had already begun the process of degeneration and disintegration: the Jewish element grafted itself onto these processes, and with the spirit, the instincts, and the methods proper to it has accelerated them and exasperated them, guiding them to that point that they would not, perhaps, have so quickly arrived. But, faithful to our resolution to keep ourselves to a pure exposition, we cannot pass here to defining the limits of validity of the anti-Jewish theses — also because, as we have said, we have already written of this elsewhere.

---

7   See the Epilogue to that book, *The Inversion of Ghibellinism*.

CHAPTER X

The Racist Conception
of Law

*The Roman-Rationalistic conception and the biological
conception of law. Positive law and "living" law. Racist
devaluation of the State. "Fidelity" and punishment.*

THE NINETEENTH PARAGRAPH of the program of the Nazi party
contains this declaration: "We demand substitution of a German
common law in place of the Roman Law serving a materialistic
world-order." The myth of race penetrates even in the juridical domain
and tends to create forms obedient to its principles. As the basis of the
regulation of social and political life, right cannot be separated from the
new ideology in the act of its translation into practice.

For the new conception of law, we refer to an exposition of Helmut
NICOLAI, which we will complete with suitable views from certain other
authors. Then we will mention the positive Nazi legislation which has followed this ideology.

The central theme of this ideology was originally more or less the following: there exists an abstract, mechanical, leveling, universalistic, and

absolutist conception of law — and, contrary to it, there exists an organic, differentiated, ethical conception which conforms to nature. The first is the conception of Roman law, as much as of the canonical ecclesiastical law; the second is the racist conception, which is supposedly an ancient Nordic tradition, which today should be reconditioned.

That, however, the use of the epithet "Roman" to characterize the first view proceeds from an arbitrary and tendentious generalization can be seen from the very views of the racist jurists in matters of history: even they recognize that Rome at its origins was "Nordic"; it knew law according to a style of virile liberty and of ethical responsibility. But the intermixing of the blood and of the races, ethnic chaos, followed the first Roman period, and above this by now rotten substance, strewn through with Jews, with Levantines and with Negroes, rose the Roman *Imperium* as an "enormous soulless statal machine" (NICOLAI). Along with it, "Roman law," no longer with any connection to the blood, took form. This law rests therefore upon a political unit exterior to peoples, and which from that exteriority dominates peoples; it develops itself on a positive-rationalistic basis, with logico-sophistic disquisitions, with abstract formulations of laws, as rigid in form as they are arbitrary in content. Every natural sentiment of law thus, through the decadence of Rome, was lost. Roman law denaturalized the living law which every people carried with itself. In a capitalistic society, it has become the convenient fetish of a handful of men who are ready to legally sanction their theft through a network of purely formal paragraphs. Roman law, however, is like a firmly immobile stone: it obstructs the way, save as it is ably avoided. With "law" and "State," two dead and stifling crusts come to suffocate the life of peoples. In possession of all powers, the "State" promotes its laws not in the name of the good and the honor of a people, of justice and of duty, but as a gift from on high, similar to love, to compassion, and to the grace of the Christians (ROSENBERG).

Let us turn now to the opposite conception of law. Here we recall an ancient Hindu saying: "Law and Unlaw do not walk around and say: We are this. Law is what Aryan men discover to be right." "This is an allusion," comments Rosenberg, "to a primordial wisdom forgotten in the present day that law is a blood related scheme. It is a system of religion and art. It is linked for eternity to a certain blood with which it appears and with which it passes away."[1] When a race lives and perpetuates itself without intermixing — adds Nicolai — together with its unadulterated blood, it possesses an innate sense of right, of justice and injustice, valid for it and not for others: a direct sentiment, which has no need to justify itself through an authority superimposed over the community and from which it draws its strength. On this basis, law and collective moral sentiment are confounded: ever supposing that the racial purity is maintained. "In *that* conception [that is, in the Roman conception]," writes Nicolai, "law is that which the arbitrarily discriminant power of the State decrees, while in *this* [in the Nordic racist conception] law is an eternal ethical greatness which stands above the powers of the State and which cannot be mutated by them. In *that* conception, whatever stands in law — the *positum*, whence positivism — is considered as law, while in *this* conception, law is only that which conforms to an eternal juridical idea. In *that* conception, whatever can justify itself with the letter of the law is legitimate, while in *this*, form gives place to content. The polestar *there* is the accomplishment of paragraphs; *here*, it is conscience."[2] "A dead science of paragraphs" — this epigraph should be writ therefore on the sepulchral stone of Roman law, save that, so far as racist law goes, in this connection it appears as nothing more than a concoction of jus-naturalism, of Protestantism, and of optimistic primitivism. At its center stands the idea that already in the state of nature a race is more or less "supernatural," that is that it possesses in the same degree of immediateness of the animal instincts, in all its members, a direct and indubitable perception of a given order of values, such that law is not the matter of discrimination, of "position," of legislation, but rather, we would almost say, of inspiration or intuition. The theory of the "natural light" of ROUSSEAU here marries therefore with the Lutheran theory of the direct experience of the divine, the miraculous

---

1   *Myth*, Book III, Chapter IV.

2   Nicolai is yet another forgotten or obscured figure from the Nazi era. I have translated his quotations from the Italian.

virtue of pure blood serving as auspex. Naturalism receives a confirmation through Rosenberg, according to which there exist two different ways of conceiving the world: that which sees it ordered by immanent and immutable natural laws, which would be the Nordic conception; and that which understands it as created from nothing and ordered from outside by a Creature, who can always intervene arbitrarily to alter its course, and this would be the conception of "the Semites, the Jews, and of Rome." The two opposite conceptions of law, the one organico-natural, the other universalistico-despotic, supposedly take as their premises precisely these two opposed conceptions.

Another point of difference is that the Roman law by nature would be individualistic. Arising in a period of "racial disgregation," according to Nicolai, it has in view naught but the individual in his relationship with the State: mechanical relations, devoid of history, atomic. The ethical connection of the individual to a given group and to a given descendance here does not constitute at all matter of right. No different is the rationalistic and positivist conception of right developed in the nineteenth and twentieth centuries: an abstract technistic conception, which begins and ends in the concept of law, and has no regard for the past and the future of a people. Once he is sorted in terms of "law" before the State, the individual is *solutus*, he can do whatever he wants. In the racist conception of right, on the other hand, which is supposed to have been effective in the ancient Teutons, the point of departure is the individual conceived not in himself, but as the member of a community and the ring of a descendance. The interest not of the individual, but precisely of this community ethnically defined, which gives to itself its own laws and wishes to maintain itself, to continue itself through time, and to strengthen itself, here becomes the true criterion for justice and injustice, legitimate and illegitimate. Teutonic racist right, contrasted with Roman, presents therefore a manifestly "social" characteristic. And its laws, or better say, its intuitions, by their nature and origin, would be valid only for a determinate people, would be unsusceptible of generalization and of universalization. Only those who have equal blood would naturally have equal rights. Finally, since by this conception, law is not something transmitted as an exterior discipline, but rather as a patrimony inherent to the blood and with the blood transmitting itself, "not just anyone can know right, but only he who is of pure race, who has been generated through a straightforward union of parents of the same kind, whose descendants have remained pure of any intermixing." Nicolai moreover is among those who are convinced that there is only a single truly pure race, the Arya race, whence he draws this singular but still consistent conclusion: "Law can be known, posited, disclosed, and pronounced, only by the Arya man, by the Nordic man. He alone can be judge, legislator, and ruler of the society of his people." From here also a direct connection to eugenics and to racial hygiene. To obtain a new German juridical conscience, new studies and new theories are not the way: it is sufficient to circumscribe the German people, isolate it, de-Judaize it, to systematically reintegrate in it the blood in Nordic-Aryan sense, and thus from this regenerated blood, this blood returned to purity, the innate German virtues will be redeemed which are now suppressed, and the right juridical sense, appropriate to the race, will automatically establish itself. The problem is therefore more or less a problem from the biological laboratory, or from a racial breeding operation.

More recently, Falk RUTTKE has specified in the following way the point of view of racist law:

> The point of departure is not the defense of the race by means of the law, but rather the defense and strengthening of order connected to the blood. Toward this end, it is necessary to adopt certain measures, first of all, so that the law is connected to the racial idea, and a juridical doctrine is created which is founded on the laws of race; in the second place, so that in the constitution of law and in its application the care of heredity and racial hygiene stand at the center of all the provisions; thirdly, so that legislators of racial quality are presupposed by the juridical order, itself conforming to race; and finally, so that the constitution and the application of the law are accompanied by a continuous education of the people in matters of racism and of heredity by means of a vision of the world based on the idea of race as the formative-educative idea, connected to an intimate sentiment of responsibility.[3]

---

3   I have had to translate Ruttke's quotations, too, from Evola's Italian.

The biological intonation of the views of this author are evident in his idea, that "only that juridical order, which is not in contradiction with the results of research in matters of race and heredity can be considered 'just' and fitting to the nature proper [*artgemäss*] of the German people." Whoever knows however precisely what a margin of uncertainty yet exists in that scientific research of a bio-racial order to which Ruttke here refers, supposing one only considers *all* the truly efficient elements in a human being, will see also that one cannot limit oneself to such simplistic ideas, and that only in a superior conception, attuned "traditionally" rather that scientistically, can the just needs contained in this battle for an antiformalistic and organic law be truly brought to count for something and to act positively.

Rosenberg writes: "Being rooted in an organic totality, the idea of duty, the vital reference, is that all this characterises the German concept of law, and all this springs from a centre of will."[4] According to the Teutonic idea, he has "right" whose honor is intact. In its turn, according to a saying of the *Saxon Code* "every honor comes from fidelity": fidelity with respect to one's own gods, one's own forebears, one's own blood and above all to the proper duties that each individual has before his community, within which this community can subsist and develop, says Nicolai. Whoever proves his "fidelity" and his "honor" participates in right, and has the "liberty" to exercise it. Thus, as a third principle to that of honor and fidelity, liberty — and here, new polemical lines against oppressive imperialisms and the denaturalization of peoples. Imperialism for Nicolai too is foreign to the German nature, and to the German conception of right, so much so that even politically the most Teutonic constitution was the federal constitution, with its partial autonomies aimed toward protecting the factor of "liberty" within the nation (autonomies which however in Germany today have been abolished by the new totalitarian Nazi legislation — something which Nicolai does not mention). Indeed, as a fourth element after honor, fidelity, and liberty, we have the juridical principle of "struggle," precisely for the defense and the affirmation of natural

---

4   *Myth*, Book III, Chapter IV.

right, which here is identified with the will of a given ethnic group to exist and to continue to exist through time. But in this connection Nicolai recognizes that before a weaker race, the stronger has the right to demand that it clears the field and abandons those lands which were necessary for the conditions of life of its descendants. Up to what point this "juridical" principle, which assumes the guise of "right to life" and openly throws contempt on the paralyzing network of abstract "international law," is reconcilable with the anti-imperialistic pretense of the Nordic nature, is something which is rather difficult to see. It is clear that here we are dealing with positions which are just in their exigencies, but which have not been thought through very well, and which moreover the development of recent events has decided to rectify. Once again, one willfully forgets that part that, not an "imperialistic" idea, but an imperial one has had in the very best German tradition.

✦

Through these ideologies the racist devaluation of the State, which we have already revealed, is confirmed, and also its devaluation of the ethical and juridical value of this State — as logical consequence, moreover, of certain optimistic-naturalistic premises: indeed, wherever a people or a race is conceived as entirely gifted with its own rationality and capable of a direct appreciation of ethical and social values, it is evident that the function of the State in its organizing, educating, and dominating function from on high, must be more or less disowned. And once again a meeting point between racism and Socialism is verified, even if it be as "national" Socialism: an armed community which wishes to be free, which at bottom does not tolerate any hierarchy, which is united in its exploitation of common goods, which posits the group before the individual and gives to itself its own laws according to the exigencies of its life. Thus, we hear the declaration: "The State does not create law, but formulates it only, administrates it, expresses in the form of the law that which is recognized as right, and whose origins stand however in the consciousness of the race." The distinction between positive and customary law is removed and conducted to a simple distinction of degrees, of clarification and formula-tion, "because the justice of law, the separation between legitimate and arbitrary law, must not be understood according to the letter of the law, but rather according to the biological-German principle of the adequacy of the conditions of existence of the race" (Nicolai). The essential task of the state is related to the aforementioned prophylactic action and to racial hygiene, and the juridical concept itself of penalty is justified, more or less, on such a basis. "Punishment is not an educative method, as our humani-tarian apostles wish us to believe. Punishment is simply the elimination of foreign elements and of heterogeneous natures. A man who does not consider his people and the honor of his people as the supreme value, has lost the right to be protected by this people." More particularly, the penal concept seems to comprehend two aspects: according to the first, attempt is made to conduct each crime back to a betrayal, to an infraction of the duty to fidelity with respect to the community ethnically defined, an infraction which renders the criminal unworthy, devoid of every right, and which banishes him. According to the other aspect, the delinquent is a failed type, inferior, degenerate, which a race, especially in inevitable intermixings, often produces, and which in name of the existence of a race should be eliminated or treated in such a way as to impede his exercise of any given action which might be collectively or hereditarily injurious.

This means that from a purely "ethical" conception of crime, which is a "social" contamination of that which, as the principle of "fidelity" — *fi-des* — might even have value in a very different society, in a feudal society, one passes to a purely "biological" conception, without arriving at a properly "juridical" conception. So soon as the purity of race has been reconditioned, one holds that every perturbation of the ethical conscience will necessarily thus be overcome. For which it remains to us to turn to the consideration of the new Nazi legislation created toward this end, that is, toward the protection of the race.

CHAPTER XI

The New Racist
Legislation

The Nazi law on hiring. The interdiction of mixed couples.
The interdiction on the Jews. Laws on racial hygiene.
Sterilization and castration.

BEFORE ANYTHING, what is the race, properly speaking, that
should be protected? For in fact the racists openly recognize that
"no European people is racially pure, not even the German." But
amongst the various races present in the German people, it is thought the
Nordic race, more than any other, has given form to German civilization.
"Even those realms wherein the Nordic race is pure today only in certain
cases, find in the Nordic race their fundamental basis. German means
Nordic, and this quality has acted in the creation of types and of civilizations amongst the Western, Dinaric, Baltico-Eastern races. Even the predominately Dinaric types have been internally formed in a Nordic way."
The primacy thus given to race should not however throw into Germany
the seeds of racial hatred, but should rather carry us to the recognition
of a "pureblood" cement for the various elements of the nation. Racial

culture will signify therefore above all "protection of the elements of the Nordic race present in our people. A German State takes as its first duty the creation of laws corresponding to this fundamental exigency."

Thus, in theory. In practice, as moreover in the concept of HITLER himself—notwithstanding certain attempts at an interracial selection and, also, a politics proper to special organizations, such as the SS, or to centers, such as the *Ordensburgen* and the *Nationalpolitische Erziehungsanstalte*—one has upheld the widest and most indeterminate idea of the "Arya race," defined essentially by exclusion: whoever is not a Jew nor of a colored race is generally considered "Arya."

This has brought the introduction of the racial element as a definition of the juridical condition of the people in the German State. In this connection, Paragraph 4 of the initial program of the Nazi Party has been adopted, which distinguished, on a biological basis, the true and proper citizen (*Reichsbürger*) from he who "belongs to the State" (*Staatsangehöriger*) in these terms: "Only a member of the race can be a citizen. A member of the race [or ancestry-companion: *Volksgenosse*] can only be one who is of German blood, without consideration of creed. Consequently, no Jew can be a member of the race." The conception of "belonging to the State" is rather only juridical: it refers to all those who are connected by a bond of belonging to the *Reich* without necessarily being of German blood or kin, and who ask therefore the condition of fidelity to the race-people and to the State.

Only the *Volkgenosse*, the "ancestry-companion," or member of the race-people, truly enjoys all civil and political rights. This, once more, corresponds to a point of the originating Nazi program — to Point 6, in which it is written, "The right to determine matters concerning administration and law belongs only to the citizen. Therefore, we demand that every public office, of any sort whatsoever, whether in the Reich, the county or municipality, be filled only by citizens." There is thus a discrimination of dignity on the basis of blood.

The biological condition to be completely a "citizen" and not merely a member of the *Reich* is to not have in one's ancestors, for three generations,

Jewish blood or other non-Arya blood. This same condition, from the point of view of the laws on heredity, would seem strictly insufficient, because according to such laws the effects of intermixings beyond the third generation would be left equally to make themselves felt. Nonetheless, it is to be observed that returning back to the third generation, one arrives at a time in which the Jews were not yet emancipated, and in which the mixed couples were exceedingly rare, for which it is held to be plausible that whoever up to that time was in good standing with race, had been so also previously.

The Jew and, in general, the non-Arya, is rather considered to be whoever descends from four Jewish or non-Arya forebears, from three forebears of such a kind and from one Aryan forebear, or, yet again, from two non-Arya forebears and two Arya forebears; these last, however, individually, having belonged to the Jewish religion on 16 October 1935 or after, or having been shown at that date, or after, married to a person of Jewish race. Moreover, he is considered Jewish who is born by extra-marital union with Jews, or who is born by successive unions of persons who at that date belonged to the Jewish community or were married with Jews or non-Arya. Thereafter the concept of *mixed being* (*Mischling*) is defined: in the first degree, if two ancestors are non-Arya; in the second degree, if only one in four is. Jews and non-Arya and "mixed breeds" — *Mischlinge* — can only belong to the State with limited rights. For these "mixed beings" there is however a graduation of rights. Moreover, certain exceptions are contemplated for reasons of State: respecting those who have special merits before the *Reich* — whence the curious qualification of *Ehrenarier*, or "honorary Arya," which however strictly should have as its counterpart that of *Ehrenjuden*, "honorary Jews," to be applied to many whom, "Arya" in their bodily race, are but little Arya in their character or spirit. These concepts having been defined, a series of laws inspired by them have been issued, and above all a law on the employees of the State, functionaries, professors, etc. This law stipulates that the non-Arya, those who in short do not enjoy the full qualification of "ancestry-companion," are without exception made redundant. A further stipulation has brought the adoption of the same provision with respect to those who, though Arya, have married or, at a given moment, would marry a member of a non-Arya race. Before the case of a *fait accomplis*, that is of a functionary, professor, official, etc., who already before the racial laws was married with a non-Arya element, the alternative is given to either divorce or to lose the position in question. Originally, certain exceptions were made with respect to combatant non-Aryans or to relatives of combatants fallen in the World War. Other exceptions can be made by the Minister of Internal Affairs, through a specialized office, with respect to functionaries abroad. In both cases, an essentially discretionary criterion holds.

With these laws, the intention is therefore to isolate a pure "Aryan" substance at the center of the State. It is ever brought into relief that in the consideration of whether a person is of Arya character or not, "no given religious faith nor name is any longer decisive, but solely heredity and descendance, that is, belonging to a given race." A further ordinance, dating to 14 November 1935, is intended to protect "the German blood and honor," with an intervention now in the sphere of private right itself: every marriage and even every extra-conjugal sexual relationship between "ancestry-companions" and non-Arya is forbidden. It is a little curious that in this connection not the least distinction between man and woman is made. That is to say, an equal right is conceived — in contrast to the view of the ancient Arya traditions — and an equal power of race in man and woman.

New laws have gradually extended the provisions of exclusion from the properly political sphere, and that of the free professions, of the press, of private teaching itself. A particular disarray has occurred in the application of the "Arya clause" in the religious field, both Catholic and Protestant. By force of this clause, the pastors and the other exponents of the two Churches who in their ancestry up to the third generation Jewish or non-Arya blood should not be recognized in their capacities, and should be impeded in their functions. For the Protestants, this represents however a manifest and unacceptable violation of Article 3 of

the profession of Lutheran faith;[1] for Catholics, worse yet, the violation
of the fundamental equality of all creatures with respect to God, and of
the super-racial character of the priesthood, which is legitimate solely in
function of a sacrament. The agitation in this field is yet severe. The only
ones to accept the new law without hesitation are the so-called Christian-
Germans, who have voted for certain laws, and who have created ten
bishops Prussia dependent on the central bishop of the Reich, who is held
to swear to the Head of the State, that is, presently, to Hitler.

It must be observed that in the racist action, and above all in the
anti-Jewish action, brought not only on the organs of the State, but on
every domain of the public German life, these legally defined provisions
are prolonged in political measures and in interventions which are now
direct and now indirect, varying on a case by case basis, and devoid of
a precise juridical basis. For example, Judaism in Germany was strongly
represented in high capitalism and in high industry. In order to act "legally" here, National Socialism would have had to confront the problem of
private right in general and, in particular, of property and of private initiative. In reality, certain extremists in this connection invoked a "second
revolutionary wave" — we ourselves have mentioned certain writers, such
as Dyrssen, who have spoken of the "anti-Western" message (the West is
here identified with the Atlantic capitalistic nations) which Bolshevism
might represent for "Prussian socialism," whence to definitively liberate
Germany from the yoke of capitalism and from the surviving traces of
economic liberalism. But all this has not been strong enough to determine
an official extremist legislation. One has thus had to make do, reaching
the same result by other routes, essentially political routes through either
direct or indirect action, without fully confronting the doctrinal problem
and radically resolving it. In schools, while at first one limited oneself to
restricting the number of non-Arya pupils to a given percentage of the
total number, in succession one proceeded to a separation, arranging for
the non-Arya to have their own non-Arya schools, which are therefore

---

1   Namely, that article which stipulates that Jesus Christ alone can bring a reconcilia-
    tion of humanity with God.

separate from the Arya schoolchildren. The same development has been seen with respect to the free professions — doctors, lawyers, etc. At first, a *numerus clausus* was adopted, which amounts to saying a given percentage which cannot be superseded of non-Arya professionals, to repulse the parasitical invasion that these had effected; then later, it has been arranged that whoever is fully Jewish or non-Arya can exercise his profession only with respect to persons of his own race.

A further stipulation, connected to those already indicated, prohibits the changing of names. One of the means for recognizing the Jews in Germany is furnished precisely by their name, and the substitution of Jewish names with German names was one of the preferred and most widely used routes of the Jews to hide their origin and to silently penetrate into German milieus.

We now turn to the second branch of Nazi legislation, that which regards the preservation of race from the point of view of heredity (eugenics or racial hygiene).

It is significant that tendencies of this kind have an *American* origin. Francis GALTON (1822–1922) is considered the father of "eugenics," and precedents to the relevant Nazi legislation are to be found above all in certain aspects of the United States, connected to certain movements, the best known of which is anti-alcoholic prohibitionism. Theoretically, the premises of this legislation are anti-individualistic and anti-humanitarian. It refuses to consider the single human being as a simple individual or even as a simple citizen, but rather it recognizes in him the carrier of determinate hereditary qualities, that the State has the right to consider in view of the future good of the collective. It is contested that the assistance of the State should extend itself indiscriminately to all the elements that compose it. In all systems of welfare, it happens that the healthiest and most capable part pays contributions to sustain, maintain, and reproduce the weak and the minorities, with the result that this work is harmful for the whole. The sentiment of pity and of humanity favor and sustain the worst elements, sick, inadequate, and delinquent heirs; and one does not realize the responsibility which the descendance of every man puts upon him, of the right to concentrate every resource toward the end of the preservation and the development of healthy elements, which are themselves the true exponents of a nation. GÜNTHER, who here takes up the "selectionist" theses of DE LAPOUGE, recalls a phrase of NIETZSCHE's: "That which is falling should also be pushed,"[2] and adds: "It is certain that a legislation intoned in this hard spirit contributes more to the health of a people, than a legislation which always and only cares for individuals, and even individuals who are hereditarily compromised." Here racism distinguishes between "the right to life" and "the right to give life": everyone has the right to life. The right to give life on the other hand is not given to him from whom one can positively expect a deranged and invalid descendant, destined to further adulterate the healthy part of the race. These ideas therefore inspire a part of the Nazi legislation, that which has caused the greatest uproar in the world, particularly in intellectual and religious circles. We are speaking of two laws, one on "sterilization" and the other on "castration." The first, issued the 4 July 1933, shows before all that the interdiction on the right to give life, that is to reproduce, does not correspond to a penal point of view, but only a hygienic-social one, as a sick heir is not considered a wrongdoer. To be a sick heir is not a shame; that which offends the ethic racist sense is only the sick heir's condemnation, by way of his own irresponsibility, of future generations. This, in official declarations. Philosophically we have however but recently seen that from a rigorous racist point of view ethic concepts are brought back to biological bases, and thus it becomes difficult to draw a neat division between the racially infirm and the guilty, at least in the sense that ethnic degeneration is conceived of as the basis of the loss of every healthy moral principle.

The text of the law is: "Whoever has hereditary illnesses may be rendered sterile with a surgical operation, if from the data of the medical science it can be expected with the greatest likelihood that also his descendants will suffer from grave hereditary defects of body or psyche. Hereditarily infirm in the terms of the law is to be considered whoever suffers from one of the following illnesses: congenital disability,

---

2   Taken from *Thus Spake Zarathustra*, Third Part, "The Old and the New Tablets."

schizophrenia, manic depression, epilepsy, hereditary chorea, hereditary deafness and blindness, grave hereditary physical deformities. Beyond which whoever exhibits advanced alcoholism can be rendered sterile." The presupposition for the application of the law is that "the illness is indisputably verified by a doctor approved by the *Reich*, even on the basis of a transient appearance of its hidden roots." In its application, the law does not restrict itself to those cases in which the infirm spontaneously request to be sterilized, although this is the case which most corresponds to the spirit of the law. The compulsory operation is not mandated: either in the infirm whose age excludes the possibility of reproduction, or in the inform who are permanently committed to sick houses, or in the infirm who by their own will and at their own expense permit themselves to be isolated in institutions of the kind in order to avoid sterilization. The law includes various stipulations to prevent abuses, admits revisions of the doctor's verdict, and assures the secrecy of the sterilization operation, so that the infirm need not feel any social harm from it. On the basis of the most recent statistics, it would appear that in Germany the law will be applied in some 412,500 cases.

It seems that the operation of sterilization is executed in such a way as to impede generation, but not the capacity for a sterile sexual union. This capacity is not removed save in those cases which fall under a second law, promulgated 24 November 1933, which contemplates the possibility of compulsory castration in the cases of dangerous habitual delinquency of a sexual nature, that is of delinquents who can be impeded in their abnormality, and so made inoffensive, only through the annulment of their sexual capacity. If the delinquent does not belong to this specifically sexually dangerous type, but is only ill in the sense of the law against morbose heredity, is treated following this law and, after the opinion if a eugenic-penal tribunal, undergoes only sterilization. For the execution of these laws, on behalf of the various political judiciary and administrative authorities, in every city and in every community the Nazi Regime has instituted designated offices for hygiene and for the protection of the race. With all these measures, racism passes therefore from theory to practice.

It plans little by little to exclude all extraneous elements, and, by elimination through selection, to reintegrate the race from a purely qualitative point of view, to the maximum health and purity, so as to establish contact with the originating forces of the Aryan blood. By adopting these ideas, National Socialism believes it has made of Germany the model from which all the peoples who yet conserve a healthy ethnic instinct should take inspiration. VON LEERS writes:

> In contrast to the history of all the other peoples of Nordic lineage, the German people has for the first time acquired a clear knowledge of race and of the destiny of race. It has scientifically verified for the first time the significance of race which — beginning from PLATO — has never been understood by any other people, neither by the Greeks, nor by the Romans [?]. After the periods of decadence and of intermixing, now a period of purification and formation is announced, which will give life to a new age of the world. Universal history does not proceed in a straight line, but along a curved line: from the age of the great primordial Nordic civilization to the age of the tombs of stone, we have descended into the deep vales of centuries of decomposition, to rise again to new heights. This will not be abandoned, but indeed — and not only for the material goods of life — it will become ever more significant; for that which we before had not yet seen, we now have gained with full knowledge: the importance of the soul of race, the non-repeatability of the race created by God as a biological and psychic reality.[3]

---

3   Translated once more from Evola's Italian.

CHAPTER XII

The Racism of Adolf Hitler

The Nazi vision of the world. The Aryan theses. The Nazi
conception of the State. State and race. The new Nazi education.
The myth of the future.

BY NOW ALL THE CONSTITUTIVE ELEMENTS of the racist theory,
beginning from its most distant antecedents, are known to the
reader. In conformity with the proposal of the present book, we
will yet consider only a single point, in which various of the motifs we
have already discussed are reunited to take on a meaning predominately
as myth, and now a "political" myth — as constituted by the conception of
Adolf HITLER.

Turning therefore to the exposition of Hitler's racist idea, we will limit
ourselves to literally reproducing its most significant expressions, not only
on account of our desire to restrict ourselves here to a purely objective exposition, but also because, considering that which we have so far learned,
there is almost nothing new, and that which therefore might interest us
is above all the form, the *pathos*. Here the motifs already known present

themselves again, and become the elements of a political creed. So far as the individual genesis of the racist idea in Hitler, it seems that it derives from an instinctive reaction which he experienced in the face of the ethnic mix of Vienna — at least in certain classes that he must above all have frequented, gathering elements of disparate and often spurious races, side by side with a strong influence of the Jewish element.

Let us begin by defining the meaning and the scope which racism has for Hitler. Racism is for him an inseparable and central part of a "vision of the world," of the National Socialistic vision of the world. To whatever is part of this "vision of the world" in his movement, the characteristics an immutable and infallible dogma are conferred. "[A] Weltanschauung," Hitler states, "is intolerant and cannot permit another to exist side by side with it. It imperiously demands its own recognition as unique and exclusive, and insists upon a complete reformation of public life in all its branches, in accordance with its views."[1] "Political parties are prone to make compromises, but a Weltanschauung never does this. A political party even reckons with opponents, but a Weltanschauung proclaims its own infallibility."[2] All of which comes therefore to be applied to racism, which Hitler professes. Regarding his principal work, wherein this racism finds expression, and from which now we will principally draw our quotations — *Mein Kampf*, that is, *My Struggle* — the official agency of the Nazi party expresses itself thus: "It contains for the present and for the future the definitive principles of the National Socialistic conception. It constitutes the very essence of that conception, and must become the Bible of the German people." The fundamental premise of racism in Hitler is presented almost in the form of theological predestination: Providence desires that men not be equal, it has predetermined a plurality of races and has fixed them with gifts and special characteristics which cannot be altered without incurring degeneration and decadence. The soil, in and of itself, has little influence: the scarce fertility of one and the same soil,

---

1   All quotations are taken from *Mein Kampf* (Ostara Publications). The present quotation is found in Volume Two, Chapter V, p. 512.

2   Volume II, Chapter V, p. 513.

while it presses a more gifted race to superior creations, to hard labor and conquest, can produce the impoverishment and misery of another. The fall of civilizations is due to cross-breeding which poisons the blood of the races that have created them. Such crossbreeding has two consequences:

1) A lowering of the level in the higher race.

2) A devolution both corporeal and spiritual, and thus the beginning of a slow but sure process of deterioration.

To accommodate such a thing, for Hitler, means nothing but "to sin against the will of the Eternal Creator," who expresses himself in the eternal laws of nature.

If one proposes the objection, "But it is precisely man who overcomes nature!" Hitler indicts this view as an "insolent objection, which is Jewish in its inspiration and is typical of the modern pacifist."[3] Before all — according to him — man has "overcome" nature in nothing, but at most has succeeded in mending some miserable scrap of the veil; he does not create, but only discovers the laws of nature, and only by obeying these laws does he dominate. Only the infantile presumption of certain mad ideologues, for Hitler, has made us forget the incommensurable epochs in which our planet has traversed the ether without men, obeying only iron natural laws. In the second place, after this recognition of typically "scientistic" ideas, Hitler observes that, the idea of "overcoming" is an idea like any other, which beyond the human mind has not existence, and which therefore, as all ideas, does not arise accidentally, but is part of the human constitution, of a temperament, in short of something conditioned by the laws of nature. Finally, Hitler, who here however does not speak any longer of overcoming, but simply of the pacifistic-humanitarian idea supposed in whomever makes the objection, says that such an idea could even have the possibility of realization, but only when a unique superior humanity has been made the unique dominator of the world: thus first difference, battle and victory, then, "perhaps," the rest.

---

3   Volume I, Chapter XI, p. 319.

After which, Hitler declares that "All that we admire in the world to-day, its Science and its art, its technical developments and discoveries, are the products of the Creative activities of a few peoples, and it may be true that their first beginnings must be attributed to one race. The existence of civilisation is wholly dependent on such peoples. Should they perish, all that makes this earth beautiful will descend with them into the grave."[4] The entirety of human progress is conditioned on the victorious march of the highest race. This is the Arya race. The Arya is the ideal archetype of that which we intend when we say "human." "He is the Prometheus of mankind, from whose shining brow the divine spark of genius has at all times flashed forth, always kindling anew that fire which, in the form of knowledge, illuminated the dark night by drawing aside the veil of mystery and thus showing man how to rise and become master over all the other beings on the earth."

Hitler, developing the ideas of CHAMBERLAIN, distinguishes between three species of races: races that "create" a civilization, races that "carry" a civilization, and races "destructive" of civilization. The first case exclusively concerns the Arya races. The Arya races have ever posited themselves the task of "a creative synthesis between the innate idea of race and the material conditions that impose themselves on this, up to the point of a crystalline conformity of end [*einer kristallklar erfüllten Zweckmässigkeit*]."[5] The second case is that of races which simply assume the civilization that the Arya have created and diffused, as, for example, is the case of those peoples of color which "Europeanize" themselves. Finally, as the prototype of a race incapable of its own civilization, and thus destructive of civilization, the Jewish race is indicated, as a parasitical and disintegrating race. The superiority of the Arya over the non-Arya more than in any other gift resides, according to Hitler, in his capacity to put all his aptitudes to the service of the community, insofar as in him the instinct of conservation idealizes and depersonalizes itself, assuming a heroic character, and

---

4   Volume I, Chapter XI, p. 322. The next quotation is from the same page.

5   I was unable to find the source of this quotation; Evola has included a portion of the German for anyone who is interested.

the I is ready to willingly subordinate itself and even to sacrifice itself, if necessary, for the good of the collective. Naturally, such a conception of the nature of the Arya is rather one-sided and appears evidently dictated by certain political National Socialistic ends which Hitler had predetermined. In the Jew, the social sense is according to Hitler only apparent, for he is substantially a vulgar egoist; his solidarity, taking its inspiration from a primitive herd instinct, lasts only so long as the common danger lasts. The Jews are not united save when and where they feel menaced, or else interested in a common profit: if they were alone in the world, "they would eat each other alive."

All this regards the general premises contained in the first part of Hitler's book. In the second part before all the conception of the deleterious effects of every cross-breeding makes its appearance:

> At all critical moments in which a person of pure racial blood makes correct decisions, that is to say, decisions that are coherent and uniform, the person of mixed blood will become confused and take half-measures.

> Hence we see that a person of mixed blood is not only relatively inferior to a person of pure blood, but is also doomed to become extinct more rapidly.

> In innumerable cases where the pure race holds its ground, the mongrel breaks down. Therein we see the corrective measures adopted by Nature; she restricts the possibilities of procreation, thus impeding the fertility of cross-breeds and dooming them to extinction.

> For instance, if an individual member of a race should mingle his blood with the member of a superior race, the first result would be a lowering of the racial level, and furthermore, the issue of this mixed marriage would be weaker than those of the people around them who had maintained their blood unadulterated.

> Where no new blood from the superior race enters the racial stream of the mongrels, and where these mongrels continue to cross-breed among themselves, the latter will either die out because they have insufficient powers of resistance.[6]

---

6   Volume Two, Chapter II, pp. 448–449. All quotations in the following paragraph are taken from the page after, save the last, which comes from Volume Two, Chapter X, p. 633.

Here the transcription of the Mendelian law on dehybridization is quite visible, and here we find the theoretical presuppositions of the entire praxis of "racial hygiene" and of the interdiction on mixed marriages. Removing the barriers of race so far as to overwhelm the last remains of the superior pure quality, one would obtain a mush: "One can breed a herd of animals, but from a mixture of this kind, men such as have created and founded civilisations would not be produced. The mission of humanity might then be considered at an end." In truth, the image chosen by Hitler here is but little fitting, because if there is a field in which already for a long time the principle of the culture of "pure" races has been efficaciously applied, it is precisely the domain of the animals, that of herd animals included. Hitler continues: "But there is only one right that is sacrosanct and that right is at the same time a most sacred duty, namely, to protect racial purity so that the best types of human beings may be preserved and thus render possible a more noble development of humanity itself." Rather than following certain commandments of the Church and certain views, for example those which result in the celibate priest, it is necessary to "actually fulfill the Will of God and do not allow His handiwork to be debarred, for it was by the Will of God that man was created in a certain image and endowed with certain characteristics and certain faculties."

The National Socialistic revolution is not a reaction. "We had no wish to resurrect from the dead the old Reich which had been ruined through its own blunders, but to build up a new State."[7] The new State is the national-racist State.

> The current political conception of the world is that the State, though it possesses a Creative force which can build up civilisations, has nothing in common with the concept of race as the foundation of the State.
>
> The State is considered rather as something which has resulted from economic necessity or is, at best, the natural outcome of political urge for power.

---

7   Volume Two, Chapter VII, p. 557.

> Such a conception together with all its logical consequences, not only ignores the primordial racial forces that underlie the State, but it also leads to a minimization of the importance of the individual.[8]

And international Marxism is nothing but the result of the translation in a specific political faith, in the world of the Jew Karl MARX, of a reality which has long existed. Marx "in a world already in a state of gradual decomposition, he used the unerring instinct of the prophetic genius to detect the essential poisons, so as to extract them and concentrate them, with the art of an alchemist, in a solution which would bring about the rapid destruction of the independent nations of the earth. All this was done in the Service of his race."

The national-racist conception of the State "recognizes the value of humanity on the basis of its originating racial elements." According to it, or better say, according to its ideal, *nation and race are one and the same thing*; it is race which, in normal circumstances, composes the nation, posited as something homogeneous, equal to itself. The State "is a community of living beings who have kindred physical and spiritual natures, organised for the purpose of ensuring the Conservation of their own kind and fulfilling those ends which Providence has assigned to that particular race or racial branch,"[9] and thus also in the nation. Having rejected the idea of the equal value of the races, "[o]n the basis of this recognition it feels bound, in conformity with the Eternal Will that dominates the universe, to postulate the victory of the better and stronger and the Subordination of the inferior and weaker thus subscribing to Nature's fundamental aristocratic principle and it believes that this law holds good even down to the last individual organism."[10] "The *völkisch* Weltanschauung differs fundamentally from the Marxist by reason of the fact that the former recognises the significance of race and therefore also of personal worth and has made these the pillars of its structure."[11]

---

8   Volume Two, Chapter I, p. 426. The subsequent quotation comes from the page after.

9   Volume One, Chapter IV, p. 168.

10 Volume Two, Chapter I, p. 427.

11 Volume Two, Chapter IV, p. 505.

Therefore, for Hitler,

> The fundamental principle is that the State is not an end in itself, but the means
> to an end. It is the preliminary condition for the development of a higher form
> of human civilisation, but not the reason for such a development, for which a
> culturally Creative race is alone responsible.

> There may be hundreds of excellent States on this earth and yet if the Aryan,
> who is the creator and Custodian of civilisation, should disappear, all culture
> corresponding to the spiritual needs of the superior nations to-day would also
> disappear.[12]

"We must make a clear-cut distinction between the vessel and its contents.
The State is only the vessel and the race is what it contains," continues
Hitler in clarifying his idea. "The vessel can have significance only if it
preserves and safeguards the contents. Otherwise it is worthless." The
supreme purpose of the national State is therefore "to guard and preserve
those racial elements which, through their work in the cultural field, create
that beauty and dignity which are characteristic of a higher mankind." On
the contrary, a State is said to not conform to its mission and to be a bad
State when, "in spite of the existence of a high cultural level, it dooms to
destruction the representatives of that culture by breaking up their racial
compositeness." And since this process of decadence is not immediately
visible, "the cultural level of a people is not the standard by which we can
judge the value of the State in which that people lives." The true criterion
is related rather to everything which furnishes a solid guarantee for the
rising of the Arya elements of a nation.

Even Hitler recognizes that Germany is not the expression of a single
pure racial stock. Various races are present, but "The process of welding
the original elements together has not gone so far as to warrant us in saying that a new race has emerged." The various elements have remained
rather in a state of simple coexistence. "Beside the Nordic type we find the
East-European type, beside the Eastern there is the Dinaric, the Western
type intermingling with both, and hybrids among them all. That is a grave

---

12   Volume Two, Chapter II, 439. The quotations in the following two paragraphs are all
      taken from the next pages, ending at page 446.

drawback to us. Through it the Germans lack that strong herd instinct which arises fr om unity of blood and saves nations from ruin in danger-ous and critical times, because on such occasions small differences disap-pear, and a united herd faces the enemy." From here, the work of national totalization on the racist basis which the Nazi government has resolutely begun, and which is even now underway. "As a State, the German Reich shall include all Germans. Its task is not only to gather in and fester the most valuable sections of our people, but to lead them slowly and surely to a dominant position in the world."

We are dealing therefore with the formation not of a ruling class in the usual sense, but rather of a "ruling racist nucleus," to be drown from the Teutonic conglomerate, and to be invested with every power and every decisive faculty. So far as the road to this end to this goes, according to the ideas presented by Hitler in his discourse, it would be defined as the power of "elective affinities." Even as the preaching of the Evangel of the international has attracted all the elements of decomposi-tion in the ethnic morass, "Jews, procurers, and sub-humans," and even as the preaching of the democratic ideal of prosperity has called to the gathering and has made the bourgeois class emerge, so the preaching of the doctrine of "Arya" heroism and of the right of blood will not fail to awaken those elements that are yet pure, bringing them to the fore-ground, permitting them to form the "ruling racist nucleus." A natural selection by means of vocation.

More generally, Hitler proposes to differentiate the whole of the ele-ments present in an Aryan nation and, in particular in Germany, accord-ing to three classes juridically defined as the "citizens of the *Reich*," the "members of the State," and the "foreigners" — which proposal has, as we have seen, been translated into reality. For him, it is a scandal that the con-sideration of race has for so long a time not been taken into account in the concept of citizenship; that the acquisition of citizenship "is not very dif-ferent from that of being admitted to membership of an automobile club": that is, that it has sufficed to make a request, so that, by the decision of a functionary, that is done "What God Himself could not do is achieved by some Theophrastus Paracelsus of a civil servant. A stroke of the pen, and a Mongolian slave is forthwith turned into a real 'German.'"[13] Racially heterogeneous elements should not live in a State other than as "foreigners." Birth should define only the status of being a "member of the State," which however does not yet give one the possibility of filling public offices nor of exercising political activity: for which the "member of the State" would be distinguished from the foreigner only because he does not belong, as this other does, to a State abroad. To become "citizens," true members of the *Reich*, a further verification would be necessary, based on the full consciousness of the race of the candidate, on his physical health and then on his loyalty, solemnly sworn and witnessed, to the Arya community and to the State. Only then might a "certificate of citizenship" be released, which would be "a bond which unites all the various classes and sections of the nation." Hitler does not hesitate to say that "[i]t must be regarded as a greater honor to be a Citizen of this Reich, even as a Street-sweeper, than to be the king of a foreign State." In which, a certain degradation of the idea of race becomes visible. According to the traditional views, only in the elites, in the aristocracies, is the true race manifested and realized.

Regarding the measures of racial hygiene, here are Hitler's ideas, from which these measures proceed: "A national State should before all bring marriage from the level of a constant outrage against race to the sacredness of an institution held to generate creatures made in the image of the Lord, and not abortions between man and monkey."[14] Every "humanitarian" or even religious protest against the consequences of these views is shunned by Hitler with the following words: "In this present State of ours, whose function it is to be the guardian of law and Order, our national bourgeoisie looks upon it as a crime to make procreation impossible for syphilitics and those who suffer from tuberculosis or hereditary diseases,

---

13 Volume Two, Chapter III, p. 493. The quotations at the end of this paragraph are from 495.

14 Volume Two, Chapter II, p. 450. The quotations following, up until the paragraph which begins "As has already been known," are taken from the subsequent pages if *Mein Kampf*, ending on p. 458.

and also for cripples and imbeciles. But the practical prevention of procreation among millions of our very best people is not considered an evil,
nor does it offend against the moral code of this hypocritical class." So far
as the Churches go,

> They talk about the Spirit, but they allow man, as the embodiment of the Spirit,
> to degenerate to the proletarian level. Then they gape with amazement when
> they realise how small is the influence of the Christian Faith in their own coun-
> try and how depraved and ungodly is this riff-raff which is physically degenerate
> and therefore morally degenerate also. To balance this state of affairs they try
> to convert the Hottentots, the Zulus and the Kaffirs and to bestow on them the
> blessings of the Church.
>
> While our European people, God be praised and thanked, are left to become the
> victims of moral depravity, the pious missionary goes out to Central Africa and
> establishes mission-stations for Negroes.
>
> Finally, sound and healthy though primitive and backward people will be
> transformed, in the name of our 'higher civilisation,' into a motley of lazy and
> brutalized mongrels.

Reacting to this, Hitler declares therefore that:

> In this field the *völkisch* State will have to repair the damage that has been
> caused by the fact that the problem is at present neglected by all the various
> parties concerned.
>
> It will be the task of the *völkisch* State to make the race the nucleus of the life
> of the community. It must make sure that the purity of the racial strain will
> be preserved.
>
> It must proclaim the truth that the child is the most valuable possession a nation
> can have.
>
> It must see to it that only those who are healthy beget children; that there is only
> one infamy, namely, for parents that are ill or show hereditary defects to bring
> children into the world and that in such cases it is a matter of honor to refrain
> from doing so.
>
> But, on the other hand, it must be considered as reprehensible to refrain from
> giving healthy children to the nation.

THE MYTH OF THE BLOOD

In this matter, the State must assert itself as the trustee of a millennial future, in the face of which the egotistic desires of the individual count for nothing and will have to give way before the ruling of the State.

In order to fulfil this duty in a practical manner the State will have to avail itself of modern medical discoveries. It must proclaim as unfit for procreation all those who are afflicted with some identifiable hereditary disease or are the carriers of it, and practical measures must be adopted to have such people rendered sterile.

On the other hand, Provision must be made for the normally fertile woman so that she will not be restricted in child-bearing through the financial and economic conditions obtaining under a regime which makes the having of children a curse to parents.

And Hitler does not hesitate to prophesy that "If, throughout a period of not more than six hundred years, all physically degenerate or mentally defective persons were sterilized, humanity would not only be delivered from an immense misfortune, but also restored to a state of general health such as we at present can hardly imagine."

It is evident that in such an order of ideas particular salience is given to the physical part of the human being, and that the problem of character is considered to stand in close relation to it:

Just as, in general, racial quality is the preliminary condition for the mental efficiency of any given human material, the training, of the individual will first of all have to be directed towards the development of sound bodily health, for the general rule is that a strong and healthy mind is found only in a strong and healthy body.

The fact that men of genius are sometimes not robust in health and stature, and are even of a sickly Constitution, is no proof of the falsity of the principle I have enunciated.

These cases are only exceptions which, as everywhere else, prove the rule. But when the bulk of a nation is composed of physical degenerates it is rare for a great man to arise from such a miserable motley, and in any case his activities would never meet with great success.

A degenerate mob will either be incapable of understanding him at all or their will-power will be so feeble that they cannot follow the soaring flight of such an eagle.

For which in the Hitlerian State, "will first of all have to base its educational work not on the mere imparting of knowledge, but rather on physical training and the development of healthy bodies." Only after, and subordinately, will the intellectual faculties be developed. And at the apex of development character should be placed, strength of will and of decision should be favored, for education should instill the joy in responsibility. Lastly, "scientific education" will come, since:

> A person whose formal education in the Sciences is relatively small, but who is physically sound and robust, of a steadfast and honest character, ready and able to make decisions and endowed with strength of will, is a more useful member of the national community than a weakling who is scholarly and refined.

> A nation composed of learned men who are physically degenerate, or weak-willed and timid pacifists, is not capable of ensuring even its own existence on this earth.

Hitler does not fail to reclaim the Hellenic ideal: "What has made the Greek ideal of beauty immortal is the wonderful union of splendid physical beauty with nobility of mind and spirit." Such a reference suffers the limitation proper to that point of view which Hitler has phrased in clarion words: even if one aims at a synthesis and an integrated, "classical" ideal of humanity, it is thought that the true way which leads to such is to awaken the spirit by rendering the body healthy: it is not that according to which, by fortifying the spirit, health and vigor might follow, beyond also a superior meaning for the body. It should also be noted that Hitler, to land a blow with his antitheses, takes as his example the "scholar" or bloodless and pusillanimous intellectual, who offers him good game. But true spirituality has little to do with all that.

As has already been made known, the eternal enemy of the Arya man, the destroyer demon of his civilization, is the Jew. "The destructive activities of Judaism in different parts of the national body can be ascribed fimdamentally to the persistent Jewish efforts at undermining the importance of personality among the nations that are their hosts and, in place of personality, substituting the domination of the masses. The constructive principle of Aryan humanity is thus displaced by the

destructive principle of the Jews. They are the ferment of decomposition'
among nations and races and, in a broad sense, the wreckers of human
civilisation."[15] In this connection, not only Marxism is indicted, the
Marxist attempt to demoralize the personality in the name of whatever
belongs to number, mass, and economy: the Jew is also described as "the
chief agitator for the complete destruction of Germany. Whenever we
read of Germany being attacked in any part of the world the Jew is always
the instigator. In peace-time as well as during the War the Jewish-Marxist
stock-exchange press systematically stirred up hatred against Germany,
until one State after another abandoned its neutrality and placed itself at
the Service of the Allies in the World War, even against the real interests
of its own people."[16] The goal of Judaism was to Bolshevize Germany after
having brought it to its knees with the war of 1914–1918. Hitler, searching
for the point wherein the Jewish effort was concentrated before the new
war, located it in France:

> In England, and also in Italy, the contrast between the better kind of na-
> tive statesmanship and the policy of the Jewish financiers often becomes
> strikingly evident.
>
> Only in France does there exist to-day, in a greater degree than ever before, a
> profound harmony between the aims of the Stock Exchange, of the Jews who
> control it and those of a chauvinistic national policy.
>
> This identity of purpose constitutes an immense danger for Germany and it is for
> this very reason that France is, and will remain, by far her most dangerous enemy.
>
> The French nation, which is becoming more and more polluted by Negro blood,
> represents a menace to the existence of the white race in Europe, because it is
> bound up with the Jewish campaign for world domination. The contamination
> caused by the influx of Negroid blood on the Rhine, in the very heart of Europe,
> is in accord with the sadistic and perverse lust for vengeance on the part of the
> hereditary enemy of our people.
>
> This suits the purpose of the cool, calculating Jew, who would use this means
> of beginning a process of bastardisation in the very centre of the European

---

15   Volume Two, Chapter IV, p. 503.

16   Volume Two, Chapter VI, p. 538.

continent and, by infecting the white race with the blood of an inferior stock, destroy the foundations of its independent existence.

France's activities in Europe to-day [Hitler wrote when the Rhineland was still occupied], spurred on by the French lust for vengeance and systematically directed by the Jew, are a criminal attack upon the existence of the white races and will one day arouse against the French people a spirit of vengeance among a generation which will recognise racial pollution as the original sin of mankind.[17]

But the Jew acts not only from outside upon Germany, but also from within. That maneuver which determined the battle between the Catholics and the Protestants in Germany is owed, Hitler believes, to the Jews:

Anyhow, the Jew has attained his ends. Catholics and Protestants are fighting one another to their heart's content, while the enemy of Aryan humanity and of all Christendom is laughing up his sleeve.

Just as it was once possible to occupy the attention of the public for several years with the struggle between federalism and unification, wearing out its energy in this mutual friction, while the Jew trafficked in the freedom of the nation and sold our country to the masters of international high finance — so in our day he has succeeded again, this time by raising strife between the two German religious denominations, while the foundations on which both rest are being eaten away and destroyed through the poison injected by international and cosmopolitan Jewry.[18]

Hitler is uninterested in conflicts of the kind:

As regards the future of the world, it does not matter which of the two triumphs, the Catholic or the Protestant faith, but it does matter whether Aryan humanity survives or perishes. […] It is the sacred duty, particularly of those who adopt a patriotic attitude, to see to it that within the framework of their own particular denomination, they do not render mere lip-service to God, but actually fulfil the Will of God and do not allow His handiwork to be debarred, for it was by the Will of God that man was created in a certain image and endowed with certain characteristics and certain faculties.

---

17   Volume Two, Chapter XIII, p. 704.

18   Volume Two, Chapter X, p. 632. The following long quotation, and the fragments in the following short paragraph, are from page 633.

Whoever ruins the work of God, profaning "noble and unique creature who was given to the world as a gift of God's grace" — meaning the man of the Arya race — "wages war against God's creation and God's will."

The National Socialist hooked cross symbolizes precisely "the mission allotted to us — the struggle for the victory of Aryan mankind and at the same time the triumph of the ideal of Creative work which in itself is, and always will be, anti-Semitic."[19]

After having repeated that "On this planet of ours human culture and civilisation are indissolubly bound up with the presence of the Aryan," and that at the decline or the disappearance of the Arya "the dark shroud of a new barbaric era would enfold the earth,"[20] Hitler closes his book, saying, "A state which in this age of racial poisoning dedicates itself to the care of its best racial elements must some day become lord of the earth."[21] The State which today, more than all others, has risen from such consciousness, for Hitler is National Socialist Germany. He writes however that "The differences between the various peoples should not prevent us from recognising the community of race which unites them, on a higher plane."[22] "Greeks and Romans find themselves immediately so near to the Germans because they have their roots in a single fundamental race, for which reason the immortal creations of the ancient peoples exercised an attraction on their racially related descendants." And finally: "Roman history, along general lines, is, and will remain, the best teacher, not only for our own time, but also for the future."

---

19   Volume Two, Chapter VII, p. 561.

20   Volume Two, Chapter I, p. 428.

21   Volume Two, Chapter XV, p. 777.

22   Volume Two, Chapter II, p. 474. The closing quotation is taken from 473–474. I have not been able to find the source of the middle quotation: on 474 Hitler says, "A civilisation is fighting for its existence. It is a civilisation that is the product of thousands of years of historical development, and the Greek as well as the German forms part of it." This is, however, quite different from Evola's quotation.

Conclusion

IN A RECENT WORK, treating of the genesis of Racism, Guéydan de ROUSSEL and Bernard FAŸ have thought it possible to consider this doctrine as a chapter of humanism — of humanism, understood in the most generic sense as a conception of the world and of life, at the center of which stands essentially man. Faÿ in particular observes that, beginning from the Renaissance, the divinity which has most impressed man, has been humanity itself; in its time Masonry leveraged itself upon this sentiment, attributing to humanity itself as a mass a kind of divine character, fitted with the halo of "progress." The confused inclination to mix the two concepts of divinity and humanity has successively found various other expressions. Faÿ states that the inexorable anti-theist crusade of Bolshevik Russia but badly hides this same will to transfer veneration from the transcendent element to the human. But also in other totalitarian movements, according to him, signs of the same tendency are evident, even if however on another basis — for example, having in view humanity as the substance of a given nation, of a given lineage, or, precisely, as biological reality, as blood, as race.

Is this the final meaning of racism? It would be hazardous to affirm it, if one takes in view all the tendencies contained in this current. The interpretation just mentioned, moreover, in part fits a racism which, having an exclusively "scientific" character, in the modern, materialistic, and positivistic sense of the term, nonetheless departs the scientific field to promote a mysticism which is *sui generis*. As the object of "science" in that sense, race cannot be other than a simply biological reality, and racism a chapter of the "natural science of man," which amounts to saying a discipline of the same, which considers man more or less on the same plane as the other animal species, affecting indifference or contempt for all those other aspects in light of which the traditional disciplines had rather always considered the human being. If, beginning from *this* racism, one penetrates into the field of the political idea, in a superior sense, and of the spirit, certain false turns are forever possible, and, at most, one might come even to that inversion characteristic of "humanism" in general: meaning that route by way of which, even as one wishes to spiritualize matter, one ends with materializing the spirit.

But this is certainly not the case for *all* racism. As has already been indicated, already in GOBINEAU its fundamentally aristocratic origin is quite visible: it affirms itself as a reaction against the morass of democratic egalitarianism and against a materialistic and anti-qualitative climate, which, at bottom, is precisely the climate wherein scientism itself has developed: from which scientism, by a most curious inversion, racism, in other of its aspects, has however borrowed various of its arms, and in which it has had to seek its alibi. Now, it is entirely possible, in the whole of racism, to discriminate and isolate precisely the superior tendency just now mentioned, understanding it as a principle of revolt against an internationalistic, leveling, rationalistic and plebeian civilization, thus finding in the return to the idea of race and above all of superior race or over-race, presentiments of a recovery of a spiritual heritage which we have forgotten.

Indeed, already at the beginning of this book we have observed that, if there is a valid racism lying almost exclusively beneath the auspice of "myth," of a force-idea which is to be evaluated in the terms of practical action; and if there is another, whose meaning does not supersede the field of modern scientist investigations — still there is yet an idea of race which takes its inspiration from the origins, from our best traditions, in which — as we have said — one spoke little of race only because one was *of* race, because the consideration of the racial element was something natural in the custom and in the law of every superior class, so much so that even following it, to say "noble" and to say "of race" in the superior sense was more or less the same thing. Now, it is possible, in contemporary racism, to bring into relief precisely this element, and to see to it that it is *this* which gives tone to the remainder of the doctrine, even in its biological and anthropological appendices. And then, evidently, the meaning of racism will be quite different from that attributed to it by Faÿ and by de Roussel.

Wherever racism betrays rather only the humanistic-materialistic component, it can well happen that, in its extremist forms, its ideal place falls decidedly toward the end of a cycle: having lost the sense of metaphysical reality and of the divine element in man, Western civilization has passed on to consider man in and of himself, and, successively, to consider man as a simple animal species; by bringing him to race, it has proceeded to make of race — conditioned only biologically — a mysticism. But wherever racism betrays the other component, the aristocratic component, which, as we have recalled, exercised a specific influence on the first theories of the "masculine," "diurnal" and "active" races, and in the general myth of the Arya race and the Nordic-Arya dominator, the place of racism is quite another; it might fall at the beginning of a new reconstructive cycle. Though borrowing, as has been said, various arms from modern science, racism would then have the possibility of using these arms against the materialistic, democratic, rationalistic conception proper to the last phases of Western decadence. By affirming, against that conception, the value of blood, of tradition, of race, and by intending to re-establish differences and hierarchies, racism might have the meaning of restoration and of recovery of higher values.

In the present volume, we have set ourselves the task — as we have already announced — of presenting with the greatest objectivity the various motifs which, up to the advent of Germanic National Socialism, have nourished the racist current. It is in our other work, *Synthesis of the Doctrine of Race*, that we have taken a position before these various motifs, toward the end of specifying that formulation of racism which answers to the second possibility, to that of the idea of race as a positive and reconstructive idea, adhering to the best of our traditions. To that book we therefore refer that reader who desires points of reference for a critique, for the discrimination and the evaluation of the various views herein presented.

Index

Darré, Walter 147–148
Darwin, Charles R. 13, 30
d'Eichtal, Gustave 14–26
Demeter 134
Deniker, J. 94
de Roussel, William Guéydan 3–6, 201–203
de Vries de Heekelingen, E. 155
d'Olivet, Fabre 14, 34, 114
Donatello 41
Dostoevsky, Fyodor 99
Driesmans, Heinrich 43–47
Dühring, K. E. 157
Duns Scotus 55
Durkheim, E. 160
Dyrssen, Carl 148, 180

E

Eckhart, J. (Meister). *See* Meister Eckhart
Ehrenfels, Chr. Von 61
Einstein, Albert 159

F

Faÿ, Bernard 201–203
Frederick William 45–47
Fichte, J. G. 1–14
Fischer, Eugen 66–88
Ford, Henry 165
Franck, W. 160
Freud, Sigmund 160
Fritsch, Th. 151–163

G

Galen xii, 5
Galton, Francis 30, 181
Garibaldi, G. 41
Gentile, Giovanni 58
Gieseler 66, 89
Gobineau, Arthur de xxi–xxvi, 9–47, 101, 113, 132, 151, 202

Grimm, Jakob 7
Gross, Walter 70
Guénon, René vii, 153, 165
Günther, Hans F. K. 2, 16, 66, 83–138, 151–158, 182

H

Haeckel, W. 30
Halfeld 158
Ham 3
Hauer 145
Haydn, J. 95
Hector 134
Hegel, G. W. F. 11
Herder, J. G. 6–8
Herodotus 23, 133
Himmler, Heinrich 145
Hindenburgm v., P. 92
Hippocrates 5
Hirschfeld, Magnus 160
Hitler, Adolf xxii–xxvi, 177–200
Hugo, Victor 41, 165

J

Jacob 107
Japheth 3–4
Jesus 55, 124, 138–139, 180
John 139
Joly 166
Julian (emperor) xii, 4, 68
Juvenal 137

K

Kant, Immanuel xxiv
Kautsky, K. 157
Klemm, G. 14, 40
Kloatsch 116
Kretschmer, P. 133

OTHER BOOKS PUBLISHED BY ARKTOS

OTHER BOOKS PUBLISHED BY ARKTOS

GREAT NECK EXXON
605 NORTHERN BLVD
GREAT NECK NY 11021

Exxonmobil
605 Northern Blvd
Great Neck NY
11021

DATE 09/14/19   12:43
TRAN# 9040961
PUMP #04
SERVICE LEVEL: FULL
PRODUCT: PLUS
GALLONS: 13.463
PRICE/G: $ 3.399
FUEL SALE $ 45.76
CREDIT $45.76

Discover
************6630
Entry Method: Swiped
Auth #: 01438R
Resp Code:
Stan: 110240945891
Invoice #: 37284
Store # 4803862
SITE ID: 135114
TERMINAL ID: 001

THANK YOU
HAVE A NICE DAY

OTHER BOOKS PUBLISHED BY ARKTOS

OTHER BOOKS PUBLISHED BY ARKTOS

ERNST VON SALOMON	*It Cannot Be Stormed*
	The Outlaws
SRI SRI RAVI SHANKAR	*Celebrating Silence*
	Know Your Child
	Management Mantras
	Patanjali Yoga Sutras
	Secrets of Relationships
GEORGE T. SHAW (ED.)	*A Fair Hearing*
OSWALD SPENGLER	*Man and Technics*
TOMISLAV SUNIC	*Against Democracy and Equality*
	Postmortem Report
	Titans are in Town
HANS-JÜRGEN SYBERBERG	*On the Fortunes and Misfortunes of Art in Post-War Germany*
ABIR TAHA	*Defining Terrorism: The End of Double Standards*
	The Epic of Arya (2nd ed.)
	Nietzsche's Coming God, or the Redemption of the Divine
	Verses of Light
BAL GANGADHAR TILAK	*The Arctic Home in the Vedas*
DOMINIQUE VENNER	*For a Positive Critique*
	The Shock of History
MARKUS WILLINGER	*A Europe of Nations*
	Generation Identity

Lightning Source UK Ltd.
Milton Keynes UK
UKHW011305220719
346610UK00003B/1358/P